MW00620688

CORNELIUS NEPOS

LCL 467

CORNELIUS NEPOS

WITH AN ENGLISH TRANSLATION BY

JOHN C. ROLFE

HARVARD UNIVERSITY PRESS

CAMBRIDGE, MASSACHUSETTS

LONDON, ENGLAND

First published (with Florus) 1929
This separate edition 1984

LOEB CLASSICAL LIBRARY® is a registered trademark
of the President and Fellows of Harvard College

ISBN 978-0-674-99514-7

Printed on acid-free paper and bound by
The Maple-Vail Book Manufacturing Group

CONTENTS

EXCERPT FROM THE BOOK ON LATIN HISTORIANS

INTRODUCTION

The Life and Works of Cornelius Nepos

Cornelius Nepos (his *praenomen* is unknown) was
born in Cisalpine Gaul, the native land of Catullus,
Vergil Livy and the Plinys. The elder Pliny speaks
of him as *Padi accola*,[1] and since we know that he was
a native of that part of Cisalpine Gaul which took its
name from the Insubres,[2] it has been conjectured
that his birthplace was Ticinum, the modern Pavia.

The dates of his birth and death are not known
with certainty. He appears to have lived from
about 99 to about 24 B.C.; for we know that he sur-
vived Atticus, who died in 32 B.C., and that he lived
to an advanced age. The elder Pliny twice refers[3]
to "Cornelius Nepos, qui divi Augusti principatu
obiit."

Nepos took up his residence in Rome early and
spent the greater part of his life there. He seems to
have had an independent fortune and to have devoted
his entire attention to literary work. He apparently
took no part in political life; at least, we know from
one of Pliny's letters that he was not of senatorial
rank.[4] He exchanged letters with Cicero[5] and he

---

[1] *N.H.* iii. 127.
[2] Pliny, *Epist.* iv. 28. 1; cf. Cicero, *ad Fam.* xv. 16. 1.
[3] *N.H.* ix. 137; x. 60.　　　　　[4] v. 3. 6.
[5] Macrob. *Sat.* ii. 1. 14; Suet. *Jul.* 55; etc.

was intimate with Atticus after the latter's return
from Athens in 65 B.C. Catullus dedicated a book
of poems to him in complimentary lines.[1]

A reference of Fronto [2] seems to indicate that
Nepos, like his friend Atticus, was a publisher, as
well as a writer, of books.

Nepos was a prolific author in several branches of
literature. The greater part of his works has been
lost and is known to us only through references of
other writers. The list is as follows:

Love Poems, mentioned by the younger Pliny in
the letter cited above.[3]

Chronica, referred to by Catullus in his dedication.
This work comprised in three books an outline
of the history of the world from the earliest
times to about 54 B.C. Like the *Liber Annalis* [4]
of Atticus, it was of a chronological character.

Exempla, a collection of anecdotes arranged under
various captions, like the *Factorum et Dictorum
Memorabilium libri IX* of Valerius Maximus, and
intended for the use of rhetoricians. A fifth
book is cited by Gellius.[5] It must have been
published after 43 B.C.[6]

A *Life of Cato*, mentioned by Nepos himself.[7]

A *Life of Cicero*,[8] apparently composed after the
death of the orator.

A treatise on Geography, known, though not by
title, from references of the elder Pliny , and
Pomponius Mela. The former speaks of it as
uncritical.[9]

[1] Catull. 1.   [2] Page 20, 6, Naber (i. p. 169, L.C.L.).
[3] v. 3. 6.   [4] Nepos, xxiii. 13. 1.   [5] vi. 18. 11.
[6] Suet. Aug. 77.   [7] xxiv. 3. 5.   [8] Gell. xv. 28. 2.
[9] *N.H.* v. 4.

INTRODUCTION

De Viris Illustribus, in at least sixteen books.[1] Nepos arranged his biographies in groups of two books each. The first book of every group included the distinguished men of foreign nations, for the most part Greeks; the second, those of Rome. From references of Nepos himself and others[2] the categories of generals, historians, kings and poets have been determined. What the other four were is uncertain; philosophers, orators, statesmen and grammarians have been suggested. The reference of Gellius[3] to Book xii with reference to a Roman historian is variously explained, some assuming an error in the text of Gellius; others, that an introductory book of a general character preceded and introduced the pairs of lives.

Of this work we have the entire book *De Excellentibus Ducibus Exterarum Gentium*, and two lives from the book *De Historicis Latinis*, besides a few fragments. The former was for a long time believed to be the work of Aemilius Probus, a grammarian of the time of Theodosius II (A.D. 408–450) on account of an epigram of his which appears in some of the manuscripts after the Life of Hannibal.

It reads as follows:

Vade, liber, nostri fato meliore memento;
   Cum leget haec dominus, te sciat esse meum.
Nec metuas fulvo strictos diademate crines,
   Ridentes blandum vel pietate oculos.

---

[1] Charisius, i. 141. 13 K., cites the sixteenth book.
[2] Nepos, x. 3. 2; xxi. 1. 1; xxiii. 13. 4; Suet. *vit. Ter.* iii. (ii. p. 457, L.C.L.).
[3] xi. 8. 5.

Communis cunctis hominem, sed regna tenere
    Se meminit; vincit hinc magis ille homines.
Ornentur steriles fragili tectura libelli;
    Theodosio et doctis carmina nuda placent.
Si rogat auctorem, paulatim detege nostrum
    Tunc domino nomen; me sciat esse Probum.
Corpore in hoc manus est genitoris avique meaeque;
    Felices, dominum quae meruere, manus.[1]

Go forth, my book, and under a better destiny be
mindful of me. When my Lord shall read this, let
him know that you are mine. Fear not the golden
diadem that binds his locks, his eyes smiling with
kindness and goodness. Gracious to all, he remembers that he is a mortal man, but a man who rules an
empire; thus he binds men the closer. Let the frail
covering of useless books be adorned, but to Theodosius and the cultured unadorned songs are pleasing.
If he ask for the author, then gradually reveal my
name to my Lord. Let him know that I am Probus.[2]
In this work is the hand of my father, my grandfather
and myself. Happy the hands that have found
favour with my Lord.

As early as the sixteenth century it was shown that
the author of the book on Great Generals must have
belonged to the later days of the Republic and the
beginning of the Empire.[3] Furthermore, the resem-
blances in language and style to the lives of Cato

---

[1] Followed in codd. A and P by " Aemilii (Emilii, P)
Probi de excellentibus ducibus exterarum gentium . liber
explicit."
[2] The Honest Man.
[3] See, for example, xviii. 8. 2; xvii. 4. 2; viii. 2. 4;
i. 6. 2.

and Atticus, which have come down to us under the name of Cornelius Nepos, are so great as to leave no doubt that they are the work of the same writer. Aemilius Probus, following in the footsteps of his grandfather and his father, was apparently the editor of a collection of Selected Lives from the *De Viris Illustribus* of Nepos.

The entire work was published before the death of Atticus in 32 B.C., probably in 34 or 35. At some time before 27 B.C. a second edition was issued,[1] in which the brief extract *On Kings* and the lives of Datames, Hamilcar and Hannibal seem to have been added to the existing collection and additions made to the biography of Atticus. Thus the first edition contained only Greeks and Romans.

According to his own statement,[2] Nepos wrote biography and not history, and it is as the oldest existing biographical work that has come down to us under the name of its author that the surviving part of the *De Viris Illustribus* may claim a modest place in the history of literature. The lives were addressed to the general public [3] rather than to scholars, and their purpose was to entertain and at the same time point a moral. They therefore should, and in the majority of instances do, belong to the Peripatetic type, represented by the *Parallel Lives* of Plutarch. Nepos falls far short of Plutarch as a biographer; he preceded him in comparing Romans with foreigners, although in this method of gratifying Roman national

---

[1] See **xxv**. 19. 1. Octavian is everywhere referred to as Caesar, never with the title Augustus, conferred on him in 27 B.C.

[2] **xvi**. 1. 1.

[3] See Praef. 1–7; **xv**. 1. 1; etc.

xi

pride he had himself been anticipated by Varro [1] and other writers of the period.[2]

Nepos was not skilled in the art of composition, and as a result his work presents a combination of nearly all possible types of biography.[3] Besides the Peripatetic biographies we have brief summaries in the Alexandrine-philological manner (*Cimon, Conon, Iphicrates, Chabrias* and *Timotheus*), and eulogies (*encomia* or *laudationes*) either in an approximation [4] to the conventional form taught in the schools of rhetoric and based on the virtues of the hero (*Epaminondas*), or with a superficial resemblance to the *Agesilaus* of Xenophon and based upon the hero's exploits (*Agesilaus*). The *Atticus*, which is also a eulogy, is unique in being originally written of a person who was still living; after his death, as has been said, it was somewhat changed. It is in the main of the type represented by Xenophon's *Agesilaus* and the brief laudation of Germanicus in Suetonius' *Caligula*.[5]

Nepos writes as a rule in the " plain " style.[6] His vocabulary is limited, and he expresses himself ordinarily in short sentences. The results of rhetorical training are shown in his attempts to adorn his narrative, especially, although not consistently,[4] in more elevated passages, when he depicts the virtues of his heroes [7] or puts speeches into their mouths. He occasionally attempts long periods, but

[1] In the *Imagines.*
[2] See, for example, Cic. *Tusc. Disp.* i. 1.
[3] Leo, p. 210.
[4] He is rarely, if ever, consistent in the use of any literary form or rhetorical device.
[5] i–vii.　　　　　　　[6] See Gellius, vi. 14.
[7] *E.g.* xv. 3.

is obviously not at home in them. His principal rhetorical devices are rhythmical *clausulae*, alliteration and antithesis. The last-named figure is used to such excess that his sentences are frequently overloaded at the beginning, and end weakly. Although he was a contemporary of Caesar and Cicero, his Latinity belongs with that of Varro and the writers of the supplements to Caesar's *Civil War*. He has some archaisms, numerous colloquial words and expressions, and some words that are common to him and writers of a later date. He has little variety in his diction; in particular he uses *nam* and *enim* to an extent which taxes the ingenuity of a translator. He is also fond of the pronoun *hic*, probably owing to the influence of the Alexandrine biographers.[1]

Although Nepos makes direct mention of Thucydides, Xenophon's *Agesilaus*, Plato's *Symposium*, Theopompus, Dinon, Timaeus, Silenus, Sosylus, Polybius, Sulpicius Blitho, Atticus and the writings of Hannibal, it is obvious that he rarely, if ever, made first-hand use of those authorities. The material which he needed for his Greek subjects was available in the biographical literature of that country,[2] such as the works of Antigonus of Carystus, Hermippus and Satyrus. In the biographies of Romans, which are lost except for the *Cato* and the *Atticus*, he may have depended to a greater extent on historical sources, although he had predecessors in Varro and Santra.

THE MANUSCRIPTS

The best manuscripts of Nepos are no longer in existence. The *codex Parcensis* (P), so named from

---

[1] See Leo, p. 217.   [2] See xv. 4. 6.

INTRODUCTION

the Abbey of Parc, was discovered and collated by
Roth. It belonged to the fifteenth century, but
represented an older tradition than the earlier
Sangallensis and *Guelferbytanus*. It found its way to
the library of Louvain, where it disappeared during
the late war. The collation of Roth is preserved in
the public library of Basle. Of about the same age
and value, so far as it goes, is a manuscript variously
known as the *codex Danielinus* or *Gifanianus* (*Dan.*
or *Gif.*), which was formerly at St. Benoît sur Loire,
but has been lost sight of since the sixteenth century.
Many of its readings have been more or less imper-
fectly preserved in the margin of the edition of
Langueil (1543). In many cases they are so similar
to those of the *codex Guelferbytanus Gudianus*, 166,
(*A*) of the twelfth or thirteenth century, that Chate-
lain [1] thought it possible that *codex A* was actually
the famous Danielinus. Other manuscripts of value
are the *Sangallensis* (*B*), of the fourteenth century,
the *Monacensis*, 88, (*M*), written at Ulm in 1482, and
a manuscript of the *Collegium Romanum* (*R*). The
Utrecht edition of 1542 (*u*) represents a special
tradition and was ranked among the manuscripts by
Roth and Halm.

For other manuscripts added by Gemss, Winsted
and Guillemin, which occasionally furnish good
readings, see the list of sigla. All the existing
codices have the same lacuna at vi.2.3 and a number
of obvious errors in common, and hence are descended
from the same archetype, assumed to be a minuscule
manuscript not earlier than the eleventh century.
They are classified as follows by Guillemin: (1) Dan.-
Gif., P, A, θ, π; (2) B, μ; (3) u; (4) R, M, F, λ

[1] *Paléographie de classiques latins,* ii. p. clxxxii.

INTRODUCTION

Owing to the lack of reliable manuscripts and the fact that Nepos has been so extensively used in the schools of ancient, as well as of modern, times, editors have been very free in making emendations and transpositions, and in assuming the existence of *lacunae*. The extremes of conservatism and the reverse are perhaps illustrated by the editions of Winsted and Guillemin. In this edition the manuscript reading has been kept wherever it seemed possible to do so ; in the words of Winsted (Praef.): "Nepotis librum limatiorem quam ipse reliquit reddere veritus sum." Deviations from the codices, except in the case of obvious and generally accepted corrections, have been indicated in the critical notes.

BIOGRAPHICAL NOTE

The *editio princeps* of Nepos was published at Venice in 1471 ; it was followed by the *editio Juntina* of 1525 and the Utrecht edition of 1542. Of critical editions may be mentioned: Lambin, *Aemilii Probi et Cornelii Nepotis quae supersunt*, Paris, 1569 ; Roth, with prolegomena of Rinck, Basle, 1841 ; Nipperdey, Berlin, 1867 ; Halm, Leipzig, 1871 ; Fleckeisen, Leipzig, 1884 ; Winsted, Oxford, 1904 ; and Guillemin, with a translation into French, Paris, 1923. The best commentary is that of Nipperdey, Berlin, 1849 (ed. 2 by Lupus, Berlin, 1879). The school editions in various languages are very numerous, such as Nipperdey's abridgment for the use of schools, of which an eleventh edition by C. Witte appeared in 1913 ; that of Browning, Oxford, 1868 (ed. 3 by Inge, 1887) ; and that of O. Wagner, Leipzig, 1922. Nepos' style is treated

INTRODUCTION

by B. Lupus, *Der Sprachgebrauch des Cornelius Nepos*, Berlin, 1876, and in the preface to the Nipperdey-Witte edition; and his branch of literature by Fr. Leo, *Die Griechisch-römische Biographie*, Leipzig, 1901, and D. R. Stuart, *Epochs of Greek and Roman Biography*, Berkeley, California, 1928.

BIBLIOGRAPHICAL ADDENDUM (1984)

Editions
Paravia: E. Malcovati, Turin 1945[2]
Budé: *Vies d'Hannibal, de Caton et d'Atticus*, M. Ruch, Paris 1968
Teubner: *Vitae*, P. K. Marshall, Leipzig 1977
Utet: *Opere di Nepote*, L. Agnes, Turin 1977
Vite e frammenti, A. Sartori, Milan 1980

Commentary
Nipperdey-Witte, Berlin 1962[12]

Studies
P. K. Marshall, *The manuscript tradition of Cornelius Nepos*, BICS Supple. 37 (1977)
E. Malcovati, 'Nuovi Studi su Cornelio Nepote,' *Athenaeum* 55 (1977) 417–421

General

A. Momigliano, *The Development of Greek Biography*, Cambridge, Mass. 1971

SIGLA

Dan.⎫
Gif. ⎬ = Codex Danielinus or Gifanianus.

P = Codex Parcensis, fifteenth century.

A = Codex Guelferbytanus Gudianus 166, twelfth to thirteenth century.

B = Codex Sangallensis, fourteenth century.

M = Codex Monacensis, 1482.

R = Codex Collegii Romani, thirteenth century.

H = Codex Haenelianus, 1469.

Leid. = Codex Leidensis Boecleri.

Leid. II = Codex Leidensis.

Can. = Codex Bodleianus Canonici Lat. 159, fifteenth century.

V = Codex Vindobonensis, fifteenth century.

Σ = Codex Strozzianus (Florence).

F = Codex Claromontanus 259, fifteenth century.

θ = Codex Parisinus 5826, fifteenth century.

μ = Codex Parisinus 6143, fifteenth century.

λ = Codex Parisinus 5837, fifteenth century.

π = Codex Parisinus (Arsenal Library), fifteenth century.

u = Utrecht edition of 1542.

Nipp. = Nipperdey.

Fleck. = Fleckeisen.

Guill. = Guillemin.

THE BOOK OF CORNELIUS NEPOS

ON THE

GREAT GENERALS OF FOREIGN NATIONS

CORNELII NEPOTIS

LIBER DE EXCELLENTIBUS DUCIBUS
EXTERARUM GENTIUM

PRAEFATIO

1 Non dubito fore plerosque, Attice, qui hoc genus
scripturae leve et non satis dignum summorum
virorum personis iudicent, cum relatum legent quis
musicam docuerit Epaminondam, aut in eius virtutibus commemorari, saltasse eum commode scien-
2 terque tibiis cantasse.   Sed hi erunt fere qui expertes
litterarum Graecarum nihil rectum, nisi · quod
3 ipsorum moribus conveniat, putabunt.   Hi si didi-
cerint non eadem omnibus esse honesta atque
turpia, sed omnia maiorum institutis iudicari, non
admirabuntur nos in Graiorum virtutibus exponendis
4 mores eorum secutos.   Neque enim Cimoni fuit
turpe, Atheniensium summo viro, sororem germanam habere in matrimonio, quippe cum cives
eius eodem uterentur instituto; at id quidem nostris
moribus nefas habetur.   Laudi in Creta[1] ducitur
adulescentulis quam plurimos habuisse amatores.

---

[1] Creta, *Valckenaer*; Graecia, *MSS.*

---

[1] See xv. 2.   In the Notes and Index the Lives are referred
to by number.
[2] v. 1. 2.

THE BOOK OF CORNELIUS NEPOS

ON THE

GREAT GENERALS OF FOREIGN NATIONS

PREFACE

I DOUBT not, Atticus, that many readers will look upon this kind of writing as trivial and unworthy of the parts played by great men, when they find that I have told who taught Epaminondas music or see it mentioned among his titles to fame that he was a graceful dancer and a skilled performer on the flute.[1] But such critics will for the most part be men unfamiliar with Greek letters, who will think no conduct proper which does not conform to their own habits. If these men can be made to understand that not all peoples look upon the same acts as honourable or base, but that they judge them all in the light of the usage of their forefathers, they will not be surprised that I, in giving an account of the merits of Greeks, have borne in mind the usage of that nation. For example, it was no disgrace to Cimon, an eminent citizen of Athens, to have his own sister to wife,[2] inasmuch as his countrymen followed that same custom; but according to our standards such a union is considered impious. In Crete it is thought praiseworthy for young men to have had the greatest possible number of love affairs.

3

Nulla Lacedaemoni vidua tam est nobilis, quae
5 non ad cenam [1] eat mercede conducta. Magnis in
laudibus tota fere fuit Graecia victorem Olympiae
citari; in scaenam vero prodire ac populo esse
spectaculo nemini in eisdem gentibus fuit turpitudini.
Quae omnia apud nos partim infamia, partim humilia
atque ab honestate remota ponuntur.
6   Contra ea pleraque nostris moribus sunt decora
quae apud illos turpia putantur. Quem enim Romanorum pudet uxorem ducere in convivium? Aut
cuius non mater familias primum locum tenet aedium
7 atque in celebritate versatur? Quod multo fit aliter
in Graecia; nam neque in convivium adhibetur nisi
propinquorum, neque sedet nisi in interiore parte
aedium, quae gynaeconitis appellatur, quo nemo
accedit nisi propinqua cognatione coniunctus.
8   Sed hic plura persequi cum magnitudo voluminis
prohibet, tum festinatio ut ea explicem quae exorsus
sum. Qua re ad propositum veniemus et in hoc
exponemus libro de vita excellentium imperatorum.

---

[1] cenam, *PA*; scenam, *the other MSS.*; obscena ineat,
O. Wagner; moeccum, *L. Havet.*

---

[1] *Cenam* is probably corrupt, but no satisfactory emendation has been proposed. The suggestion of Wagner, "to
indulge in promiscuous intercourse," seems the best one; see
the critical note.

[2] The reference is primarily to the *atrium*, but also to
other rooms to which guests were admitted; *primum locum*
is contrasted with *interiore parte*.

At Lacedaemon no woman without a husband, however distinguished she may be, refuses to go to a
dinner-party as a hired entertainer.[1] Almost everywhere in Greece it was deemed a high honour to
be proclaimed victor at Olympia; even to appear
on the stage and exhibit oneself to the people was
never regarded as shameful by those nations. With
us, however, all those acts are classed either as
disgraceful, or as low and unworthy of respectable
conduct.

On the other hand, many actions are seemly
according to our code which the Greeks look upon
as shameful. For instance, what Roman would
blush to take his wife to a dinner-party? What
matron does not frequent the front rooms[2] of her
dwelling and show herself in public? But it is very
different in Greece; for there a woman is not
admitted to a dinner-party, unless relatives only are
present, and she keeps to the more retired part
of the house called "the women's apartment," to
which no man has access who is not near of kin.

But further enlargement of this topic is impossible,
not only because of the extent of my proposed work,
but also by my haste to treat the subject that I
have chosen. I shall therefore come to the point
and shall write in this book of the lives of celebrated
commanders.

I. MILTIADES

1. Miltiades, Cimonis filius, Atheniensis, cum et antiquitate generis et gloria maiorum et sua modestia unus omnium maxime floreret eaque esset aetate ut non iam solum de eo bene sperare, sed etiam confidere cives possent sui talem eum futurum qualem cognitum iudicarunt, accidit ut Athenienses Cherso-
2 nesum colonos vellent mittere. Cuius generis cum magnus numerus esset et multi eius demigrationis peterent societatem, ex his delecti Delphos deliberatum missi sunt,[1] quo potissimum duce uterentur. Namque tum Thraeces eas regiones tenebant, cum
3 quibus armis erat dimicandum. His consulentibus nominatim Pythia praecepit ut Miltiadem imperatorem sibi sumerent: id si fecissent, incepta prospera futura.
4 Hoc oraculi responso Miltiades cum delecta manu classe Chersonesum profectus, cum accessisset Lemnum et incolas eius insulae sub potestatem redigere

---

[1] *The MSS. except Leid. add* qui consulerent Apollinem.

---

[1] He claimed descent from Aeacus, son of Zeus; for similar family-trees cf. Suet. *Galba* 2; *Vesp.* 12.
[2] A general term for a peninsula; here the Thracian Chersonesus is meant, the modern Gallipoli peninsula.
[3] In chapters 1 and 2 Nepos confuses Miltiades with his uncle of the same name. The responses of the oracle were

I. MILTIADES

1. MILTIADES, the Athenian, son of Cimon, because of the antiquity of his family,[1] the fame of his ancestors, and his own unassuming nature, was the most distinguished man of his day. He had reached a time of life when he not only inspired high hopes in his fellow-citizens, but even gave them confidence that he would be the kind of man that they found him on longer acquaintance, when it chanced that the Athenians wished to send a colony to the Chersonesus.[2] Since the number of eligible citizens was large and many wished to take part in that migration, a deputation from their number was sent to Delphi, to inquire who would be the best leader to choose. For at that time the Thracians were in control of those regions, and a contest with them was inevitable. To the envoys who consulted her the Pythia named Miltiades[3] and bade them take him as their commander, declaring that if they did so, their enterprise would be successful.

It was owing to that response of the oracle that Miltiades, accompanied by a carefully selected band, set sail with a fleet for the Chersonesus. Having reached Lemnos[4] and wishing to bring the

usually vague or ambiguous, like the well-known *aio te, Aeacide, Romanos vincere posse,* given to King Pyrrhus of Epirus.

[4] Nepos everywhere has the Latin forms of Greek names and uses the Roman names for the Greek gods.

vellet Atheniensium, idque Lemnii sua sponte[1]
5 facerent postulasset, illi irridentes responderunt
tum id se facturos, cum ille, domo navibus proficiscens, vento aquilone venisset Lemnum; hic
enim ventus, ab septentrionibus oriens, adversum
6 tenet Athenis proficiscentibus. Miltiades, morandi
tempus non habens, cursum derexit quo tendebat,
pervenitque Chersonesum.

2. Ibi brevi tempore barbarum[2] copiis disiectis,
tota regione quam petierat potitus, loca castellis
idonea communiit, multitudinem quam secum duxerat
in agris conlocavit crebrisque excursionibus locuple-
2 tavit. Neque minus in ea re prudentia quam
felicitate adiutus est; nam cum virtute militum
devicisset hostium exercitus, summa aequitate res
constituit atque ipse ibidem manere decrevit. Erat
3 enim inter eos dignitate regia, quamvis carebat
nomine, neque id magis imperio quam iustitia consecutus; neque eo setius Atheniensibus, a quibus
erat profectus, officia praestabat. Quibus rebus
fiebat ut non minus eorum voluntate perpetuum[3]
imperium obtineret qui miserant, quam illorum cum
quibus erat profectus.

4 Chersoneso tali modo constituta Lemnum revertitur et ex pacto postulat ut sibi urbem tradant. Illi
enim dixerant, cum vento borea domo profectus eo

[1] sponte ut, *u*; idque ut, *Cobet.*
[2] barbarum, *Dan. PA*; *the other MSS. have* barbarorum.
[3] perpetuum *Pluygers*; perpetuo, *MSS.*

---

[1] There were two cities on Lemnos, Hephaistia and Myrina.

8

inhabitants of that island under the sway of the Athenians, he demanded of the Lemnians that they should voluntarily accept that condition. They replied ironically that they would do so, whenever he should set sail from his home and come to Lemnos driven by Aquilo. But that wind, since it blows from the north, is dead ahead for those who sail from Athens. Miltiades, having no time to lose, kept on to his destination and arrived at the Chersonesus.

2. There he soon dispersed the forces of the barbarians, and having gained possession of the entire region that he had in view, he fortified strategic points with strongholds, settled on farms the company which he had brought with him, and enriched them by frequent raids. In that whole enterprise his success was due not less to statesmanship than to good fortune; for when, thanks to the valour of his soldiers, he had vanquished the enemy, he organized the colony with the utmost impartiality and decided to make his own home there. As a matter of fact, he enjoyed the rank of king among the colonists without having that title, an honour which he owed to his justice no less than to his position of authority. Nevertheless, he continued to do his duty by the Athenians, who had sent him to Thrace; and as a result he retained permanent authority, no less with the consent of those who had sent him than of those who had taken part in the expedition.

After the Chersonesus was thus organized, Miltiades returned to Lemnos and demanded the surrender of the city [1] according to the agreement. For they had said that they would give themselves

pervenisset, sese dedituros; se autem domum
5 Chersonesi habere. Cares, qui tum Lemnum incolebant, etsi praeter opinionem res ceciderat, tamen
non dicto, sed secunda fortuna adversariorum capti,
resistere ausi non sunt atque ex insula demigrarunt.
Pari felicitate ceteras insulas quae Cyclades nomin-
antur sub Atheniensium redegit potestatem.

3. Eisdem temporibus Persarum rex Darius ex
Asia in Europam exercitu traiecto Scythis bellum
inferre decrevit. Pontem fecit in Histro flumine,
qua copias traduceret. Eius pontis, dum ipse
2 abesset, custodes reliquit principes quos secum ex
Ionia et Aeolide duxerat; quibus singulis illarum [1]
urbium perpetua dederat imperia. Sic enim facillime putavit se Graeca lingua loquentes qui Asiam
incolerent sub sua retenturum potestate, si amicis
suis oppida tuenda tradidisset; quibus se oppresso
nulla spes salutis relinqueretur. In hoc fuit tum
3 numero Miltiades.[2] Hic, cum crebri adferrent nuntii
male rem gerere Darium premique a Scythis, hortatus
est[3] pontis custodes ne a fortuna datam occasionem
4 liberandae Graeciae dimitterent. Nam si cum iis
copiis quas secum transportarat interisset Darius,
non solum Europam fore tutam, sed etiam eos qui
Asiam incolerent Graeci genere liberos a Persarum
futuros dominatione et periculo. Id [4] facile effici

---

[1] illarum, *Andresen*; ipsarum, *MSS.*
[2] Miltiades, *Halm*; M. cui illa custodia crederetur, *MSS.*
[3] *Most MSS. have* Miltiades *before* hortatus est.
[4] id, *Halm*; id et, *Mu*; et, *the other MSS.*

---

[1] Only Hephaistia surrendered without opposition.
[2] Nepos' statement is inaccurate. Lemnos is not one of
the Cyclades, and it was Conon who reduced the islands of
the Aegean.

up whenever he left his home and came to them before a north wind; but now, as he reminded them, he had his home in the Chersonesus. To the Carians, who at that time dwelt in Lemnos, the situation was an unexpected one; nevertheless, since they were trapped not so much by their promise as by the good fortune of their opponents, they did not dare to resist,[1] but left the island. Miltiades had equal success in bringing the remaining islands known as the Cyclades into the power of the Athenians.[2]

3. At that same period of time King Darius B.C. 513 decided to lead an army from Asia into Europe and make war on the Scythians. He built a bridge over the river Hister for the transport of his troops and entrusted the guard of that bridge during his absence to men of rank whom he had brought with him from Ionia and Aeolis. To each of those men he had given the permanent rule of a city in the region from which each had come. For in that way he hoped most easily to retain under his sway the Greek-speaking peoples dwelling in Asia, if he entrusted the charge of their towns to friends of his, who would have no hope of safety in case he were overthrown. Among these at that time was Miltiades. He, learning from numerous sources that Darius was meeting with no success and was hard pressed by the Scythians, urged the defenders of the bridge not to lose the opportunity that fortune had given them of freeing Greece. For if Darius and the forces which he had taken with him should perish, not only would Europe be safe, but also the dwellers in Asia who were of Greek descent would be freed from the Persian yoke and menace. That result

posse: ponte enim rescisso, regem vel hostium ferro
vel inopia paucis diebus interiturum.

5 Ad hoc consilium cum plerique accederent, Histiaeus Milesius ne res conficeretur obstitit, dicens non
idem ipsis, qui summas imperii tenerent, expedire
et multitudini, quod Darii regno ipsorum niteretur
dominatio; quo exstincto, ipsos, potestate expulsos,
civibus suis poenas daturos. Itaque adeo se abhor-
rere a ceterorum consilio, ut nihil putet ipsis utilius
6 quam confirmari regnum Persarum. Huius cum
sententiam plurimi essent secuti, Miltiades, non
dubitans tam multis consciis ad regis aures consilia
sua perventura, Chersonesum reliquit ac rursus
Athenas demigravit. Cuius ratio etsi non valuit,
tamen magno opere est laudanda, cum amicior
omnium libertati quam suae fuerit dominationi.

4. Darius autem, cum ex Europa in Asiam redisset, hortantibus amicis ut Graeciam redigeret in
suam potestatem, classem quingentarum navium
comparavit eique Datim praefecit et Artaphernem
iisque ducenta peditum, decem milia equitum
dedit, causam interserens se hostem esse Atheniensibus, quod eorum auxilio Iones Sardis expugnassent
2 suaque praesidia interfecissent. Illi praefecti regii
classe ad Euboeam appulsa celeriter Eretriam ceperunt omnesque eius gentis cives abreptos in Asiam

---

[1] He did not return until some years later, in 493 B.C.
[2] This was in 499 B.C. during the Ionian revolt, before
Darius' Scythian expedition.

could easily be accomplished; for the bridge once destroyed, within a few days the king would fall victim either to the enemy's steel or to famine.

That plan met with the approval of a great many, but Histiaeus of Miletus opposed its execution, pointing out that he and his colleagues, who held high command, were not in the same situation as the common people, since their authority was bound up with the sovereignty of Darius; if the king should be killed, their power would be wrested from them and they would be exposed to the vengeance of their fellow-citizens. Therefore he was so far from approving the plan proposed by the rest that he believed nothing to be more to their advantage than the maintenance of the Persian rule. When the opinion of Histiaeus met with general approval, Miltiades, feeling sure that with so many witnesses his proposal would come to the king's ears, left the Chersonesus and returned to Athens.[1] His design, although it failed, is none the less deserving of high praise, since he was more interested in the public freedom than in maintaining his own power.

4. Now Darius, having returned from Europe to Asia and being urged by his friends to reduce Greece to submission, got ready a fleet of five hundred ships and put it under the command of Datis and Artaphernes, giving them in addition two hundred thousand foot and ten thousand horsemen. He alleged as a pretext for his hostility to the Athenians that it was with their help that the Ionians had taken Sardis and slain his garrison.[2] Those officers of the king, having landed on Euboea, 490 B.C. quickly took Eretria, carried off all the citizens of

ad regem miserunt. Inde ad Atticam accesserunt ac suas copias in campum Marathona deduxerunt; is est ab [1] oppido circiter milia passuum [2] decem.

3 Hoc tumultu Athenienses tam propinquo tamque magno permoti, auxilium nusquam nisi a Lacedaemoniis petiverunt Phidippumque, cursorem eius generis qui hemerodromoe vocantur, Lacedaemonem miserunt, ut nuntiaret quam celeri opus esse auxilio.
4 Domi autem creant decem praetores, qui exercitui praeessent, in iis Miltiadem; inter quos magna fuit contentio, utrum moenibus se [3] defenderent an
5 obviam irent hostibus acieque decernerent. Unus Miltiades maxime nitebatur ut primo quoque tempore castra fierent: id si factum esset, et civibus animum accessurum, cum viderent de eorum virtute non desperari, et hostes eadem re fore tardiores, si animadverterent auderi [4] adversus se tam exiguis copiis dimicari.

5. Hoc in tempore nulla civitas Atheniensibus auxilio fuit praeter Plataeenses; ea mille misit militum. Itaque horum adventu decem milia armatorum completa sunt, quae manus mirabili flagrabat pugnandi cupiditate. Quo factum est ut plus quam collegae Miltiades valeret. Eius ergo auctoritate impulsi, Athenienses copias ex urbe eduxerunt locoque idoneo castra fecerunt. Dein postero die

---

[1] abest, *R*; abest ab, *Aldus.*
[2] passuum, *u*; passus, *MSS.*
[3] se, *added by Lambin.*
[4] auderi, *Lambin and some inferior MSS; the best MSS.* have audere.

---

[1] Couriers who could run for whole days and cover great distances. Phidippides, which was the correct form of the

that place, and sent them to the king in Asia. Then they kept on to Attica and led their forces into the plain of Marathon, which is distant about ten miles from Athens.

The Athenians, though greatly alarmed by this hostile demonstration, so near and so threatening, asked help only from the Lacedaemonians, sending Phidippus, a courier of the class known as " all-day runners,"[1] to report how pressing was their need of aid. But at home they appointed ten generals to command the army, including Miltiades; among these there was great difference of opinion, whether it were better to take refuge within their walls or go to meet the enemy and fight a decisive battle. Miltiades alone persistently urged them to take the field at the earliest possible moment; stating that if they did so, not only would the citizens take heart, when they saw that their courage was not distrusted, but for the same reason the enemy would be slower to act, if they realized that the Athenians dared to engage them with so small a force.

5. In that crisis no city gave help to the Athenians except the Plataeans. They sent a thousand soldiers, whose arrival raised the number of combatants to ten thousand.[2] It was a band inflamed with a marvellous desire for battle, and their ardour gave Miltiades' advice preference over that of his colleagues. Accordingly, through his influence the Athenians were induced to lead their forces from the city and encamp in a favourable position. Then,

name, is said to have covered the 140 miles between Athens and Sparta in 48 hours.

[2] This is what Nepos seems to say; but there were 10,000 Athenians and 1000 Plataeans.

sub montis radicibus acie regione [1] instructa non
apertissuma [2]—namque arbores multis locis erant
rarae [3]—proelium commiserunt hoc consilio, ut et
montium altitudine tegerentur et arborum tractu
4 equitatus hostium impediretur, ne multitudine
clauderentur.

Datis etsi non aequum locum videbat suis, tamen
fretus numero copiarum suarum confligere cupiebat,
eoque magis quod, priusquam Lacedaemonii subsidio venirent, dimicare utile arbitrabatur. Itaque
5 in aciem peditum centum, equitum decem milia
produxit proeliumque commisit. In quo tanto plus
virtute valuerunt Athenienses, ut decemplicem
numerum hostium profligarint, adeoque perter-
ruerint ut Persae non castra, sed naves petierint.
Qua pugna nihil adhuc exstitit [4] nobilius; nulla enim
umquam tam exigua manus tantas opes prostravit.

6. Cuius victoriae non alienum videtur quale
praemium Miltiadi sit tributum docere, quo facilius
2 intellegi possit eandem omnium civitatum esse
naturam. Ut enim populi Romani honores quondam
fuerunt rari et tenues ob eamque causam gloriosi,
nunc autem effusi atque obsoleti, sic olim apud
3 Athenienses fuisse reperimus. Namque huic Miltiadi, quia Athenas totamque Graeciam liberarat,
talis honos tributus est: in porticu, quae Poecile
vocatur, cum pugna depingeretur Marathonia, ut

---

[1] regione, *Roth*; e regione, *MSS.*
[2] non apertissuma, *Roth*; nona (nova, *Dan. π*; nana, *A θ*)
partis (partem, *π*) summa, *Dan. P A θ π u*; non apertis
summa, *B*; nova arte vi summa, *M*; in parte montis summa, *R.*
[3] namque . . . rarae *follows* commiserunt *in the MSS.*
[4] exstitit, *Halm*; est his (hiis), *MSS.*

---

[1] Pentelicon.

on the following day, the army was drawn up at the foot of the mountain [1] in a part of the plain that was not wholly open—for there were isolated trees in many places—and they joined battle. The purpose was to protect themselves by the high mountains and at the same time prevent the enemy's cavalry, hampered by the scattered trees, from surrounding them with their superior numbers.

Although Datis saw that the position was not favourable to his men, yet he was eager to engage, trusting to the number of his troops; and the more so because he thought it to his advantage to give battle before the Lacedaemonian reinforcements arrived. Therefore he led out his hundred thousand foot and ten thousand horse and began the battle. In the contest that ensued the Athenians were so superior in valour that they routed a foe of tenfold their own number and filled them with such fear that the Persians fled, not to their camp, but to their ships. A more glorious victory was never before won; for never did so small a band lay low so great a power.

6. It does not seem out of place to tell what reward was given to Miltiades for that victory, in order that it may the more readily be understood that the nature of all states is the same. For just as among the people of Rome distinctions were formerly few and slight and for that reason glorious, while to-day they are lavish and worthless, so we find it to have been at Athens in days gone by. For the sole honour that our Miltiades received for having won freedom for Athens and for all Greece was this: that when the picture of the battle of Marathon was painted in the colonnade called

in decem praetorum numero prima eius imago
4 poneretur isque hortaretur milites proeliumque
committeret. Idem ille populus, postea quam maius
imperium est nactus et largitione magistratuum
corruptus est, trecentas statuas Demetrio Phalereo
decrevit.

7. Post hoc proelium classem LXX navium
Athenienses eidem Miltiadi dederunt, ut insulas
quae barbaros adiuverant bello persequeretur. Quo
imperio plerasque ad officium redire coegit, non-
2 nullas vi expugnavit. Ex his Parum insulam opibus
elatam cum oratione reconciliare non posset, copias
e navibus eduxit, urbem operibus clausit omnique
3 commeatu privavit; dein vineis ac testudinibus
constitutis, propius muros accessit. Cum iam in eo
esset ut oppido potiretur, procul in continenti lucus
qui ex insula conspiciebatur nescio quo casu nocturno
tempore incensus est. Cuius flamma ut ab oppidanis
4 et oppugnatoribus est visa, utrisque venit in opinionem signum a classiariis regis datum. Quo factum
est ut et Parii a deditione deterrerentur et Miltiades,
timens ne classis regia adventaret, incensis operibus
quae statuerat, cum totidem navibus atque erat
profectus Athenas magna cum offensione civium
suorum rediret.
5 Accusatus ergo est proditionis, quod, cum Parum
expugnare posset, a rege corruptus infectis rebus

---

[1] Literally, "the many-coloured colonnade" (sc. *stoa*).
It was adorned with paintings by Polygnotus and other
great artists, and later was the place of meeting of the Stoics.

[2] Nepos confuses Athenian and Roman customs. At
Athens such largess came from the state and not from the
magistrates.

[3] Nepos substitutes for μηχανήματα in the account of
Ephorus the Roman devices in use in his own time.

Poicile,[1] his portrait was given the leading place among the ten generals and he was represented in the act of haranguing the troops and giving the signal for battle. But that same people, after it had gained greater power and was corrupted by the largess of the magistrates,[2] voted three hundred statues to Demetrius of Phalerum.

7. After that battle the Athenians again 489 B.C. entrusted Miltiades with a fleet of seventy ships, in order to make war on the islands that had given help to the barbarians. While holding that command he compelled many of the islands to return to their allegiance, but with some he had to resort to force. Among the latter the island of Paros was so confident of its strength that it could not be brought to terms by argument. Therefore Miltiades disembarked his troops, invested the city with siege-works, and completely cut off its supplies. Then he set up his mantlets and tortoise-sheds [3] and advanced against the walls. He was on the point of taking the town, when a grove, which was some distance off on the mainland but visible from the island, by some chance caught fire one night. When the flames were seen by the besiegers and the towns-people, both parties thought it a signal given by the king's marines. The result was that the Parians were kept from surrendering, while Miltiades, fearing that the king's fleet was approaching, set fire to the works that he had constructed, and returned to Athens with all the ships which he had taken with him, to the great vexation of his fellow-citizens.

In consequence, he was accused of treason, on the ground that, when he might have taken the city, he had been bribed by the king and had left without

discessisset. Eo tempore aeger erat vulneribus, quae in oppugnando oppido acceperat. Itaque quoniam [1] ipse pro se dicere non posset, verba fecit
6 frater eius Stesagoras.[2] Causa cognita, capitis absolutus pecunia multatus est, eaque lis quinquaginta talentis aestimata est, quantus in classem sumptus factus erat. Hanc pecuniam quod solvere in praesentia non poterat, in vincla publica coniectus est ibique diem obiit supremum.

8. Hic etsi crimine Pario est accusatus, tamen alia causa fuit damnationis. Namque Athenienses propter Pisistrati tyrannidem, quae paucis annis ante fuerat, nimiam [3] civium suorum potentiam
2 extimescebant. Miltiades, multum in imperiis magnisque [4] versatus, non videbatur posse esse privatus,
3 praesertim cum consuetudine ad imperii cupiditatem trahi videretur. Nam Chersonesi [5] omnes illos quos habitarat annos perpetuam obtinuerat dominationem tyrannusque fuerat appellatus, sed iustus. Non erat enim vi consecutus, sed suorum voluntate, eamque potestatem bonitate retinebat. Omnes autem et dicuntur et habentur tyranni, qui potestate sunt
4 perpetua in ea civitate quae libertate usa est. Sed in Miltiade erat cum summa humanitas tum mira communitas, ut nemo tam humilis esset cui non ad

[1] cum, *u.*
[2] Stesagoras, *Longueil*; Sagoras, etc., *MSS.*
[3] nimiam, *Gemss*; omnium, *MSS.*
[4] magistratibusque, *M R u.*
[5] Chersonesi, *some inferior MSS.*; Chersonesso, *A B P R u Can*; in Chersoneso, *Fleck.*

---

[1] The truth of the statement is doubtful. Herodotus says nothing about it.

accomplishing his purpose. At the time Miltiades was disabled by wounds which he had suffered in the attack on the town, and since for that reason he could not plead his own cause, his brother Stesagoras spoke in his behalf. When the trial was concluded, Miltiades was not condemned to capital punishment, but to pay a fine, the amount of which was fixed at five hundred talents, the sum which had been spent on the fleet under his command. Since he could not pay the fine at once, he was put in the state prison, and there met his end.[1]

8. Although it was the affair of Paros that led to the accusation of Miltiades, there was another reason for his condemnation; for the Athenians, because of the tyranny which Pisistratus had held some years before,[2] dreaded excessive power in the hands of any citizen. They did not think it possible that Miltiades, who had held so many and such important military commands, would be able to conduct himself as a private citizen, especially since habit seemed to have given him a taste for power. In the Chersonesus, for example, during all the years of his residence there he had enjoyed uninterrupted sovereignty. He had been called tyrant, but he was a just one, since he owed his power, not to force, but to the consent of his subjects, and retained it as a result of his virtue. But all men are called tyrants, and regarded as such, who hold permanent rule in a city which has enjoyed a democratic form of government. But in Miltiades there was not only the greatest kindliness, but also such remarkable condescension that no one was so

[2] Pisistratus and his sons Hippias and Hipparchus were tyrants from 560 to 510 B.C.

eum aditus pateret; magna auctoritas apud omnis
civitatis, nobile nomen, laus rei militaris maxima.
Haec populus respiciens maluit illum innoxium plecti
quam se diutius esse in timore.

II. THEMISTOCLES

1. Themistocles, Neocli filius, Atheniensis. Huius
vitia ineuntis adulescentiae· magnis sunt emendata
virtutibus, adeo ut anteferatur huic nemo, pauci
2 pares putentur. Sed ab initio est ordiendus. Pater
eius Neocles generosus fuit. Is uxorem Acarnanam
civem duxit, ex qua natus est Themistocles. Qui
cum minus esset probatus parentibus, quod et
liberius vivebat et rem familiarem neglegebat, a
3 patre exheredatus est. Quae contumelia non fregit
eum, sed erexit; nam cum iudicasset sine summa
industria non posse eam exstingui, totum se dedidit
rei publicae, diligentius amicis famaeque serviens.
Multum in iudiciis privatis versabatur, saepe in
contionem populi prodibat; nulla res maior sine eo
gerebatur; celeriter quae opus erant reperiebat,
4 facile eadem oratione explicabat, neque minus in
rebus gerendis promptus quam excogitandis erat,
quod et de instantibus, ut ait Thucydides, verissime
iudicabat et de futuris callidissime coniciebat. Quo
factum est ut brevi tempore illustraretur.

humble as not to be admitted to his presence. He had great influence with all the Greek states, a famous name, and great renown as a soldier. Having in mind these advantages of his, the people preferred that he should suffer, though innocent, rather than that they should continue to be in fear.

II. THEMISTOCLES

1. Themistocles, son of Neocles, the Athenian. This man's faults in early youth gave place to such great merits that no one is ranked above him and few are thought to be his equals. But we must begin our account of his life at the beginning. His father Neocles was of high birth. He married an Acarnanian woman possessing the rights of citizenship, who became the mother of Themistocles. The son displeased his parents by living too lawlessly and neglecting his property, and in consequence was disinherited by his father. But this affront, instead of breaking his spirit, aroused his ambition. For believing that such a disgrace could be wiped out only by the greatest industry, he devoted all his time to public life, doing his best to gain friends and distinction. He took a prominent part in civil suits, and often came forward to speak in the public assembly; no business of importance was transacted without him; he was quick to see what was needed and able to express his views clearly. Furthermore, he was no less active in carrying out his plans than he had been in devising them, because, as Thucydides expresses it, he judged present events with great exactness and divined the future with remarkable skill. As a result he soon became famous.

2. Primus autem gradus fuit capessendae rei publicae bello Corcyraeo; ad quod gerendum praetor a populo factus, non solum praesenti bello, sed etiam 2 reliquo tempore ferociorem reddidit civitatem. Nam cum pecunia publica, quae ex metallis redibat, largitione magistratuum quotannis interiret, ille persuasit populo ut ea pecunia classis centum navium 3 aedificaretur. Qua celeriter effecta, primum Corcyraeos fregit, deinde maritimos praedones consectando mare tutum reddidit. In quo cum divitiis ornavit, tum etiam peritissimos belli navalis fecit Athenienses. 4 Id quantae saluti fuerit universae Graeciae bello cognitum est Persico. Nam cum Xerxes et mari et terra bellum universae inferret Europae cum 5 tantis copiis [1] quantas neque ante nec postea habuit quisquam—huius enim classis mille et ducentarum navium longarum fuit, quam duo milia onerariarum sequebantur; terrestres autem exercitus $\overline{\text{DCC}}$ 6 peditum, equitum $\overline{\text{CCCC}}$ fuerunt;—cuius de adventu cum fama in Graeciam esset perlata et maxime Athenienses peti dicerentur propter pugnam Marathoniam, miserunt Delphos consultum quidnam facerent de rebus suis.

7   Deliberantibus Pythia respondit ut moenibus ligneis se munirent. Id responsum quo valeret cum intellegeret nemo, Themistocles persuasit consilium esse Apollinis, ut in naves se suaque conferrent: 8 eum enim a deo significari murum ligneum. Tali consilio probato, addunt ad superiores totidem naves

---

[1] copiis eam invasit (eam copiis, $M F \lambda$; eam *omitted by* R), M R u F λ; copiis venit, μ V *and other inferior MSS.*

---

[1] The silver mines at Laurium, in the southern part of Attica.

[2] See note 2, p. 18.

2. The first step in his public career came in connection with the war with Corcyra; chosen general by the people to carry on that contest, he inspired the Athenians with greater courage, not only at that time, but also for the future. For while the public funds which came in from the mines [1] every year were being squandered by the magistrates [2] in largess, he persuaded the people to use that money to build a fleet of a hundred ships. The fleet was quickly built, and with it he first humbled the Corcyreans, and then made the sea safe by ridding it of pirates. In that way he made the Athenians not only rich, but highly skilled also in naval warfare. How much this meant to the safety of all Greece became evident during the Persian invasion; for when Xerxes was making war 480 B.C. upon all Europe by land and sea with greater forces than any man ever possessed before or since—he had a fleet of twelve hundred ships of war, attended by two thousand transports, together with a land force of seven hundred thousand foot and four hundred thousand horse;—after the news of his coming had reached Greece, and it was said that Athens was the special object of his attack because of the battle of Marathon, the people sent to Delphi to inquire what measures they ought to take.

The Pythia replied to the envoys that they must defend themselves by wooden walls. When no one could understand what the oracle meant, Themistocles convinced the people that Apollo's advice was that they should take to their ships with all their possessions; for that was what the god meant by a wooden wall. Having adopted that plan, they added to the fleet already mentioned an equal

25

triremes suaque omnia quae moveri poterant partim
Salamina,[1] partim Troezena[2] deportant; arcem
sacerdotibus paucisque maioribus natu ad[3] sacra
procuranda tradunt, reliquum oppidum relinquunt.

3. Huius consilium plerisque civitatibus displicebat
et in terra dimicari magis placebat. Itaque missi
sunt delecti cum Leonida, Lacedaemoniorum rege,
qui Thermopylas occuparent longiusque barbaros
progredi non paterentur. Hi vim hostium non
2 sustinuerunt eoque loco omnes interierunt. At
classis communis Graeciae trecentarum navium, in
qua ducentae erant Atheniensium, primum apud
Artemisium inter Euboeam continentemque terram
cum classiariis regis conflixit. Angustias enim
Themistocles quaerebat, ne multitudine circuiretur.
3 Hic etsi pari proelio discesserant, tamen eodem loco
non sunt ausi manere, quod erat periculum ne, si
pars navium adversariorum Euboeam superasset,
4 ancipiti premerentur periculo. Quo factum est ut
ab Artemisio discederent et exadversum Athenas
apud Salamina classem suam constituerent.

4. At Xerxes, Thermopylis expugnatis, protinus
accessit astu[4] idque nullis defendentibus, interfectis
2 sacerdotibus quos in arce invenerat, incendio delevit.
Cuius flamma perterriti classiarii cum manere non
auderent et plurimi hortarentur ut domos suas
discederent moenibusque se defenderent, Themisto-

---

[1] Salaminam, *MSS., and so elsewhere.*
[2] Troezenam, *MSS.*
[3] ad, *an unknown critic in Lambin*; ac, *MSS.*
[4] astu, *Mon.* 433; astum, *A B M P R u*; ad astu, *suggested by Halm.*

number of triremes, and transported all their movable property either to Salamis or Troezene. The citadel they left in charge of the priests and a few of the older citizens, who were to attend to the sacred rites; the rest of the city they abandoned.

3. Many of the states did not approve of Themistocles' plan, but preferred to fight on land. Accordingly, a band of picked men was sent with Leonidas, king of the Lacedaemonians, to hold Thermopylae and prevent any further advance of the barbarians. They, however, could not resist the enemy's attack, but in that pass they all perished. But the common fleet of Greece, consisting of three hundred ships, of which two hundred belonged to Athens, first engaged with the king's marines off Artemisium, between Euboea and the mainland. For Themistocles chose a narrow place, in order not to be surrounded by superior numbers. Although the result of that battle was indecisive, the Greeks nevertheless did not venture to hold their ground, because there was reason to fear that if a part of the ships of their opponents should round Euboea, they would be exposed to attack on both sides. They therefore retired from Artemisium and stationed their fleet at Salamis, over against Athens.

4. Now Xerxes, having forced the pass at Thermopylae, at once marched upon Athens, and since it was without defenders, he massacred the priests whom he found on the citadel and destroyed the city by fire. The flames of the burning town so terrified the soldiers on the fleet, that they did not dare to hold their position, but the greater number recommended withdrawing to their homes and taking refuge within their walls. Themistocles

cles unus restitit et universos pares esse posse aiebat,
dispersos testabatur perituros, idque Eurybiadi, regi
Lacedaemoniorum, qui tum summae imperii prae-
3 erat, fore adfirmabat. Quem cum minus quam
vellet moveret, noctu de servis suis quem habuit
fidelissimum ad regem misit, ut ei nuntiaret suis
4 verbis adversarios eius in fuga esse: qui si discessissent, maiore cum labore et longinquiore tempore
bellum confecturum, cum singulos consectari coge-
retur; quos si statim aggrederetur, brevi universos
oppressurum. Hoc eo valebat, ut ingratiis ad
5 depugnandum omnes cogerentur. Hac re audita,
barbarus, nihil doli subesse credens, postridie alienis-
simo sibi loco, contra opportunissimo hostibus, adeo
angusto mari conflixit, ut eius multitudo navium
explicari non potuerit. Victus ergo est magis etiam
consilio Themistocli [1] quam armis Graeciae.

5. Hic etsi male rem gesserat, tamen tantas
habebat reliquias copiarum, ut etiam tum iis opprimere posset hostes. Iterum ab eodem gradu
depulsus est. Nam Themistocles, verens ne bellare
perseveraret, certiorem eum fecit id agi, ut pons
quem ille in Hellesponto fecerat dissolveretur ac
2 reditu in Asiam excluderetur, idque ei persuasit.
Itaque qua sex mensibus iter fecerat, eadem minus

---

[1] Themistocli, *A*; -clei, *P*; Themistoclis, *the other MSS.*

---

[1] In xvii. 4. 4 Nepos gives the time as a year. It actually
was four months (Hdt. viii. 51) and the return took forty-five
days (*id.* viii. 115).

alone objected, saying that united they could be a match for the Persians, but insisting that if they should separate, they would all be lost; and he assured Eurybiades, king of the Lacedaemonians, who held the chief command at the time, that what he said was true. And when he had less influence on the Spartan than he hoped, he sent the most faithful of his slaves by night to the king, to take word to him in the name of Themistocles that his enemies were on the point of flight: if they should disperse, it would require longer time and greater effort to end the war, since he would be obliged to attack each city separately; but if he advanced upon them at once, he would quickly destroy them all. Themistocles' design was to compel all the Greeks to fight a decisive battle against their will. When the barbarian received the message, he did not suspect any deception, and although the position was most unfavourable for him, but highly advantageous for the enemy, he joined battle on the following day in so narrow a part of the sea that it was impossible to manœuvre his immense number of ships. Hence he was defeated, thanks to Themistocles' strategy even more than to the arms of Greece.

5. Although the king lost that battle, he still had so many troops left that with them he might even then have overwhelmed the Greeks. A second time he was baffled by the same man; for Themistocles, fearing that Xerxes would continue the war, informed him that a plan was on foot to destroy the bridge which he had made over the Hellespont and thus cut off his return to Asia. The king was convinced of the truth of the report, and so, while he had taken six months to make the journey,[1] he

diebus triginta in Asiam reversus est seque a Themistocle non superatum, sed conservatum iudicavit.
3 Sic unius viri prudentia Graecia liberata est Europaeque succubuit Asia. Haec altera victoria, quae cum Marathonio possit comparari tropaeo. Nam pari modo apud Salamina parvo numero navium maxima post hominum memoriam classis est devicta.

6. Magnus hoc bello Themistocles fuit neque minor in pace. Cum enim Phalerico portu neque magno neque bono Athenienses uterentur, huius consilio triplex Piraei portus constitutus est iisque[1] moenibus circumdatus ut ipsam urbem dignitate
2 aequiperaret, utilitate superaret. Idem muros Atheniensium restituit praecipuo suo periculo. Namque Lacedaemonii, causam idoneam nacti propter barbarorum excursiones qua negarent oportere extra Peloponnesum ullam urbem muros[2] habere, ne essent loca munita, quae hostes possi-
3 derent, Athenienses aedificantes prohibere sunt conati. Hoc longe alio spectabat atque videri volebant. Athenienses enim duabus victoriis, Marathonia et Salaminia, tantam gloriam apud omnes gentis erant consecuti, ut intellegerent Lacedaemonii
4 de principatu sibi cum iis certamen fore. Qua re eos quam infirmissimos esse volebant. Postquam autem audierunt muros instrui, legatos Athenas miserunt, qui id fieri vetarent. His praesentibus

---

[1] iisque, *Scheffer*; isque, *MSS.*
[2] muros, *B, Leid. II*; *the other MSS. omit.*

---

[1] That is, the first rank among the Greek states and the chief command in time of war, then held by the Lacedaemonians.

returned to Asia over the same route in less than
thirty days, convinced that he had not been conquered, but saved, by Themistocles.

Thus through the cleverness of one man the
liberty of Greece was assured and Asia succumbed
to Europe. This is a second victory which may be
matched with the triumph at Marathon; for at
Salamis in like manner a small number of ships
completely vanquished the greatest fleet within the
memory of man.

6. Themistocles showed greatness in that war
and no less greatness when peace came. For while
the Athenians were using the harbour of Phalerum,
which was neither large nor good, through his advice
the triple port of the Piraeus was constructed, and
fortified with such strong walls that it equalled
Athens herself in splendour and surpassed her in
utility. Themistocles also rebuilt the walls of Athens 479-8
at great personal risk. For the Lacedaemonians, B.C.
having found a specious reason in the invasions of
the barbarians for saying that no city outside of the
Peloponnesus ought to have walls, namely, that
there might be no fortified places for the enemy to
get into their hands, tried to interrupt the Athenians
in their work. Their motive was not at all what
they wished it to appear. The fact was that the
Athenians by their two victories at Marathon and
Salamis had gained such prestige all over Greece
that the Lacedaemonians knew that it was with
them that they must contend for the hegemony.[1]
Therefore they wished the Athenians to be as weak
as possible, and as soon as they learned that the
walls were rising, they sent envoys to Athens, to
put a stop to the work. While the deputation was

5 desierunt ac se de ea re legatos ad eos missuros
dixerunt. Hanc legationem suscepit Themistocles
et solus primo profectus est; reliqui legati ut tum
exirent, cum satis alti tuendo muri exstructi viderentur,[1] praecepit: interim omnes, servi atque liberi
opus facerent neque ulli loco parcerent, sive sacer
sive privatus esset sive publicus,[2] et undique quod
idoneum ad muniendum putarent congererent. Quo
factum est ut Atheniensium muri ex sacellis
sepulcrisque constarent.

7. Themistocles autem ut Lacedaemonem venit,
adire ad magistratus noluit et dedit operam ut
quam longissime tempus duceret, causam inter-
2 ponens se collegas exspectare. Cum Lacedaemonii
quererentur opus nihilo minus fieri eumque in ea re
conari fallere, interim reliqui legati sunt consecuti.
A quibus cum audisset non multum superesse
munitionis, ad ephoros Lacedaemoniorum accessit,
penes quos summum erat imperium, atque apud eos
contendit falsa iis esse delata: qua re aequum esse
illos viros bonos nobilesque mittere quibus fides
haberetur, qui rem explorarent; interea se obsidem
3 retinerent. Gestus est ei mos, tresque legati functi
summis honoribus Athenas missi sunt. Cum his
collegas suos Themistocles iussit proficisci iisque
praedixit ut ne prius Lacedaemoniorum legatos
dimitterent quam ipse esset remissus.

[1] satis . . . viderentur, *Heerwagen*; satis altitudo muri
extructa videretur, *MSS.*

[2] sive sacer sive prophanus sive privatus esset sive publicus,
M and some inferior MSS.

[1] *Sacer* is contrasted with *privatus* and *publicus* (= *pro-
fanus*), but perhaps the reading of cod. M (see crit. note) i
right; cf. Cic. *Verr.* iv. 2 and v. 1.

present, the Athenians desisted, saying that they would send envoys to Lacedaemon to discuss the matter. That mission Themistocles undertook and set out at first alone, giving orders that the rest of the envoys should not follow until the walls seemed to have risen high enough to defend: that in the meantime all, bond and free, should push the work, sparing no place, whether sacred or public or private,[1] but getting together from every hand whatever they thought suitable for a fortification. That is the reason why the walls of Athens were made of shrines and tombs.

7. But when Themistocles came to Lacedaemon, he at first refused to appear before the magistrates, and did his best to gain as much time as possible, pretending that he was waiting for his colleagues. While the Lacedaemonians were protesting that the work was going on just the same, and that he was trying to deceive them about it, meanwhile the rest of the envoys arrived. When Themistocles heard from them that not much of the fortification remained unfinished, he went before the ephors of the Lacedaemonians, in whose hands was the supreme power, and declared in their presence that they had been misinformed: therefore it was just that they should send reliable men of high position, in whom they had confidence, to investigate the matter; in the meantime they might hold him as a hostage. His proposition was accepted, and three deputies, who had held the highest offices, were sent to Athens. Themistocles directed his colleagues to return with them and charged them not to allow the envoys of the Lacedaemonians to return, until he himself had been sent back.

4 Hos postquam Athenas pervenisse ratus est, ad
magistratum senatumque Lacedaemoniorum adiit
et apud eos liberrime professus est Athenienses suo
consilio, quod communi iure gentium facere possent,
deos publicos suosque patrios ac Penates, quo
facilius ab hoste possent defendere, muris saepsisse
5 neque in eo quod inutile esset Graeciae fecisse.
Nam illorum urbem ut propugnaculum oppositum
esse barbaris, apud quam iam bis classes regias
6 fecisse naufragium. Lacedaemonios autem male et
iniuste facere, qui id potius intuerentur quod ipsorum
dominationi quam quod universae Graeciae utile
esset. Qua re, si suos legatos recipere vellent quos
Athenas miserant, se remitterent; aliter illos
numquam in patriam essent recepturi.

8. Tamen non effugit civium suorum invidiam.
Namque ob eundem quo damnatus erat
Miltiades testularum suffragiis e civitate eiectus,
2 Argos habitatum concessit. Hic cum propter multas
eius virtutes magna cum dignitate viveret, Lacedaemonii legatos Athenas miserunt, qui eum absentem

---

¹ Here and in iv. 4. 3 Nepos uses the singular *magistratum*
of the college of five ephors or "overseers." The "senate"
is the γερουσία, the corresponding body at Sparta, consisting
of twenty-eight elders (γέροντες) and the two kings. Other
Roman terms applied to Greek institutions are *nobiles* (7. 2)
and *honoribus* (7. 3).

² An institution established by Cleisthenes after the
expulsion of the Pisistratidae. The Prytanies and the
popular assembly (ἐκκλησία) must first determine whether
such a step was necessary. If they decided in the affirmative,
each citizen wrote on a potsherd (ὄστρακον, whence the
term "ostracism") the name of the man whom he wished
to banish. The one who had the greatest number of votes
recorded against him, provided the total number of voters
was 6000, was obliged to leave the city within ten days for an

As soon as he thought that the deputation had reached Athens, he appeared before the magistrates [1] and the senate of the Lacedaemonians and confessed to them with the utmost frankness that the Athenians, by his advice, and taking advantage of the rights granted by the common law of nations, had encircled with walls the gods of all Greece, of their native city and of their homes, in order the more easily to defend them against the enemy; and that in so doing they had acted for the best interests of Greece. For their city, he said, was like an outpost in the path of the barbarians, and upon it the king's fleets had already twice suffered shipwreck. But the Lacedaemonians were acting wrongfully and unjustly in having in view rather what contributed to their own supremacy than to the welfare of Greece as a whole. Therefore, if they wished to recover their envoys which they had sent to Athens, they must let him go; otherwise they would never get them back again in their native land.

8. In spite of all, Themistocles could not escape the distrust of his fellow-citizens; but because of the same feeling of apprehension that had led to the condemnation of Miltiades he was banished from the city by the shard-vote [2] and went to live in Argos. There because of his many accomplishments he lived in great distinction, until the Lacedaemonians sent envoys to Athens,[3] to accuse him

exile of ten, later of five, years, but without loss of rank or property. If the number of votes did not amount to 6000, no action was taken. Cf. v. 3. 1, where the Greek name ὀστρακισμός is given.

[3] In 471 B.C., or according to others in 468 or 467.

accusarent, quod societatem cum rege Perse ad
3 Graeciam opprimendam fecisset. Hoc crimine
absens proditionis damnatus est.

Id ut audivit, quod non satis tutum se Argis
videbat, Corcyram demigravit. Ibi cum cives[1] principes animadvertisset timere ne propter se bellum
iis Lacedaemonii et Athenienses indicerent, ad
Admetum, Molossum regem, cum quo ei hospitium
4 erat, confugit. Huc cum venisset et in praesentia
rex abesset, quo maiore religione se receptum
tueretur, filiam eius parvulam adripuit et cum ea
se in sacrarium quod summa colebatur caerimonia
coniecit. Inde non prius egressus est, quam rex
5 eum data dextra in fidem reciperet, quam praestitit.
Nam cum ab Atheniensibus et Lacedaemoniis
exposceretur publice, supplicem non prodidit monuit-
que ut consuleret sibi: difficile enim esse in tam
propinquo loco tuto eum versari. Itaque Pydnam
eum deduci iussit et quod satis esset praesidii dedit.
6 Hic in navem omnibus ignotus nautis escendit.
Quae cum tempestate maxima Naxum ferretur,
ubi tum Atheniensium erat exercitus, sensit Themistocles, si eo pervenisset, sibi esse pereundum. Hac
necessitate coactus domino navis quis sit aperit,

---

[1] cives, *H. J. Müller*; eius, *MSS.*; eius principes civitatis,
u M.

---

[1] This imposed a sacred and binding obligation to protect
a guest against his enemies. Thucydides says that Admetus
was not a friend of Themistocles, whence some editors insert
non after *erat*.

[2] Thucydides says that it was a son, and some editors
change *filiam* to *filium*; but the deviations of Nepos from
the historical sources are too numerous to mention in detail.

[3] In 473 B.C., warring against the cities that had revolted
from the Athenian league.

behind his back of having conspired with the king of Persia to enslave Greece. On this charge he was found guilty of high treason without a hearing.

As soon as he learned of this, Themistocles decided that he was not sufficiently safe in Argos and withdrew to Corcyra. When he perceived that the leading citizens of that place were fearful that the Lacedaemonians and Athenians would declare war upon them because of his presence, he took refuge with Admetus, king of the Molossians, with whom he had relations of guest-friendship.[1] Having arrived there when Admetus was away from home, in order that his host might be under the greater obligation to receive and protect him he caught up the king's little daughter[2] and hastened with her into the household shrine, which was regarded with the greatest veneration; and he would not come out again until the king gave him his right hand and received him under his protection. And Admetus kept his promise; for when the Athenians and Lacedaemonians made an official demand for Themistocles, Admetus did not surrender the suppliant; he advised him, however, to take measures to protect himself, saying that it would be difficult for him to remain in safety in a place so near to Greece. Accordingly, the king had him taken to Pydna, giving him such escort as he deemed sufficient.

There Themistocles embarked on a ship without being known to any of the crew. When the vessel was driven by a violent storm towards Naxos, where the Athenian army was at the time,[3] Themistocles understood that if he landed there he was lost. Therefore of necessity he made himself known to the captain of the ship, adding many promises if he

7 multa pollicens, si se conservasset. At ille clarissimi viri captus misericordia, diem noctemque procul ab insula in salo navem tenuit in ancoris neque quemquam ex ea exire passus est. Inde Ephesum pervenit ibique Themistoclen exponit. Cui ille pro meritis postea gratiam rettulit.

9. Scio plerosque ita scripsisse, Themistoclen Xerxe regnante in Asiam transisse. Sed ego potissimum Thucydidi credo, quod aetate proximus de iis qui illorum temporum historiam reliquerunt, et eiusdem civitatis fuit. Is autem ait ad Artaxerxen eum venisse atque his verbis epistulam misisse:

2 " Themistocles veni ad te, qui plurima mala omnium Graiorum in domum tuam intuli, quam diu mihi necesse fuit adversum patrem tuum bellare patriam-

3 que meam defendere. Idem multo plura bona feci, postquam in tuto ipse et ille in periculo esse coepit; nam cum in Asiam reverti vellet, proelio apud Salamina facto, litteris eum certiorem feci id agi, ut pons quem in Hellesponto fecerat dissolveretur atque ab hostibus circumiretur; quo nuntio ille

4 periculo est liberatus. Nunc autem confugi ad te, exagitatus a cuncta Graecia, tuam petens amicitiam; quam si ero adeptus, non minus me bonum amicum habebis, quam fortem inimicum ille expertus est. Te [1] autem rogo, ut de iis rebus, quas tecum conloqui volo, annuum mihi tempus des eoque transacto ad te venire patiaris."

---

[1] te, *Fleck*; id *B, Leid. II*; ea, *the other MSS.*

---

[1] i. 137. 3 ff.
[2] Artaxerxes Macrochir; see xxi. 1. 3.
[3] Thucydides says, διὰ τὴν σὴν φιλίαν, " because of my friendship for you."

would save his life. The sailor, filled with pity for so distinguished a man, for a day and a night kept his ship at anchor out at sea far off from the island, and would not allow anyone to leave her. Then he went on to Ephesus and there landed Themistocles, who afterwards requited him for his services

9. I am aware that many have written that Themistocles passed over into Asia during the reign of Xerxes, but I prefer to believe Thucydides, because among the writers who have left a history of those times he was most nearly contemporary with Themistocles, besides being a native of the same city. Now he says [1] that it was to Artaxerxes [2] that Themistocles came, and that he sent a letter to the king in the following words: " I, Themistocles, have come to you, the man of all the Greeks who brought the most ills upon your house, so long as it was necessary for me to war against your father and defend my native land. But I also did him many more favours, so soon as I began to find myself in safety and he was in danger. For when he wished to return to Asia after having fought the battle at Salamis, I informed him by letter of the enemy's plot to destroy the bridge which he had made over the Hellespont and to cut off his retreat; and it was that message which saved him from danger. But now I have sought refuge with you, hounded as I am by all Greece, seeking your friendship; [3] if I obtain it, you will have in me as good a friend as I was a courageous foeman of Xerxes. But with regard to the matters about which I wish to confer with you, I ask you to allow me a year's delay and let me come to you at the end of that time."

CORNELIUS NEPOS

10. Huius rex animi magnitudinem admirans cupiensque talem virum sibi conciliari, veniam dedit. Ille omne illud tempus litteris sermonique Persarum se dedidit; quibus adeo eruditus est, ut multo commodius dicatur apud regem verba fecisse quam 2 ii poterant qui in Perside erant nati. Hic cum multa regi esset pollicitus gratissimumque illud, si suis uti consiliis vellet, illum Graeciam bello oppressurum, magnis muneribus ab Artaxerxe donatus, in Asiam rediit domiciliumque Magnesiae sibi con- 3 stituit. Namque hanc urbem ei rex donarat, his quidem verbis, quae ei panem praeberet—ex qua regione quinquaginta talenta quotannis redibant— Lampsacum autem, unde vinum sumeret, Myunta,[1] ex qua obsonium haberet.

Huius ad nostram memoriam monumenta manserunt duo: sepulcrum prope oppidum, in quo est 4 sepultus, statua[2] in foro Magnesiae. De cuius morte multimodis apud plerosque scriptum est, sed nos eundem potissimum Thucydidem auctorem probamus, qui illum ait Magnesiae morbo mortuum neque negat fuisse famam, venenum sua sponte sumpsisse, cum se quae regi de Graecia opprimenda 5 pollicitus esset praestare posse desperaret. Idem ossa eius clam in Attica ab amicis sepulta, quoniam legibus non concederetur, quod proditionis esset damnatus, memoriae prodidit.

---

[1] Myunta, *Aldus*; *the MSS. usually have corruptions of proper names, which will not always be noted.*
[2] statua, *Fleck*; statuae, *MSS.*

---

[1] This is one of Nepos' frequent exaggerations; cf. Thuc. i. 138 and Plut. *Them.* 29.
[2] Used in the Roman sense of a part of Asia Minor.
[3] *Obsonium* included everything that was eaten with bread by way of relish; with the Greeks, especially fish.

10. The king, admiring his high spirit, and eager to win the friendship of such a man, granted his request. Themistocles devoted all that time to the literature and language of the Persians, in which he became so well versed that he is said to have spoken in much better style before the king than those could who were natives of Persia.[1] Themistocles made many promises to the king, of which the most welcome was, that if Artaxerxes would consent to follow his advice, the king's arms would subjugate Greece. Then, after receiving many presents from the monarch, he returned to Asia[2] and took up his residence at Magnesia; for the king had given him that city, with the remark that it would furnish him with bread (the annual revenue of the district was five hundred talents), also Lampsacus, to supply him with wine, and Myus, to furnish the rest of his fare.[3]

Two memorials of this man have endured to our own day: his tomb near the town in which he was buried,[4] and his statue in the Forum at Magnesia. Of his death many different accounts are given by numerous writers, but once more I prefer to accept the testimony of Thucydides. That historian says that Themistocles died a natural death at Magnesia, admitting, however, that there was a report that he had poisoned himself, because he despaired of being able to keep his promises to the king with regard to the subjugation of Greece. Thucydides has also stated that Themistocles' bones were buried in Attica by his friends secretly, since his interment there was contrary to law, because he had been found guilty of treason.

---

[4] That is, Magnesia.

CORNELIUS NEPOS

III. ARISTIDES

1. Aristides, Lysimachi filius, Atheniensis, aequalis fere fuit Themistocli itaque cum eo de principatu 2 contendit; namque obtrectarunt inter se. In his autem cognitum est quanto antistaret eloquentia innocentiae. Quamquam enim adeo excellebat Aristides abstinentia, ut unus post hominum memoriam, quem quidem nos audierimus, cognomine Iustus sit appellatus, tamen a Themistocle conlabefactus, testula illa exsilio decem annorum multatus est. 3 Qui quidem cum intellegeret reprimi concitatam multitudinem non posse, cedensque animadvertisset quendam scribentem ut patria pelleretur, quaesisse ab eo dicitur qua re id faceret aut quid Aristides 4 commisisset cur tanta poena dignus duceretur. Cui ille respondit se ignorare Aristiden, sed sibi non placere quod tam cupide elaborasset ut praeter 5 ceteros Iustus appellaretur. Hic decem annorum legitimam poenam non pertulit. Nam postquam Xerxes in Graeciam descendit, sexto fere anno quam erat expulsus, populi scito in patriam restitutus est.

2. Interfuit autem pugnae navali apud Salamina, quae facta est prius quam poena liberaretur. Idem praetor fuit Atheniensium apud Plataeas in proelio quo Mardonius fusus barbarorumque exercitus inter-2 fectus est. Neque aliud est ullum huius in re

---

[1] See note 2, p. 34.

[2] According to one version of the story, the man could not write and Aristides wrote his own name for him on the shard.

III. ARISTIDES

1. Aristides the Athenian, son of Lysimachus, was of about the same age as Themistocles, and consequently disputed with him the first rank in the state; for they were rivals. In fact, the history of these two men makes clear the extent to which eloquence has the advantage of integrity. For although Aristides so excelled in honesty that he is the only one within the memory of man—at least, so far as we have heard—who was given the title of "the Just," yet his influence was undermined by Themistocles and he was exiled for ten years by that well-known process known as the shard-vote.[1] Aristides himself, when he realized that the excited populace could not be quieted, and, as he was withdrawing, saw a man in the act of voting that he should be banished, is said to have asked him why he did so, and what Aristides had done to be thought deserving of such a punishment. To which the man replied that he did not know Aristides, but that he was displeased because he had worked so hard to be distinguished from other men by the surname of "the Just."[2] Aristides did not complete the legal penalty of ten years; for when Xerxes descended upon Greece, in about the sixth year of his exile, he was restored to his native land by decree of the people.

2. Aristides took part besides in the naval battle at Salamis, although it was fought before his recall. He was also general of the Athenians at Plataea 479 B.C. in the battle in which Mardonius was defeated and the army of the barbarians was slaughtered. Although there is no other brilliant exploit in his

43

militari illustre factum quam huius[1] imperii memoria,
iustitiae vero et aequitatis et innocentiae multa, in
primis quod eius aequitate factum est, cum in communi classe esset Graeciae simul cum Pausania—
quo duce Mardonius erat fugatus—ut summa
imperii maritimi ab Lacedaemoniis transferretur ad
3 Athenienses; namque ante id tempus et mari et
terra duces erant Lacedaemonii. Tum autem et
intemperantia Pausaniae et iustitia factum est
Aristidis, ut omnes fere civitates Graeciae ad
Atheniensium societatem se applicarent et adversus
barbaros hos duces deligerent sibi.

3. Quos quo facilius repellerent, si forte bellum
renovare conarentur, ad classis aedificandas exercitusque comparandos quantum pecuniae quaeque
civitas daret Aristides delectus est qui constitueret,
eiusque arbitrio quadringena et sexagena talenta
quotannis Delum sunt conlata; id enim commune
aerarium esse voluerunt. Quae omnis pecunia
2 postero tempore Athenas translata est. Hic qua
fuerit abstinentia, nullum est certius indicium quam
quod,[2] cum tantis rebus praefuisset, in tanta pauper-
3 tate decessit, ut qui efferretur vix reliquerit. Quo
factum est ut filiae eius publice alerentur et de
communi aerario dotibus datis conlocarentur. Decessit autem fere post annum quartum quam
Themistocles Athenis erat expulsus.

----

[1] eius, *Halm.*
[2] quod, *added by Lambin.*

----

[1] He was one of the generals at Marathon, and later
against the Persians in Cyprus and on the Hellespont; cf.
iv. 2. 1.

military career except the memory of that command,[1] there are many instances of his justice, equity and integrity; in particular, that it was due to his equity, when he was on the fleet of the Greek allies in company with Pausanias, the general who had routed Mardonius, that the supremacy of the sea passed from the Lacedaemonians to the Athenians. Until then, indeed, the Lacedaemonians had held the lead on land and sea, but at that time the arrogance of Pausanias and the justice of Aristides led almost all the Greek cities to seek alliance with the Athenians and choose them as their leaders against the barbarians.

3. In order to repel the Persians more easily, if by any chance they should attempt to renew the war, Aristides was appointed to determine how much money each state should contribute for the purpose of building fleets and raising armies; and in accordance with his decision four hundred and sixty talents were deposited each year at Delos. That place was selected as the treasury of the league, but later [2] all that money was transported to Athens. There is no more certain proof of Aristides' integrity than the fact that, although he was entrusted with the management of such important affairs, he left so little money at his death, that there was hardly enough to pay his funeral expenses. The result was that his daughters were supported by the state and, when they married, were provided with dowries from the public treasury. Aristides died about four years after Themistocles had been 468 B.C. banished from Athens.

---

[2] In the time of Pericles; *quae omnis pecunia* means the contributions as a whole, except what had been expended.

CORNELIUS NEPOS

IV. PAUSANIAS

1. Pausanias Lacedaemonius magnus homo, sed varius in omni genere vitae fuit; nam ut virtutibus 2 eluxit, sic vitiis est obrutus. Huius illustrissimum est proelium apud Plataeas. Namque illo duce Mardonius, satrapes regius, natione Medus, regis gener, in primis omnium Persarum et manu fortis et consilii plenus, cum CC milibus peditum, quos viritim legerat, et XX equitum haud ita magna manu Graeciae fugatus est, eoque ipse dux cecidit 3 proelio. Qua victoria elatus, plurima miscere coepit et maiora concupiscere. Sed primum in eo est reprehensus, quod[1] ex praeda tripodem aureum Delphis posuisset epigrammate scripto,[2] in quo haec erat sententia: suo ductu barbaros apud Plataeas esse deletos eiusque victoriae ergo Apollini id[3] donum dedisse. Hos versus Lacedaemonii exsculpserunt neque aliud scripserunt quam nomina earum civitatum quarum auxilio Persae erant victi.

2. Post id proelium eundem Pausaniam cum classe communi Cyprum atque Hellespontum miserunt, ut ex iis regionibus barbarorum praesidia 2 depelleret. Pari felicitate in ea re usus, elatius se gerere coepit maioresque appetere res. Nam cum Byzantio expugnato cepisset complures Persarum

---

[1] quod, *u and some inferior MSS.*; quod cum, *A B M P R*; cum, *Nipp.*

[2] inscripto, *cod. Vat.* 3170, *Fleck.*

[3] id, *added by Fleck.*

---

[1] In reality he was a Persian and son-in-law of Darius, father of Xerxes.

[2] The bronze serpents that supported the tripod, inscribed on their coils with the names of the cities, are now in Con-

IV. PAUSANIAS

1. Pausanias the Lacedaemonian was a great man, but untrustworthy in all the relations of life; for while he possessed conspicuous merits, yet he was overloaded with defects. His most famous exploit was the battle of Plataea; for it was under his command that Mardonius, a Mede by birth, satrap and son-in-law of the king,[1] among the first of all the Persians in deeds of arms and wise counsel, with an army of two hundred thousand foot-soldiers that he himself had selected man by man, and twenty thousand horsemen, was routed by a comparatively small force of Greeks; and in that battle the leader himself fell. Puffed up by this victory, Pausanias began to engage in numerous intrigues and form ambitious designs. But first of all he incurred criticism by consecrating at Delphi from the spoils a golden tripod, on which was a metrical inscription to this purport: that it was under his lead that the barbarians had been destroyed at Plataea and that because of that victory he gave that gift to Apollo. Those verses the Lacedaemonians erased and put in their place only the names of the cities with whose help the Persians had been defeated.[2]

2. After that battle Pausanias again commanded the allied Greeks, being sent with a fleet to Cyprus and the Hellespont to dislodge the garrisons of the barbarians from those regions. Having enjoyed equal good fortune in that expedition, he began to act still more arrogantly and to entertain still loftier ambitions. In fact, having at the taking of Byzantium captured several Persian nobles, including some

stantinople. Thucydides (i. 132. 2) does not say that the tripod was of gold; that adjective is from Diodorus (xi. 33).

nobiles atque in his nonnullos regis propinquos, hos clam Xerxi remisit, simulans ex vinclis publicis effugisse, et cum his Gongylum Eretriensem, qui litteras regi redderet, in quibus haec fuisse scripta

3 Thucydides memoriae prodidit: "Pausanias, dux Spartae, quos Byzanti ceperat, postquam propinquos tuos cognovit, tibi muneri misit seque tecum adfinitate coniungi cupit; qua re, si tibi videtur, des ei

4 filiam tuam nuptum. Id si feceris, et Spartam et ceteram Graeciam sub tuam potestatem se adiuvante te[1] redacturum pollicetur. His de rebus si quid geri volueris, certum hominem ad eum mittas face, cum quo conloquatur."

5 Rex, tot hominum salute tam sibi necessariorum magno opere gavisus, confestim cum epistula Artabazum ad Pausaniam mittit, in qua eum conlaudat ac[2] petit ne cui rei parcat ad ea efficienda quae

6 pollicetur: si perfecerit, nullius rei a se repulsam laturum. Huius Pausanias voluntate cognita, alacrior ad rem gerendam factus, in suspicionem cecidit Lacedaemoniorum. Quo[3] facto domum revocatus, accusatus capitis absolvitur, multatur tamen pecunia; quam ob causam ad classem remissus non est.

3. At ille post non multo sua sponte ad exercitum rediit et ibi non callida, sed dementi[4] ratione cogitata patefecit; non enim mores patrios solum, sed

---

[1] te, *added by Bosius*; se adiuvante se, *Can.*
[2] ac, *added by Fleck*; petit, *omitted by Gemss.*
[3] quo, *u*; in quo, *MSS.*
[4] non stolida sed dementi, *MSS.*; non callida *without* sed dementi, *Gemss*; non modo non c. sed d., *Wagner.*

---

[1] That is, without being appointed commander.

relatives of the king, he secretly sent them back to Xerxes, pretending that they had escaped from the state prison; and with them he dispatched Gongylus the Eretrian, who was to deliver to the king a letter. which, as Thucydides has told us, contained the following message: " Pausanias, the Spartan general, as soon as he learned that certain prisoners that he took at Byzantium were your relatives, has sent them to you as a gift, and desires to ally himself with your family. Therefore, if it please you, give him your daughter to wife. If you do so, he guarantees that with your help he will bring Sparta and all Greece under your sway. If you desire to consider this proposal, see that you send him a trustworthy man with whom he may confer."

The king, greatly pleased at the recovery of so many intimate relatives, at once sent Artabazus to Pausanias with a letter, in which he thanked the Spartan and begged him to spare no pains to accomplish what he promised, saying that if he succeeded, there was nothing that the king would refuse him. When Pausanias knew the monarch's intentions, he devoted himself with greater energy to perfecting his plans, and thus excited the suspicions of the Lacedaemonians. In consequence, he was recalled and tried for his life, and although he escaped death, he was compelled to pay a fine, and because of that he was not sent back to the fleet.

3. But not long afterwards Pausanias returned to the army on his own account,[1] and there he revealed his designs in a manner that was rather insane than adroit.[2] For he abandoned, not only the customs

---

[2] Nepos' striving for antithesis carries him too far, but no change seems necessary; cf. the crit. note.

2 etiam cultum vestitumque mutavit. Apparatu regio
utebatur, veste Medica; satellites Medi et Aegyptii
sequebantur; epulabatur more Persarum luxuriosius
3 quam qui aderant perpeti possent; aditum petenti-
bus conveniundi non dabat, superbe respondebat,
crudeliter imperabat. Spartam redire nolebat; Colo-
nas, qui locus in agro Troade est, se contulerat; ibi
consilia cum patriae tum sibi inimica capiebat.
4 Id postquam Lacedaemonii rescierunt, legatos cum
clava ad eum miserunt, in qua more illorum erat
scriptum: nisi domum reverteretur, se capitis eum
5 damnaturos. Hoc nuntio commotus, sperans se
etiam tum pecunia et potentia instans periculum
posse depellere, domum rediit. Huc ut venit, ab
ephoris in vincla publica est coniectus; licet enim
legibus eorum cuivis ephoro hoc facere regi. Hinc
tamen se expedivit, neque eo magis carebat suspicione; nam opinio manebat eum cum rege habere
societatem.
6 Est genus quoddam hominum quod Hilotae vocatur, quorum magna multitudo agros Lacedaemoniorum colit servorumque munere fungitur. Hos
7 quoque sollicitare spe libertatis existimabatur. Sed
quod harum rerum nullum erat apertum crimen quo

---

¹ The σκυτάλη, a means of secret communication used by
the Spartan ephors. When a king or general left home, he
was given a staff, or cylindrical piece of wood, exactly similar
to one in the possession of the ephors. When they wished
to communicate with him, they wound a narrow strip of
leather in a spiral around the staff, and wrote their message
on it along the length of the staff. When the thong was
unrolled, only detached letters or fragments of words were
seen; but the person addressed could read the message by
using his staff. See Gellius, xvii. 9. 6 ff.

of his country, but even its manner of life and dress. He assumed royal splendour, the Medic garb; Persian and Egyptian attendants followed him. He dined in the Persian fashion, more extravagantly than his associates could tolerate. He refused to give audience to those who wished to meet him, returned haughty answers, and exercised his authority cruelly. He refused to return to Sparta, but went to Colonae, a place in the region of the Troad; there he nourished plans that were ruinous not only to his country but to himself.

As soon as the Lacedaemonians learned of his conduct, they sent envoys to him with the staff,[1] on which it was written after their fashion that if he did not return home, they would condemn him to death. Troubled by this message, and hoping that even then he could avert the threatening danger by his money and his prestige, he returned to Sparta. On his arrival he was imprisoned by the ephors; for according to the laws of Sparta any ephor [2] may so treat a king.[3] However, he succeeded in effecting his release, but he was none the less under suspicion; for the opinion persisted that he had an understanding with the Persian king.

There is a class of men called Helots, who are very numerous; they till the fields of the Lacedaemonians and perform the duties of slaves. These too Pausanias was believed to be tempting by the promise of freedom. But because, in spite of these circumstances, there was no direct charge which

[2] It could be done only by the entire college of ephors (five in number), and at the time when Nepos wrote there were no kings at Sparta.

[3] Pausanias was guardian of the young king Pleistachus, and hence acting as regent.

coargui posset, non putabant de tali tamque claro
viro suspicionibus oportere iudicari et exspectandum, dum se ipsa res aperiret.

4. Interim Argilius quidam adulescentulus, quem
puerum Pausanias amore venerio dilexerat, cum
epistulam ab eo ad Artabazum accepisset eique in
suspicionem venisset aliquid in ea de se esse scriptum, quod nemo eorum redisset qui super tali causa [1]
eodem missi erant, vincla epistulae laxavit signoque
detracto cognovit, si pertulisset, sibi esse pereun-
2 dum.   Erant in eadem epistula quae ad ea pertine-
bant quae inter regem Pausaniamque convenerant.
Has ille litteras ephoris tradidit.

3   Non est praetereunda gravitas Lacedaemoniorum
hoc loco; nam ne huius quidem indicio impulsi sunt
ut Pausaniam comprehenderent, neque prius vim
adhibendam putaverunt, quam se ipse indicasset.
Itaque huic indici quid fieri vellent praeceperunt.

4 Fanum Neptuni est Taenari, quod violari nefas
putant Graeci. Eo ille index [2] confugit in araque
consedit. Hanc iuxta locum fecerunt sub terra,
ex quo posset exaudiri, si quis quid loqueretur cum
5 Argilio. Huc ex ephoris quidam descenderunt.
Pausanias ut audivit Argilium confugisse in aram,
perturbatus venit eo. Quem cum supplicem dei
videret in ara sedentem, quaerit causae quid sit

---

[1] (cum) suber(a)t ali(qua) causa, *Wagner*.
[2] index, *omitted by Heerwagen*.

---

[1] *Super*, = *de*, is suspicious; Wagner's emendation
("whenever there was any occasion") is attractive; see
crit. note.

could be brought against him, the Lacedaemonians thought that a man of his position and distinction ought not to be brought to trial because of mere suspicions, but that they ought to wait until the truth revealed itself.

4. Meanwhile a young man of Argilus, with whom when a boy Pausanias had had a love affair, having received from him a letter for Artabazus, suspected that it contained some allusion to himself, since none of the messengers who had been sent on similar errands [1] had ever returned. Accordingly, he loosened the cord of the letter, broke the seal, and found that if he should deliver it, he was doomed to death; the letter also contained references to the agreement between Pausanias and the king. This letter the young man handed over to the ephors.

We must not fail to observe the deliberateness of the Lacedaemonians on this occasion. Even this man's testimony did not lead them to arrest Pausanias, but they thought that no violence ought to be offered him until he actually betrayed himself. Accordingly, they made known to this informer what he was to do. There is at Taenarum a temple of Neptune, which the Greeks deem it impious to violate. To this that informer fled and seated himself upon the altar. Near by they made a subterranean chamber, from which anyone who talked with the Argilian could be overheard, and there some of the ephors concealed themselves. When Pausanias heard that the Argilian had taken refuge at the altar, he went there in a state of great anxiety; and finding him seated on the altar in the attitude of a suppliant of the god, he asked his reason for

tam repentini consilii. Huic ille quid ex litteris
6 comperisset aperit. Modo[1] magis Pausanias perturbatus orare coepit ne enuntiaret nec se meritum
de illo optime proderet: quod si eam veniam sibi
dedisset tantisque implicatum rebus sublevasset,
magno ei praemio futurum.

5. His rebus ephori cognitis, satius putarunt in
urbe eum comprehendi. Quo cum essent profecti
et Pausanias placato Argilio, ut putabat, Lacedaemonem reverteretur, in itinere, cum iam in eo esset
ut comprehenderetur, ex vultu cuiusdam ephori,
qui eum admoneri cupiebat, insidias sibi fieri intel-
2 lexit. Itaque paucis ante gradibus quam qui eum
sequebantur, in aedem Minervae quae Chalcioicos
vocatur confugit. Hinc ne exire posset, statim
ephori valvas eius aedis obstruxerunt tectumque
3 sunt demoliti, quo celerius sub divo interiret. Dicitur
eo tempore matrem Pausaniae vixisse eamque iam
magno natu, postquam de scelere filii comperit, in
primis ad filium claudendum lapidem ad introitum
4 aedis attulisse. Hic cum semianimis de templo
elatus esset, confestim animam efflavit.[2] Sic Pausanias magnam belli gloriam turpi morte maculavit.
5 Cuius mortui corpus cum eodem nonnulli dicerent

---

[1] tanto *or* multo, *Lambin*; quo, *Fleck.*
[2] Hic . . . efflavit *after* maculavit *in MSS.*; *transposed
by Fleck.*

---

[1] For this use of *modo* Halm compared Sallust, *Jug.* 47. 3
and 75. 1; or it may simply mean " then " (" now " transferred to the past).
[2] Since they did not venture to violate the shrine; see 4. 4.
[3] Lady of the Brazen House, so called because her temple
was overlaid with plates of bronze. The goddess was Athena,

such a sudden determination. The youth told him what he had learned from the letter. Pausanias, still more [1] disturbed, began to beg him not to betray one who had always deserved well of him; adding that if he would do him that favour and aid him in the great difficulty in which he found himself, he would reward him generously.

5. Upon getting this evidence the ephors thought it would be better to arrest him in Sparta.[2] When they had left the place, and Pausanias, having won over the Argilian, as he thought, was on his way to Lacedaemon, in the course of the journey, just as he was on the point of being arrested, from the expression of one of the ephors, who wished to warn him, he perceived that they had designs upon him. Accordingly, he took refuge in the temple of Minerva, surnamed Chalcioikos,[3] outstripping his pursuers by only a few steps. To prevent his leaving the place, the ephors at once blocked up the doors of the temple and destroyed its roof,[4] in order that he might the sooner die from exposure to the open heavens. It is said that Pausanias' mother was living at the time, and that having learned of her son's guilt, in spite of her great age she was among the first to bring a stone to the entrance of the temple, to immure her own child. He was half dead when taken from the precinct and at once breathed his last. Thus it was that Pausanias dishonoured his glorious career by a shameful end. After his death some said that his body

but Nepos, as usual, uses the Roman equivalent; see note 4, p. 373.

[4] According to Thucydides (i. 134), it was not the temple, but a building within the sacred precinct, in which Pausanias sought asylum.

inferri oportere quo ii qui ad supplicium essent dati, displicuit pluribus, et procul ab eo loco infoderunt quo erat mortuus. Inde posterius dei [1] Delphici responso erutus atque eodem loco sepultus est [2] ubi vitam posuerat.

V. CIMON

1. Cimon, Miltiadis filius, Atheniensis, duro admodum initio usus est adulescentiae; nam cum pater eius litem aestimatam populo solvere non potuisset ob eamque causam in vinclis publicis decessisset, Cimon eadem custodia tenebatur neque legibus Atheniensium [3] emitti poterat, nisi pecuniam qua 2 pater multatus erat solvisset. Habebat autem in matrimonio sororem germanam suam, nomine Elpinicen, non magis amore quam more ductus; namque Atheniensibus licet eodem patre natas uxores ducere. 3 Huius coniugii cupidus Callias quidam, non tam generosus quam pecuniosus, qui magnas pecunias ex metallis fecerat, egit cum Cimone ut eam sibi uxorem daret: id si impetrasset, se pro illo pecuniam 4 soluturum. Is cum talem condicionem aspernaretur, Elpinice negavit se passuram Miltiadis progeniem in vinclis publicis interire, quoniam prohibere posset,

[1] dei, *added by Lambin.*   [2] est, *added by Fleck.*
[3] Atheniensium, *Lambin*; Atheniensibus, *MSS.*

[1] A ravine near Sparta, called καιάδας.
[2] The passage is obscure and perhaps corrupt. Since Thucydides says that Pausanias was first buried near the καιάδας, *procul* may mean " hard by," as in Horace, *Sat.* ii. 6. 105 and *Epist.* i. 7. 32, and *quo erat mortuus* may be a gloss. The death of Pausanias took place soon after the condemnation of Themistocles; see ii. 8. 2, and note 3.

ought to be taken to the spot set apart for the burial of criminals;[1] but the majority opposed this, and he was buried at a distance from the place where he had died.[2] Later, in consequence of an oracle of Delphic Apollo, he was exhumed and interred on the very spot where he had ended his life.

V. CIMON

1. Cimon, the Athenian, son of Miltiades, in his early youth suffered great trouble; for since his father had been unable to pay the fine imposed upon him by the people, and therefore had died in the state prison,[3] the son also was kept in confinement; and the laws of Athens did not allow him to be set at liberty unless he paid the amount of his father's fine.[4] Now, he had married his own sister Elpinice, led as much by the custom of his country as by affection;[5] for it is lawful for the Athenians to marry sisters born of the same father.[6] His wife's hand was sought by a certain Callias, who was rich but not of high birth and had made a great deal of money from the mines.[7] He pleaded with Cimon to give Elpinice to him as his wife, saying that on that condition he would pay the fine. Callias scorned such a proposal, but Elpinice declared that she would not allow the son of Miltiades to die in the state prison, when she had the power to pre-

---

[3] See i. 7. 6, and the note.

[4] This is not true; he suffered ἀτιμία, which deprived him of most of the privileges of citizenship.

[5] It seems impossible to reproduce the word-play, *amore . . . more.*

[6] Cf. Praef. 4.   [7] See note 1, p. 24.

seque Calliae nupturam, si ea quae polliceretur praestitisset.

2. Tali modo custodia liberatus, Cimon celeriter ad principatum pervenit. Habebat enim satis eloquentiae, summam liberalitatem, magnam prudentiam cum iuris civilis tum rei militaris, quod cum patre a puero in exercitibus fuerat versatus. Itaque hic et populum urbanum in sua tenuit potestate et apud exercitum plurimum valuit auctoritate.

2 Primum imperator apud flumen Strymona magnas copias Thraecum fugavit, oppidum Amphipolim constituit eoque decem milia Atheniensium in coloniam misit. Idem iterum apud Mycalen Cypriorum et Phoenicum ducentarum navium classem devictam cepit eodemque die pari fortuna in terra usus est.

3 Namque hostium navibus captis, statim ex classe copias suas eduxit barbarorumque maximam vim

4 uno concursu prostravit. Qua victoria magna praeda potitus cum domum reverteretur, quod iam nonnullae insulae propter acerbitatem imperii defecerant, bene animatas confirmavit, alienatas ad officium redire

5 coegit. Scyrum,[1] quam eo tempore Dolopes incolebant, quod contumacius se gesserant, vacuefecit, sessores veteres urbe insulaque eiecit, agros civibus divisit. Thasios opulentia fretos suo adventu fregit.

---

[1] Scyrum, *u, and some inferior MSS.*; Cyprum, *MSS.*

---

[1] This was not at Mycale, but at the river Eurymedon in Pamphylia in 468 B.C.; the victory at Mycale was won by Leotychides and Xanthippus in 479 B.C.

vent it, but that she would marry Callias, if he would keep his promise.

2. Having in this way gained his freedom, Cimon quickly rose to the first rank in the state; for he had a fair amount of eloquence, extreme generosity, and wide knowledge both of civil law and of the military art, since from boyhood he had accompanied his father on his campaigns. He therefore gained control over the city populace and had great influence with the army.

In his first command he routed a large force of Thracians at the river Strymon, and founded the town of Amphipolis, to which he sent ten thousand Athenians to establish a colony. On a second occasion, off Mycale,[1] he totally defeated a fleet of two hundred Cypriote and Phoenician ships, and captured them. On the same day he had equal good fortune on land; for after taking the ships of the enemy, he at once landed his soldiers and in a single onset annihilated a huge force of barbarians. As he was on his way home, having acquired a great amount of booty by his victory, he found that some of the islands had already revolted because of the severity of the Athenian rule; whereupon he assured the loyalty of those that were well disposed and compelled the disaffected to renew their allegiance. Scyros, which at that time was inhabited by *c.* 473 the Dolopians, he emptied of its population, because B.C. of their arrogant conduct, driving the earlier occupants from the city and from the island and dividing their lands among citizens of Athens. He broke the power of the Thasians, self-confident because of their wealth, by his mere arrival,[2] and from the proceeds

---

[2] As a matter of fact they resisted from 467 to 465 B.C.

His ex manubiis arx Athenarum, qua [1] ad meridiem vergit, est ornata.

3. Quibus rebus cum unus in civitate maxime floreret, incidit in eandem invidiam quam pater suus ceterique Atheniensium principes; nam testarum suffragiis, quod illi ὀστρακισμὸν vocant, X annorum 2 exsilio multatus est. Cuius facti celerius Athenienses quam ipsum paenituit; nam cum ille animo forti invidiae ingratorum civium cessisset bellumque Lacedaemonii Atheniensibus indixissent, confestim notae 3 eius virtutis desiderium consecutum est. Itaque post annum quintum quam expulsus erat in patriam revocatus, est. Ille, quod hospitio Lacedaemoniorum utebatur, satius existimans contendere [2] Lacedaemonem, sua sponte est profectus pacemque inter 4 duas potentissimas civitates conciliavit. Post, neque ita multo, Cyprum cum ducentis navibus imperator missus, cum eius maiorem partem insulae devicisset, in morbum implicitus in oppido Citio est mortuus.

4. Hunc Athenienses non solum in bello, sed etiam in pace diu desideraverunt. Fuit enim tanta liberalitate, cum compluribus locis praedia hortosque haberet, ut numquam in iis custodem posuerit [3] fructus servandi gratia, ne quis impediretur quo minus eius rebus, quibus quisque vellet, frueretur. 2 Semper eum pedisequi cum nummis sunt secuti, ut,

---

[1] qua, *Magius*; quae, *MSS.*

[2] concedere, *B²*; verbis contendere, *Sloane 327 and Cantabr.*; concedere quam armis contendere, *Halm*; verbis quam armis contendere, *Gitlbauer.*

[3] posuerit, *Cobet*; imposuerit, *MSS.*

---

[1] On the difference between *praeda* and *manubiae* see Gellius xiii. 25.

[2] See note 2, p. 34   [3] See note 1, p. 36

of the booty[1] he fortified the south side of the Athenian Acropolis.

3. Having become through these exploits the most distinguished man of his city, he incurred the same *c.* 461 distrust as his father and the other leading men of B.C. Athens, and by the shard-vote,[2] which they call ostracism, he was banished for a term of ten years. But the Athenians repented of their action sooner than he did himself; for after he had shown his fortitude by yielding to the suspicions of his ungrateful fellow-citizens, the Lacedaemonians began war with the Athenians, who at once felt the need of Cimon's well-known prowess. Therefore Cimon was recalled to his native land only four years after his banishment. Then, having a guest-friendship[3] with the Lacedaemonians, and thinking it better to go to Lacedaemon, he set out on his own responsibility and brought about peace between two powerful states.[4] Afterwards, but not much later, being sent as commander-in-chief to Cyprus with two hundred ships, after conquering the greater part of the island he was taken ill and died in the town of Citium.[5]

4. For a long time the Athenians missed Cimon, not only in war, but in peace as well. For he was so generous that, having estates and gardens in numerous places, he never set a guard over them to protect the fruits, since he did not wish to prevent anyone from enjoying any part of his property that he wished.[6] Pages always followed him with money,

[4] Cimon's recall was in 457 B.C., the peace with Lacedaemon not until 451.

[5] It was during the siege of that town in 449 B.C.

[6] The same story is told by Aristotle, 'Αθ. Πολ. 27. 3, who says that this liberality was a political device, to strengthen him against his chief rival, Pericles.

si quis opis eius indigeret, haberet quod statim daret,
ne differendo videretur negare. Saepe, cum aliquem
offensum fortuna [1] videret minus bene vestitum, suum
3 amiculum dedit. Cotidie sic cena ei coquebatur, ut,
quos invocatos vidisset in foro, omnis devocaret, quod
facere nullo die [2] praetermittebat. Nulli fides eius,
nulli opera, nulli res familiaris defuit; multos locupletavit; complures pauperes mortuos, qui unde effer-
4 rentur non reliquissent, suo sumptu extulit. Sic se
gerendo minime est mirandum, si et vita eius fuit
secura et mors acerba.

VI. LYSANDER

1. Lysander Lacedaemonius magnam reliquit sui
famam, magis felicitate quam virtute partam;
Atheniensis enim in Peloponnesios sexto et vicesimo
2 anno bellum gerentes confecisse apparet. Id qua
ratione consecutus sit haud [3] latet; non enim virtute
sui exercitus, sed immodestia factum est adversariorum, qui, quod dicto audientes imperatoribus
suis non erant, dispalati in agris relictis navibus in
hostium venerunt potestatem. Quo facto Athenienses se Lacedaemoniis dediderunt.

[1] fortunae, *Fleck.*; fortuito, *Nipperdey*; forte tunica, *O.
Wagner.*
[2] nullo die, *Nipperdey*; nullum diem, *MSS.*
[3] haud *added by Halm*; neque id qua . . . latet, *Nipperdey*; latet neminem, *Kellerbauer.*

---

[1] Another exaggeration; according to Plut. *Cim.* 10, he
entertained only the poor of his own deme (Lakiadai) who
came to Athens; cf. Aristotle, *l.c.*

so that if anyone had need of immediate help he might have something to give at once, for fear that by delay he might seem to refuse. Often, when he chanced to have met a man who was ill-treated by fortune and poorly clad, he gave him his cloak. Every day he had such an abundant dinner prepared that he could entertain all whom he saw in the market-place who had not been invited by others [1]; and this he never failed to do each day. No one asked in vain for his protection, no one for his services, no one for his financial aid; he enriched many, and buried at his own expense a great number who had died so poor that they had left nothing to pay for their funerals. Such being his conduct, it is not surprising that his life was free from trouble and his death deeply regretted.

VI. LYSANDER

1. Lysander the Lacedaemonian left a great reputation, gained rather by good fortune than by merit. There is no doubt, indeed, that he put an end to the power of the Athenians, who had been warring against the Peloponnesians for twenty-six years,[2] but how it was that he effected it is no secret. As a matter of fact, it was due, not to the valour of his army, but to the lack of discipline of his opponents, who did not obey their generals, but, leaving their ships and scattering about the country, fell into the power of the enemy.[3] As a result, the Athenians surrendered to the Lacedaemonians.

---

[2] It was the twenty-seventh year of the war.
[3] At the battle of Aegospotamoi, 404 B.C.

3 Hac victoria Lysander elatus, cum antea semper factiosus audaxque fuisset, sic sibi indulsit, ut eius opera in maximum odium Graeciae Lacedaemonii 4 pervenerint. Nam cum hanc causam Lacedaemonii dictitassent [1] sibi esse belli, ut Atheniensium impotentem dominationem refringerent, postquam apud Aegos flumen Lysander classis hostium est potitus, nihil aliud molitus est quam ut omnes civitates in sua teneret potestate, cum id se Lacedaemoniorum 5 causa facere simularet. Namque undique qui Atheniensium rebus studuissent eiectis, decem delegerat in una quaque civitate, quibus summum imperium potestatemque omnium rerum committeret. Horum in numerum [2] nemo admittebatur, nisi qui aut eius hospitio contineretur aut se illius fore proprium fide confirmarat.

2. Ita decemvirali potestate in omnibus urbibus constituta, ipsius nutu omnia gerebantur. Cuius de crudelitate ac perfidia satis est unam rem exempli gratia proferre, ne de eodem plura enumerando 2 defatigemus lectores. Victor ex Asia cum reverteretur Thasumque divertisset, quod ea civitas praecipua fide fuerat erga Athenienses, proinde ac si non [3] iidem firmissimi solerent esse amici qui constantes fuissent 3 inimici, pervertere eam concupivit. Vidit autem, nisi in eo occultasset voluntatem, futurum ut Thasii dilaberentur consulerentque rebus suis. . . .[4]

3. Itaque hi decemviralem illam [5] potestatem ab

---

[1] dictitassent, *u*; dictassent, *MSS.*

[2] numerum, *u*; numero, *MSS.*

[3] non, *u in the margin*; *the MSS. omit.*

[4] *u indicates a lacuna.*

[5] illam, *P u*; *omitted by Halm*; pot. illam, *Leid.*; suam pot., *A B R F θ*; suam pot. sui, *M.*

Lysander was elated by that victory, and while even before that he had always been reckless and given to intrigue, he now went so far that owing to him the Lacedaemonians came to be bitterly hated by all Greece. For although they had insisted that their reason for making war was to put an end to the tyrannical rule of Athens, no sooner had Lysander captured the enemy's fleet at Aegospotamoi [1] than it became his sole aim to hold all the Greek states under his control, pretending that he was acting in the interests of the Lacedaemonians. To that end, having everywhere expelled those who favoured the Athenians, he had chosen in each state ten men to be entrusted with the chief power and the direction of all affairs; among that number only those were included who were connected with Lysander by ties of hospitality, or had taken oath that they would be his men.

2. When decemviral authority had thus been established in all the cities, everything was done in accordance with Lysander's will. Of his cruelty and treachery it is enough to cite a single instance by way of illustration, rather than weary my readers by enumerating more of the same kind. When he was returning from Asia after his victory, he turned aside to go to Thasos, because that city had been especially loyal to the Athenians; and quite forgetting that those who have been the most determined enemies are usually the strongest friends, he wished to destroy the city. But he realized that unless he concealed his design, the Thasians would take flight and try to save their property. . . .

3. Therefore the Lacedaemonians abolished that

---

[1] Or Goat's River.

illo constitutam sustulerunt. Quo dolore incensus, iniit consilia reges Lacedaemoniorum tollere. Sed sentiebat id se sine ope deorum facere non posse, quod Lacedaemonii omnia ad oracula referre consuerant.

2 Primum Delphicum [1] corrumpere est conatus. Cum id non potuisset, Dodonam adortus est. Hinc quoque repulsus, dixit se vota suscepisse quae Iovi Hammoni solveret, existimans se Afros facilius corrupturum.

3 Hac spe cum profectus esset in Africam, multum eum antistites Iovis fefellerunt; nam non solum corrumpi non potuerunt, sed etiam legatos Lacedaemonem miserunt, qui Lysandrum accusarent quod sacerdotes fani corrumpere conatus esset.

4 Accusatus hoc crimine iudicumque absolutus sententiis, Orchomeniis missus subsidio occisus est a Thebanis apud Haliartum.

5 Quam vere de eo foret iudicatum, oratio indicio fuit quae post mortem in domo eius reperta est, in qua suadet Lacedaemoniis ut regia potestate dissoluta ex omnibus dux deligatur ad bellum gerendum, sed sic [2] scripta, ut deum videretur congruere sententiae, quam ille se habiturum pecunia fidens non dubitabat. Hanc ei scripsisse Cleon Halicarnasius dicitur.

4. Atque hoc loco non est praetereundum factum Pharnabazi, satrapis regii. Nam cum Lysander praefectus classis in bello multa crudeliter avareque

---

[1] Delphicum, *Roth*; Delphi, *Dan. A B M P R F* λ; Delphos, *u μ*; Delphicos, *θπ*.
[2] sic, *Wölfflin*; *the MSS. omit.*

---

[1] This happened after the battle at Aegospotamoi in 404 B.C.

66

decemviral government which he had established; whereupon, inflamed with anger, he plotted to abolish the royal power at Lacedaemon. He was aware, however, that success was impossible without the help of the gods, since it was the custom of the Lacedaemonians to consult the oracles on all matters of state. First he attempted to bribe the Delphic oracle. Failing in that, he made an attempt on Dodona. There too suffering repulse, he alleged that he had made vows which he must pay to Jupiter Hammon, supposing that he could succeed better with the Africans. In that hope he went to Africa, but the priests of Jupiter greatly disappointed him; for far from allowing themselves to be seduced, they even sent envoys to Lacedaemon, to accuse Lysander of attempting to bribe the priests of the temple. Arraigned on that charge, he was acquitted by the vote of the jurors; but being sent to help the people of Orchomenos, he was slain by the Thebans near 396 B.C. Haliartus.

How well founded the charge against him was is shown by a speech which was found in his house after his death. In it he advises the Lacedaemonians to abolish the rule of kings and select a military leader from the whole body of citizens; but the speech was so worded that it appeared to be in conformity with the advice of the gods; and that advice he felt sure of securing, trusting to the power of money. The speech is said to have been written for him by Cleon of Halicarnasus.

4. In this connection I must not fail to mention what was done by Pharnabazus, satrap of the king.[1] After Lysander, while commander of the fleet, had committed many acts of cruelty and greed, and sus-

fecisset deque eis rebus suspicaretur ad cives suos
esse perlatum, petiit a Pharnabazo ut ad ephoros sibi
testimonium daret, quanta sanctitate bellum gessisset
sociosque tractasset, deque ea re accurate scriberet:
magnam enim eius auctoritatem in ea re futuram.
2 Huic ille liberaliter pollicetur; librum grandem
verbis multis conscripsit, in quibus summis eum
effert [1] laudibus. Quem cum hic legisset probasset-
que, dum signatur, alterum pari magnitudine, tanta
similitudine ut discerni non posset, signatum sub-
iecit, in quo accuratissime eius avaritiam perfidiam-
3 que accusarat. Hinc [2] Lysander domum cum redisset,
postquam de suis rebus gestis apud maximum
magistratum quae voluerat dixerat, testimonii loco
librum a Pharnabazo datum tradidit. Hunc submoto
Lysandro cum ephori cognossent, ipsi legendum
dederunt. Ita ille imprudens ipse suus fuit accusator.

VII. ALCIBIADES

1. Alcibiades, Cliniae filius, Atheniensis. In hoc
quid natura efficere possit videtur experta; constat
enim inter omnes qui de eo memoriae prodiderunt
nihil illo fuisse excellentius vel in vitiis vel in
2 virtutibus. Natus in amplissima civitate summo
genere, omnium aetatis suae multo formosissimus;
ad omnes res aptus consiliique plenus—namque

---

[1] effert, *B M R*; fert, *Dan. P A u.*
[2] hinc, *M*; hunc, *the other MSS.*; *deleted by Fleck.*

pected that news of them had reached the ears of his countrymen, he asked Pharnabazus to give him a letter to present to the ephors, testifying to the scrupulous manner in which he had conducted the war and treated the allies, with a detailed account of his conduct; for he declared that the satrap's influence would carry great weight. The Persian readily gave him his promise and wrote a weighty scroll in many words, praising Lysander in the highest terms. This the Spartan read and approved, but while it was being sealed, another scroll of equal size, so similar that the two could not be distinguished, had already been sealed and was substituted for the first one; and this contained a fully detailed account of Lysander's avarice and treachery. When Lysander had returned home from Asia and had submitted his own account of his conduct before the chief magistrates,[1] by way of proof he proffered the letter given him by Pharnabazus. When the ephors, after dismissing Lysander, had read the satrap's screed, they gave it to him to peruse. Thus the man, without knowing it, was his own accuser.

VII. ALCIBIADES

1. Alcibiades, the Athenian, son of Clinias. In this man Nature seems to have tried to see what she could accomplish; for it is agreed by all who have written his biography that he was never excelled either in faults or in virtues. Born in the most famous of cities of a very noble family, he was by far the handsomest man of his time. He was skilled in every accomplishment and of abundant

[1] See note 1, p. 34.

imperator fuit summus et mari et terra—disertus,
ut in primis dicendo valeret, quod tanta erat com-
mendatio oris atque orationis, ut nemo ei posset [1]
3 resistere; dives; cum tempus posceret, laboriosus,
patiens [2]; liberalis, splendidus non minus in vita
quam victu; affabilis, blandus, temporibus calli-
4 dissime serviens: idem, simul ac se remiserat neque
causa suberat qua re animi laborem perferret,
luxuriosus, dissolutus, libidinosus, intemperans reperiebatur, ut omnes admirarentur in uno homine
tantam esse dissimilitudinem tamque diversam
naturam.

2. Educatus est in domo Pericli—privignus enim
eius fuisse dicitur—eruditus a Socrate. Socerum
habuit Hipponicum, omnium Graeca lingua loquentium [3] ditissimum; ut, si ipse fingere vellet, neque
plura bona eminisci [4] neque maiora posset consequi,
2 quam vel natura vel fortuna tribuerat. Ineunte
adulescentia amatus est a multis amore Graecorum,
in iis Socrate, de quo mentionem facit Plato in
Symposio. Namque eum induxit commemorantem
se pernoctasse cum Socrate neque aliter ab eo
3 surrexisse ac filius a parente debuerit. Posteaquam
robustior est factus, non minus multos amavit, in
quorum amore, quoad licitum est odiosa,[5] multa

---

[1] posset, *Nipp.*; dicendo posset, *MSS.*; dicenti, *Bardili.*
[2] cum . . . patiens, *put after* idem *by Guill.*
[3] Graeca lingua loquentium, *Heusinger*; Graecae linguae
eloquentia, *MSS.*
[4] eminisci, *Heusinger*; reminisci, *MSS.*; comminisci, *Nipp.*
[5] quoad . . . odiosa (odiose, *u*) *put after* referremus *by*
Guill.

---

[1] The relationship was not so close as that.

ability (for he was a great commander both on land and sea); in eloquence he was numbered among the best orators, since his delivery and his style were so admirable that no one could resist him. He was rich; energetic too, when occasion demanded, and capable of endurance; generous, magnificent not only in public, but in private, life; he was agreeable, gracious, able to adapt himself with the greatest tact to circumstances : but yet, so soon as he relaxed his efforts and there was nothing that called for mental exertion, his extravagance, his indifference, his licentiousness and his lack of self-control were so evident, that all men marvelled that one man could have so varied and contradictory a character.

2. He was brought up in the home of Pericles (for he is said to have been his step-son[1]), his teacher was Socrates. His father-in-law was Hipponicus, the richest man of all Greek-speaking lands. In fact, if he himself had tried to determine the conditions of his life, he could not have imagined more blessings, or acquired greater advantages, than either Nature or Fortune had bestowed upon him. In early youth he was beloved by many, after the Greek fashion, including Socrates, as Plato mentions in his *Banquet.* For Plato represented him as saying that he had spent the night with Socrates, and had left his bed as a son ought to leave that of his father. When he grew older, he had an equally great number of love affairs, in which he showed great elegance and wit, so far as that was possible in hateful practices;[2] I

---

[2] Guill.'s transfer of this phrase after *referremus* is ingenious, but calls for *licet* instead of *licitum est; odiosa* is doubtless corrupt.

delicate iocoseque fecit; quae referremus, nisi maiora potiora haberemus.

3. Bello Peloponnesio huius consilio atque auctoritate Athenienses bellum Syracusanis indixerunt. Ad quod gerendum ipse dux delectus est, duo praeterea 2 collegae dati, Nicias et Lamachus. Id cum appararetur, prius quam classis exiret, accidit ut una nocte omnes Hermae qui in oppido erant Athenis deicerentur praeter unum, qui ante ianuam erat Andocidi [1]—itaque ille postea Mercurius Andocidi [2] vocitatus est. 3 Hoc cum appareret non sine magna multorum consensione esse factum, quae non ad privatam, sed publicam rem pertineret, magnus multitudini timor est iniectus ne qua repentina vis 4 in civitate exsisteret, quae libertatem opprimeret populi.

Hoc maxime convenire in Alcibiadem videbatur, quod et potentior et maior quam privatus existimabatur; multos enim liberalitate devinxerat, plures 5 etiam opera forensi suos reddiderat. Qua re fiebat ut omnium oculos, quotienscumque in publicum prodisset, ad se converteret neque ei par quisquam in civitate poneretur. Itaque non solum spem in eo habebant maximam, sed etiam timorem, quod et obesse plurimum et prodesse poterat. Aspergebatur

---

[1] Andocidi, *Bosius*; *the MSS. have various corruptions.*
[2] Andocidi, *Halm*; *cf. note* 1.

---

[1] Square pillars surmounted by a bust of Hermes, as god of traffic, and placed on the streets in various parts of the city.

would give an account of these if I did not have other and more important topics.

3. In the Peloponnesian war it was due to his influence and advice that the Athenians declared war on Syracuse; and to conduct that war he himself was appointed general, along with two colleagues, Nicias and Lamachus. In the midst of the preparations, before the fleet sailed, it happened that on one and the same night all the Hermes-pillars [1] in the city of Athens were thrown down except one; that one was before the door of Andocides, and hence it was afterwards called the Mercury [2] of Andocides. Since it was obvious that such an outrage could have been committed only by the common effort of numerous accomplices, and since this seemed to be directed rather against the state than against individuals, the people were filled with great apprehension, fearing the outbreak of some sudden disturbance in the state, designed to overthrow their freedom.

These suspicions seemed to point especially to Alcibiades, because he was regarded as too powerful and too great to be content with a private station; for he had won the devotion of many men by his generosity, and had made a still greater number his debtors by help in the courts. The result was, that whenever he appeared in public, he drew all eyes upon himself, and no one of the citizens was considered his equal. And so he not only filled them with the highest hopes, but also with profound apprehension, because he was capable of doing a great deal of harm, as well as a great deal of good. His reputa-

---

[2] The Roman god who was identified with Hermes; cf. note 4, p. 7.

etiam infamia, quod in domo sua facere mysteria
dicebatur, quod nefas erat more Atheniensium;
idque non ad religionem, sed ad coniurationem pertinere existimabatur.

4. Hoc crimine in contione [1] ab inimicis compella-
batur. Sed instabat tempus ad bellum proficiscendi.
Id ille intuens neque ignorans civium suorum consuetudinem, postulabat, si quid de se agi vellent,
potius de praesente quaestio haberetur quam absens
2 invidiae crimine accusaretur. Inimici vero eius
quiescendum in praesentia, quia noceri ei [2] non
posse intellegebant, et illud tempus exspectandum
decreverunt quo is [3] exisset, ut absentem aggre-
3 derentur; itaque fecerunt. Nam postquam in
Siciliam eum pervenisse crediderunt, absentem quod
sacra violasset reum fecerunt.

Qua de re cum ei nuntius a magistratu in Siciliam
missus esset, ut domum ad causam dicendam rediret,
essetque in magna spe provinciae bene administran-
dae, non parere noluit et in trierem quae ad eum erat
4 deportandum missa ascendit. Hac Thurios in Italiam
pervectus, multa secum reputans de immoderata
civium suorum licentia crudelitateque erga nobiles,
utilissimum ratus impendentem evitare tempestatem,
clam se ab custodibus subduxit et inde primum

---

[1] *The best MSS. have* contentione (-em).

[2] noceri ei, *Bardili;* nocere, *M u;* noceri, *the other MSS.*

[3] quo, *Lambin, omitting* is; quo si, *MSS.;* quo classis,
Fleck.

---

[1] The Eleusinian mysteries, which were celebrated at
Eleusis in Attica with great secrecy, in honour of Demeter
and Persephone.

[2] That is, he used the secrecy of the meetings for plots of
revolution.

tion was also assailed because it was said that he celebrated the mysteries [1] in his own house, which was impious by the tradition of the Athenians; and it was thought that he did so, not from religious, but revolutionary, motives.[2]

4. It was this charge that was brought against him by his enemies in the public assembly. But the time was at hand for beginning the campaign, and Alcibiades, having that circumstance in mind, and knowing the ways of his fellow-citizens,[3] begged them, in case they intended to take any action against him, to conduct the investigation while he was present, rather than bring forward in his absence charges inspired by malice. His enemies, however, thought it best to keep quiet for the present, since they knew that they could not harm him, and wait for the time of his departure, in order to attack him behind his back. And that is what they did; for as soon as they believed that he had reached Sicily, they charged him in his absence with profanation of sacred rites.

Because of this, a message was sent to Alcibiades in Sicily by the authorities, ordering him to return home and present his defence; and although he had high hopes of success in his mission, he was unwilling to disobey the order and embarked on the trireme that had been sent to bring him back. In this he was taken to Thurii in Italy, and there pondering deeply on the unbridled licence of his fellow-citizens, and their cruelty to men of high rank, he deemed it best to avoid the threatening storm; so he eluded his guards and made his escape, first to Elis, and

[3] Cf. i. 8 and ii. 8. 1.

5 Elidem, dein Thebas venit. Postquam autem se
capitis damnatum bonis publicatis audivit, et, id
quod usu [1] venerat, Eumolpidas [2] sacerdotes a populo
coactos ut se devoverent, eiusque devotionis quo
testatior esset memoria, exemplum in pila lapidea
incisum esse positum in publico, Lacedaemonem
demigravit.

6 Ibi, ut ipse praedicare consuerat, non adversus
patriam, sed inimicos suos bellum gessit, qui [3] iidem
hostes essent civitati; nam cum intelligerent se plurimum prodesse posse rei publicae, ex ea eiecisse plusque

7 irae suae quam utilitati communi paruisse. Itaque
huius consilio Lacedaemonii cum Perse rege amicitiam fecerunt, dein Deceleam in Attica munierunt,
praesidioque ibi perpetuo posito, in obsidione Athenas
tenuerunt. Eiusdem opera Ioniam a societate averterunt Atheniensium. Quo facto multo superiores
bello esse coeperunt.

5. Neque vero his rebus tam amici Alcibiadi sunt
facti quam timore ab eo alienati; nam cum acerrimi
viri praestantem prudentiam in omnibus rebus cogno-
scerent, pertimuerunt ne caritate patriae ductus
aliquando ab ipsis desciceret et cum suis in gratiam
rediret. Itaque tempus eius interficiundi quaerere

2 instituerunt. Id Alcibiades [4] diutius celari non
potuit; erat enim ea sagacitate ut decipi non posset,

---

[1] quod numquam antea usu, *Cobet.*
[2] Eumolpidas, *u*; Olympidas, *etc., MSS.*
[3] qui, *P*; quod, *the other MSS.*
[4] Alcibiades, *Gesner*; Alcibiadi, *MSS.*

---

[1] Priests employed in the Eleusinian mysteries, descendants
of Eumolpus, the reputed founder of the mysteries.

then to Thebes. But as soon as he learned that he
had been condemned to death and his property confiscated, and that the priests known as Eumolpidae[1]
—an action for which there was precedent—had been
compelled by the people to pronounce a curse upon
him, and that to perpetuate the memory of that
curse a copy had been inscribed upon a stele of stone
and set up in a public place, he went to live in
Lacedaemon.

There, as he himself used to declare, Alcibiades
waged war, not against his country, but against his
personal enemies, since they were also the enemies
of their country; for although they knew that he
could be of great service to the state, they had
caused his banishment, having an eye rather to their
own resentment than to the public welfare. Thus
it was by his advice that the Lacedaemonians made 412 B.C.
friends with the king of Persia, and then fortified
Decelea in Attica and placed a permanent garrison 413 B.C.
there, thus holding Athens in a state of siege. It
was through him too that the Lacedaemonians
separated the Ionian cities from their alliance with
the Athenians, after which Sparta began to have
great advantage in the war.

5. Yet by these services the Lacedaemonians were
not so much attached to Alcibiades as they were
led to fear and dislike him. Indeed, realizing the
surpassing and many-sided ability of that most
energetic of men, they feared that one day, led by
love of country, he might turn from them and
become reconciled with his own citizens. They
therefore resolved to seek an opportunity for
assassinating him. That design could not long be
concealed from Alcibiades; for his keenness was

77

praesertim cum animum attendisset ad cavendum.
Itaque ad Tissaphernem, praefectum regis Darii, se
3 contulit. Cuius cum in intimam amicitiam pervenisset et Atheniensium, male gestis in Sicilia rebus,
opes senescere, contra Lacedaemoniorum crescere
videret, initio cum Pisandro praetore, qui apud
Samum exercitum habebat, per internuntios conlo-
quitur et de reditu suo facit mentionem. Erat
enim eodem quo Alcibiades sensu, populi potentiae
4 non amicus et optimatium fautor. Ab hoc destitutus,
primum per Thrasybulum, Lyci filium, ab exercitu
recipitur praetorque fit apud Samum; post, suffragante Theramene, populi scito restituitur parique
absens imperio praeficitur simul cum Thrasybulo et
Theramene.
5 Horum in imperio tanta commutatio rerum facta
est, ut Lacedaemonii, qui paulo ante victores vigue-
rant, perterriti pacem peterent. Victi enim erant
quinque proeliis terrestribus, tribus navalibus, in
quibus ducentas naves triremes amiserant, quae
6 captae in hostium venerant potestatem. Alcibiades
simul cum collegis receperat Ioniam, Hellespontum,
multas praeterea urbes Graecas, quae in ora sitae
sunt Asiae,[1] quarum expugnarant complures, in iis
Byzantium, neque minus multas consilio ad amicitiam adiunxerant, quod in captos clementia fuerant
7 usi. Ita praeda onusti, locupletato exercitu, maximis
rebus gestis, Athenas venerunt.

[1] Thraciae, *Nipp.*

---

[1] He was governor of Lydia and Caria under Darius Nothus
(424–405 B.C.).

such that he could not be deceived, especially when he had made up his mind that he must be on his guard. Accordingly, he took refuge with Tissaphernes, one of the prefects of king Darius.[1] Having won the Persian's intimate friendship, and perceiving that the power of Athens was waning after the reverse in Sicily, while that of Lacedaemon was growing, he first conferred through intermediaries with Pisander, a general who had an army at Samos, hinting at the possibility of his return to Athens; for Pisander held the same political opinions as Alcibiades, being no friend to popular government but favouring the aristocrats. Meeting with no encouragement from him, Alcibiades was first 411 B.C. received by the army through Thrasybulus, son of Lycus, and made general at Samos; later, with the support of Theramenes, he was restored by vote of the people and in his absence was given equal powers with Thrasybulus and Theramenes.

During the command of these three men such a change of fortune took place that the Lacedaemonians, who shortly before were flushed with success, now in terror sued for peace. In fact, they had lost 410 B.C. five battles on land and three on the sea, and the latter had cost them two hundred triremes, which were captured and came into the hands of the enemy. Alcibiades, acting with his colleagues, had recovered Ionia, the Hellespont, and, besides, many Greek cities situated on the coast of Asia; several of these they had stormed, including Byzantium; but of quite as many they had secured the alliance by their good judgment in showing mercy to their prisoners. So, ladened with booty, and having enriched the army, they returned to Athens in triumph. 408 B.C.

6. His cum obviam universa civitas in Piraeum descendisset, tanta fuit omnium exspectatio visendi Alcibiadis, ut ad eius triremem vulgus conflueret, 2 proinde ac si solus advenisset. Sic enim populo erat persuasum, et adversas superiores et praesentes secundas res accidisse eius opera. Itaque et Siciliae amissum [1] et Lacedaemoniorum victorias culpae suae tribuebant, quod talem virum e civitate expulissent. Neque id sine causa arbitrari videbantur; nam postquam exercitui praeesse coeperat, neque terra 3 neque mari hostes pares esse potuerant. Hic ut e navi egressus est, quamquam Theramenes et Thrasybulus iisdem rebus praefuerant simulque venerant in Piraeum, tamen unum omnes illum prosequebantur,[2] et, id quod numquam antea usu venerat nisi Olympiae victoribus, coronis aureis [3] taeniisque [4] vulgo donabatur. Ille lacrimans talem benevolentiam civium suorum accipiebat, reminiscens pristini temporis acerbitatem.

4 Postquam astu [5] venit, contione advocata sic verba fecit, ut nemo tam ferus fuerit quin eius casui inlacrimarit [6] inimicumque iis se ostenderit quorum opera patria pulsus fuerat, proinde ac si alius populus,

---

[1] amissum imperium, π V Σ, Voss. A; exercitum in S. amissum, *Fleck.*

[2] prosequebantur, *Muretus*; persequebantur, *MSS.*

[3] laureis, *Westermann.*

[4] taeniisque, *Muretus*; aeneisque, *MSS.*; *see note*, p. 81 *Perhaps we should read* coronis aureis aeneisque statuis (*cf.* xvi. 5. 5).

[5] astu, M θ μ; astum (hastum), *Dan. A B P R u F* λ; in astu, *Nipp.*

[6] casui (causam, *u*; casum, Dan. *P A B R*) inlacrumarit (lacrumarit, *Dan. P u*; lacrimarit, *A B*; lachrymarit, *R*), *Halm*; casu illacumarit, *Nipp.*

6. The whole city went down to the Piraeus to meet them; but so strong and so universal was the desire of seeing Alcibiades that the people gathered about his trireme exactly as if he had come alone. In fact, the people were convinced that it was to him that their former disasters and their present successes were due. Consequently, they blamed themselves for the loss of Sicily [1] and the victories of the Lacedaemonians, because they had banished so great a man from the state. And they seemed to have grounds for that opinion; for no sooner had he been put in command of the army than the enemy had been outmatched by land and by sea. When Alcibiades disembarked, although Thrasybulus and Theramenes had shared in the command and had come to the Piraeus with him, it was Alcibiades alone that all the people escorted, and crowns of gold and fillets [2] were showered upon him everywhere, a thing which had never happened before except to victors at Olympia. He received these tokens of his fellow-citizens' devotion with tears in his eyes, as he recalled their cruelty in the past.

As soon as he arrived in the city, the assembly was convoked and he spoke in such terms that there was none so hard-hearted as not to weep at his lot and give vent to their anger against those who had caused his exile—just as if it had been

---

[1] *Amissus,* "loss," does not occur elsewhere, and perhaps some word or phrase has been lost; see the crit. note.

[2] All the editors, so far as I know, read either *coronis aureis aeneisque,* or *coronis laureis taeniisque.* Since Plutarch (*Alc.* 33) says that golden crowns were given him in the assembly, and since fillets (or ribbons; Suet. *Nero* 25. 2) were common offerings, while bronze crowns are not mentioned anywhere, I have read *coronis aureis taeniisque;* see crit. note.

non ille ipse qui tum flebat, eum sacrilegii damnasset.
5 Restituta ergo huic sunt publice bona, eidemque illi
Eumolpidae sacerdotes rursus resacrare sunt coacti
qui eum devoverant, pilaeque illae in quibus devotio
fuerat scripta in mare praecipitatae.

7. Haec Alcibiadi laetitia non nimis fuit diuturna.
Nam cum ei omnes essent honores decreti totaque
res publica domi bellique tradita, ut unius arbitrio
gereretur, et ipse postulasset ut duo sibi collegae
darentur, Thrasybulus et Adimantus, neque id nega-
tum esset, classe in Asiam profectus, quod apud
Cymen minus ex sententia rem gesserat, in invidiam
recidit; nihil enim eum non efficere posse ducebant.
2 Ex quo fiebat ut omnia minus prospere gesta culpae
tribuerent, cum aut eum neglegenter aut malitiose
fecisse loquerentur, sicut tum accidit; nam corruptum a rege capere Cymen noluisse arguebant.
3 Itaque huic maxime putamus[1] malo fuisse nimiam
opinionem ingenii atque virtutis; timebatur enim
non minus quam diligebatur, ne secunda fortuna
magnisque opibus elatus, tyrannidem concupisceret.
Quibus rebus factum est ut absenti magistratum
abrogarent et alium in eius locum substituerent.
4   Id ille ut audivit, domum reverti noluit et se

---

[1] putamus, *u*; imputamus, *MSS.*

---

[1] This city was in Asia Minor, near Lesbos. Although it
was an ally of Athens, Alcibiades had attacked it and plundered its territories; but he had been unable to take the
city itself.

another people, and not those who were then shedding tears, that had condemned him for impiety. Accordingly, his goods were restored to him at the state's expense, and the Eumolpidae, the same priests who had pronounced the curse upon him, were compelled to retract it, while the pillars upon which the curse had been inscribed were thrown into the sea.

7. But this joy of Alcibiades was of none too long duration. When all possible honours had been voted him and all the business of the state at home and abroad had been entrusted to him alone, to be managed as he wished, and he had asked that two colleagues, Thrasybulus and Adimantus, be given him and his request was granted, he set out for Asia with a fleet; and having been less successful at Cyme [1] than was hoped, he again fell into disfavour; for 407 B.C. the people thought that there was nothing that he could not accomplish. Consequently, they attributed all reverses to his fault, declaring that he had shown either negligence or treachery. And that was what happened in this instance; for they said that he had not tried to take Cyme, because he had been bribed by the king. Therefore I am convinced that nothing was more to his disadvantage than the excessive confidence in his ability and valour; for his countrymen feared him no less than they loved him, thinking that he might be carried away by good fortune and great power, and wish to become tyrant. The result of this was, that while he was away from Athens, they deprived him of his office and appointed another [2] in his place.

As soon as Alcibiades heard of that action, he

---

[2] Namely, Conon.

Pactyen[1] contulit ibique tria castella communiit,
Ornos, Bizanthen, Neontichos, manuque conlecta,
primus Graecae[2] civitatis in Thraeciam introiit,
gloriosius existimans barbarorum praeda locupletari
5 quam Graiorum. Qua ex re creverat cum fama tum
opibus, magnamque amicitiam sibi cum quibusdam
regibus Thraeciae pepererat.

8. Neque tamen a caritate patriae potuit recedere.
Nam cum apud Aegos flumen Philocles, praetor
Atheniensium, classem constituisset suam neque
longe abesset Lysander, praetor Lacedaemoniorum,
qui in eo erat occupatus ut bellum quam diutissime
duceret, quod ipsis pecunia a rege suppeditabatur,
contra Atheniensibus exhaustis praeter arma et
2 naves nihil erat super, Alcibiades ad exercitum venit
Atheniensium ibique praesente vulgo agere coepit:
si vellent, se coacturum Lysandrum dimicare aut
pacem petere spopondit[3]; Lacedaemonios eo nolle
classe confligere, quod pedestribus copiis plus quam
3 navibus valerent; sibi autem esse facile Seuthem,
regem Thraecum, deducere ut eum terra depelleret;
quo facto, necessario aut classe conflicturum aut
bellum compositurum.

4 Id etsi vere dictum Philocles animadvertebat,
tamen postulata facere noluit, quod sentiebat se,

---

[1] Pactyen, *Ortel*; Ornos, *Lipsius*; Bizanthen, Neontichos,
Is. Voss. The MSS. have various corruptions.

[2] Graecae, *u*; Graeciae, *MSS.*

[3] spopondit, *Heerwagen*; spondet, *Wiggers*; respondit,
A P; responderet (-ent, *M*) *B M R θ λ*; *u and Cobet omit.*

gave up any thought of returning home and went to Pactye, where he fortified three strongholds, Orni, Bizanthe and Neontichos; then gathering a band of followers, he was the first member of a Greek state to penetrate Thrace, thinking it more glorious to enrich himself by pillaging the barbarians than the Greeks. Through this enterprise he increased both in fame and in wealth, besides gaining the intimate friendship of some of the kings of Thrace.

8. In spite of all, Alcibiades could not renounce his love for his country; indeed, when Philocles, the Athenian general, had brought his fleet to anchor near Aegospotamoi, and Lysander, the Lacedaemonian commander, who was not far off, was making every effort to prolong the war, because money was being supplied to his countrymen by the Persian king, while the Athenians, at the end of their resources, had nothing left but their arms and their ships, Alcibiades came to the Athenian army. There, in the presence of the common soldiers, he began to plead with them, pledging himself, if they wished, to compel Lysander either to fight or sue for peace; he said that the Lacedaemonians did not wish a naval battle, because their land forces were stronger than their fleet; but that it would be easy for him to induce Seuthes, king of the Thracians, to drive Lysander from the land; and that would oblige the Spartan either to engage with his fleet or end the war.

Although Philocles [1] understood that what Alcibiades said was true, he nevertheless did not choose to

---

[1] There were five other generals, including Conon, but Philocles held the chief command on that day; Diodorus xiii. 106. 1.

Alcibiade recepto, nullius momenti apud exercitum futurum et, si quid secundi evenisset, nullam in ea re suam partem fore, contra ea, si quid adversi accidisset, se unum eius delicti futurum reum. Ab hoc discedens, Alcibiades " Quoniam," inquit, " victoriae patriae repugnas, illud moneo, ne[1] iuxta hostem castra habeas nautica; periculum est enim, ne immodestia militum vestrorum[2] occasio detur Lysandro vestri opprimendi exercitus." Neque ea res illum fefellit; nam Lysander cum per speculatores comperisset vulgum Atheniensium in terram praedatum exisse navesque paene inanes relictas, tempus rei gerendae non dimisit eoque impetu bellum totum delevit.

9. At Alcibiades, victis Atheniensibus non satis tuta eadem loca sibi arbitrans, penitus in Thraeciam se supra Propontidem abdidit, sperans ibi facillime suam fortunam occuli posse. Falso. Nam Thraeces, postquam eum cum magna pecunia venisse senserunt, insidias fecerunt qui ea quae apportarat abstulerunt, ipsum capere non potuerunt. Ille, cernens nullum locum sibi tutum in Graecia propter potentiam Lacedaemoniorum, ad Pharnabazum in Asiam transiit, quem quidem adeo sua cepit humanitate, ut eum nemo in amicitia antecederet. Namque ei Grynium dederat, in Phrygia castrum, ex quo quinquagena talenta vectigalis capiebat.

---

[1] ne, *added by Ridenauer; omitted in MSS.*
[2] vestrorum . . . vestri, *Dan.* P A θ π μ; nostrorum . . . nostri (nostrorum militum, *R*), *the other MSS.*

do what he asked, because he saw that if the exile were taken back, he himself would be of no importance in the army; also that in the event of success he would be given no credit, while if any reverse was suffered, he alone would be held responsible. As he left him, Alcibiades said: " Since you do not wish victory for your country, I give you this bit of advice; do not keep your naval camp near the enemy; for there is reason to fear that the lack of discipline of your soldiers may give Lysander an opportunity of crushing your army." And he was not mistaken; for when Lysander had learned through scouts that a great part of the Athenian soldiers had gone ashore to pillage, leaving the ships almost empty, he did not let the chance for action slip, and by his attack he brought the whole war to an end.

9. But Alcibiades, thinking that after the defeat of the Athenians he was not altogether safe in his present residence, withdrew far into Thrace and went into hiding beyond the Propontis, thinking that there his existence might most easily be concealed. But he was mistaken; for as soon as the Thracians learned that he had come there with a large amount of money, they laid a trap for him; and they were successful in carrying off what he had brought with him, although they could not take the man himself. Then, perceiving that no place in Greece was safe for him because of the power of the Lacedaemonians, he took refuge in Asia with Pharnabazus, whom he so captivated by his personal charm, that he became the Persian's dearest friend. In fact Pharnabazus gave him Grynium, a stronghold of Phrygia, from which he received a yearly revenue of fifty talents.

4 Qua fortuna Alcibiades non erat contentus neque Athenas victas Lacedaemoniis servire poterat pati. Itaque ad patriam liberandam omni ferebatur cogi- 5 tatione. Sed videbat id sine rege Perse non posse fieri ideoque eum amicum sibi cupiebat adiungi, neque dubitabat facile se consecuturum, si modo eius conveniundi habuisset potestatem. Nam Cyrum fratrem ei bellum clam parare Lacedaemoniis adiu- vantibus sciebat; id si aperuisset, magnam se initurum gratiam videbat.

10. Hoc cum moliretur peteretque a Pharnabazo ut ad regem mitteretur, eodem tempore Critias ceterique tyranni Atheniensium certos homines ad Lysandrum in Asiam miserant, qui eum certiorem facerent, nisi Alcibiadem sustulisset, nihil earum rerum fore ratum, quas ipse Athenis constituisset; qua re, si suas res gestas manere vellet, illum perse- 2 queretur. His Laco rebus commotus statuit accu- ratius sibi agendum cum Pharnabazo. Huic[1] ergo renuntiat quae regi cum Lacedaemoniis essent, nisi Alcibiadem vivum aut mortuum sibi tradidisset. 3 Non tulit hunc satrapes et violare clementiam quam regis opes minui maluit.

Itaque misit Susamithren et Bagaeum ad Alci- biadem interficiendum, cum ille esset in Phrygia 4 iterque ad regem compararet. Missi clam vicinitati

---

[1] huic societatem, *MSS.*; societatem *deleted by Schott*, huic *by Leutsch.*

---

[1] This was now Artaxerxes II, surnamed Mnemon (405– 362 B.C.).
[2] See vi. 1. 5.   [3] See 4. 7.

Alcibiades, however, was not contented with his present lot, nor could he endure the idea that Athens was vanquished and enslaved to the Lacedaemonians. In consequence, all his thoughts were set upon freeing his country. It was clear to him, however, that he could accomplish nothing without the aid of the Persian king,[1] and for that reason he desired to win his friendship. And he felt confident of so doing, if only he could have the opportunity of meeting him. For he knew that the king's brother Cyrus was secretly planning to make war upon Artaxerxes with the help of the Lacedaemonians, and he perceived that if he should give information of that plot, he would win great gratitude.

10. At the very time that Alcibiades was making this plan and urging Pharnabazus to send him to the king, Critias and the other tyrants of Athens had sent trusty messengers to Asia, to inform Lysander that unless he got rid of Alcibiades, none of the arrangements which he had made at Athens [2] would be permanent. Therefore, if he wished what he had done to be lasting, he must try to capture the fugitive. These threats disturbed the Laconian, who made up his mind that he must deal more decidedly with Pharnabazus; he therefore threatened to renounce the agreement between the king and the Lacedaemonians,[3] unless Pharnabazus would deliver Alcibiades into his hands alive or dead. The satrap could not hold out against him, and preferred to do violence to the laws of humanity rather than see the king's power lessened.

Pharnabazus therefore sent Susamithres and Bagaeus to kill Alcibiades, while he was in Phrygia and was preparing to go to the king. These emis-

in qua tum Alcibiades erat dant negotium ut eum
interficiant. Illi, cum ferro aggredi non auderent,
noctu ligna contulerunt circa casam eam,[1] in qua
quiescebat, eamque succenderunt, ut incendio con-
5 ficerent, quem manu superari posse diffidebant. Ille
autem ut sonitu flammae est excitatus, etsi gladius
ei erat subductus, familiaris sui subalare telum
eripuit. Namque erat cum eo quidam ex Arcadia
hospes, qui numquam discedere voluerat. Hunc
sequi se iubet et id quod in praesentia vestimen-
torum fuit adripit. His in ignem eiectis, flammae
6 vim transiit. Quem ut barbari incendium effugisse
viderunt, telis eminus missis interfecerunt caputque
eius ad Pharnabazum rettulerunt. At mulier quae
cum eo vivere consuerat muliebri sua veste con-
tectum, aedificii incendio mortuum cremavit quod
ad vivum interimendum erat comparatum. Sic
Alcibiades annos circiter XL natus diem obiit
supremum.

11. Hunc infamatum a plerisque tres gravissimi
historici summis laudibus extulerunt: Thucydides,
qui eiusdem aetatis fuit, Theopompus, post aliquanto
natus, et Timaeus; qui quidem duo maledicentissimi
nescio quo modo in illo uno laudando consenserunt.[2]
2 Namque ea quae supra scripsimus de eo praedicarunt
atque hoc amplius: cum Athenis, splendidissima

---

[1] casam eam, *Shoppius*; sammeam, *Dan. A P θ*; samineam,
M R λ; sarmeam, *B*.
[2] consenserunt, *R*; conscierunt, *M u*; consuerunt, *Dan.
A u in margin*; consueverunt, *P*; consentiunt, *Halm*; etc.

---

[1] Lit., " a weapon carried under the arm."
[2] This friend is mentioned by Nepos alone; cf. Plut. *Alc*. 31.
[3] He was at least forty-five.

saries secretly instructed those who dwelt near the place where Alcibiades then was to slay him. They, however, did not dare to attack him openly, but by night piled wood about the house in which he slept and set fire to it, in order to destroy in that way a man whom they had no hope of being able to overcome by arms. But when Alcibiades was awakened by the crackling flames, although his sword had been filched from him, he seized a dagger [1] belonging to a friend; for he had with him a guest-friend from Arcadia, who had always refused to leave him.[2] This man Alcibiades ordered to follow him, and catching up whatever clothing there was at hand, he threw it upon the fire and dashed through the raging flames. When the barbarians saw that he had escaped the fire, they hurled weapons at him from a distance and thus killed him; then they took his head to Pharnabazus. But a woman who used to live with him covered the corpse with one of her robes and burned it in the fire which consumed the house, the very fire that had been designed to burn the occupant alive. Thus Alcibiades met his end at the age of about forty years.[3] 404 B.C.

11. Although his reputation has been assailed by many writers, Alcibiades has been highly praised by three authoritative historians: Thucydides, who belonged to the same period, Theopompus, who was born somewhat later than he, and Timaeus. These last two, who are strongly inclined to abuse, somehow agree in praising that one man. For it is they that are my authority for what I have previously [4] written about him, as well as for the following appraisement: although he was a native of Athens, most

[4] In chapters 1 and 2.

civitate, natus esset, omnes splendore ac dignitate
3 superasse vitae; postquam inde expulsus Thebas
venerit, adeo studiis eorum inservisse, ut nemo eum
labore corporisque viribus posset aequiperare—omnes
enim Boeotii [1] magis firmitati corporis quam ingenii
4 acumini inserviunt;—eundem apud Lacedaemonios,
quorum moribus summa virtus in patientia pone-
batur, sic duritiae se dedisse, ut parsimonia victus
atque cultus omnes Lacedaemonios vinceret; fuisse
apud Thraecas, homines vinolentos rebusque veneriis
5 deditos: hos quoque in his . rebus antecessisse;
venisse ad Persas, apud quos summa laus esset
fortiter venari, luxuriose vivere: horum sic imitatum
consuetudinem, ut illi ipsi eum in iis maxime admira-
6 rentur. Quibus rebus effecisse ut, apud quoscumque
esset, princeps poneretur habereturque carissimus.
Sed satis de hoc; reliquos ordiamur.

VIII. THRASYBULUS

1. Thrasybulus, Lyci filius, Atheniensis. Si per
se virtus sine fortuna ponderanda sit, dubito an hunc
primum omnium ponam; illud sine dubio: neminem
huic praefero fide, constantia, magnitudine animi, in
2 patriam amore. Nam quod multi voluerunt paucique
potuerunt ab uno tyranno patriam liberare, huic
contigit ut a triginta oppressam tyrannis e servitute

---

[1] Boetii, *MSS., here and elsewhere.*

magnificent of cities, he surpassed all his fellow-citizens in the elegance and distinction of his manner of life. When he was banished and went to Thebes, he so adapted himself to the ways of that city that no one could equal him in bodily strength and endurance (for the Boeotians as a whole aim to excel in strength of body rather than in keenness of intellect). At Lacedaemon, where custom assigned the greatest merit to endurance, this same man cultivated austerity to such a degree that he surpassed all the Lacedaemonians in the plainness of his table and the simplicity of his life. Among the Thracians, a people given to drunkenness and lust, he surpassed even the Thracians in those vices. He came to the Persians, where the highest renown was gained by being a daring hunter and an extravagant liver, and there he so adapted himself to their customs that even the natives were filled with admiration of his success in these things. It was in this way that he held the first rank wherever he lived, as well as being greatly beloved. But enough of him; let us pass to the other men.

VIII. THRASYBULUS

1. Thrasybulus, the Athenian, son of Lycus. If merit were to be estimated absolutely, without reference to fortune, I rather think that I should rank this man first of all. Thus much is certain: I put no one above him in sense of honour, in steadfastness, in greatness of soul and in love of country. For while many have wished, and a few have been able, to free their country from a single tyrant, it was his good fortune to restore his native land from slavery to freedom when it was under the heel of

3 in libertatem vindicaret. Sed nescio quo modo, cum eum nemo anteiret his virtutibus, multi nobilitate praecucurrerunt. Primum Peloponnesio bello multa hic sine Alcibiade gessit, ille nullam rem sine hoc; quae ille universa naturali quodam bono fecit lucri.

4 Sed illa tamen omnia communia imperatoribus cum militibus et fortuna, quod in proelii concursu abit res a consilio ad vices vimque pugnantium.[1] Itaque iure suo nonnulla ab imperatore miles, plurima vero fortuna vindicat seque hic [2] plus valuisse quam ducis prudentiam vere potest praedicare.

5 Quare illud magnificentissimum factum proprium est Thrasybuli; nam cum triginta tyranni praepositi a Lacedaemoniis servitute oppressas tenerent Athenas, plurimos civis, quibus in bello parserat fortuna, partim patria expulissent partim interfecissent, plurimorum bona publicata inter se divisissent, non solum princeps, sed etiam solus initio, bellum iis indixit.

2. Hic enim cum Phylen confugisset, quod est castellum in Attica munitissimum, non plus habuit secum triginta de suis. Hoc initium fuit salutis Atticorum, hoc robur libertatis clarissimae civitatis.

2 Neque vero hic non contemptus est primo a tyrannis atque eius solitudo. Quae quidem res et illis con-

---

[1] ad vices vimque p., *scripsi*; ad vices rerum vimque p., *Ortmann*; ad vires vimque p., *P A B M u*; ad vires usque (undique) p., *Leid. M*; ad vires nostrum cuiusque p., *R*; virtutemque p., *Lambin*; ad vires casusque, *omitting* p., *Guill.*

[2] hic, *Lambin*; his, *MSS.*

---

[1] The phrase *ad . . . pugnantium*, as it stands in the MSS., is undoubtedly corrupt; for various emendations see the crit. note.

thirty tyrants. But somehow or other, while no one surpassed him in the virtues that I have named, many men have outstripped him in renown. To begin with, in the Peloponnesian war he often won victories without the aid of Alcibiades, the latter never without his help; but Alcibiades by some innate gift gained the credit for everything.

But after all, commanders share every such success with their soldiers and with Fortune, since after battle has been joined, the issue depends rather on the luck and the fighting spirit of the soldiers than on skill.[1] Hence the soldier justly claims some share in his commander's glory, and Fortune, a large share; in fact, she can fairly boast that more was due to her in such cases than to the commander's ability. That is why the glorious deed of which I am going to speak belongs wholly to Thrasybulus. Thirty tyrants, appointed by the Lacedaemonians, held Athens in a condition of slavery. Of the citizens whom fate had spared during the war, they had driven a great many from their native land or put them to death; of many they had confiscated and shared the property. Thrasybulus was not only the first to make war upon them, but in the beginning he was the only one.

2. Now, when he had taken refuge in Phyle, which is a well-fortified stronghold in Attica, he had with him not more than thirty followers. This was the cradle of salvation for the people of Attica, this was the citadel of the liberty of a glorious state. In fact, Thrasybulus was at first an object of contempt to the tyrants, as well as his handful of followers; and it was that very fact that

temnentibus perniciei et huic despecto saluti fuit;
haec enim illos segnes ad persequendum, hos autem,
tempore ad comparandum dato, fecit robustiores.
3 Quo magis praeceptum illud omnium in animis esse
debet, nihil in bello oportere contemni neque sine
4 causa dici matrem timidi flere non solere. Neque
tamen pro opinione Thrasybuli auctae sunt opes;
nam iam tum illis temporibus fortius boni pro liber-
5 tate loquebantur quam pugnabant. Hinc in Piraeum
transiit Munychiamque munivit. Hanc bis tyranni
oppugnare sunt adorti, ab eaque turpiter repulsi,
protinus in urbem, armis impedimentisque amissis,
refugerunt.
6 Usus est Thrasybulus non minus prudentia quam
fortitudine; nam cedentes violari vetuit—cives enim
civibus parcere aequum censebat—neque quisquam
est vulneratus nisi qui prior impugnare voluit.
Neminem iacentem veste spoliavit, nil attigit nisi
arma quorum indigebat, quaeque ad victum pertine-
7 bant. In secundo proelio cecidit Critias, dux tyrannorum, cum quidem adversus Thrasybulum fortissime
pugnaret.
3. Hoc deiecto Pausanias venit Atticis auxilio, rex
Lacedaemoniorum. Is inter Thrasybulum et eos
qui urbem tenebant fecit pacem his condicionibus:
ne qui praeter triginta tyrannos et decem, qui
postea praetores creati superioris more crudelitatis
erant usi, adficerentur exsilio neve bona publi-

---

1 *Quidem* implies that valour would not be expected from
Critias.
2 He was king from 408 to 394 B.C.

proved the ruin of those who scorned him and won the safety of the object of their contempt; for it made his enemies slow to attack and strengthened his forces by giving them time for preparation. From this it follows that all men ought to bear in mind this thought, that in war nothing should be scorned, and that it is a true saying that the mother of one who knows what fear is seldom has cause to weep. And yet Thrasybulus' forces did not grow so rapidly as he hoped, for even then in those days good citizens were readier to speak for liberty than to fight for it. From Phyle he went to the Piraeus and fortified Munychia. That place the tyrants twice tried to take, but they suffered an ignominious repulse and at once fled to the city with the loss of their arms and baggage.

Thrasybulus showed no less judgment than courage; for he forbade injuring those who had surrendered (he thought it right for citizen to spare citizen), and no one was wounded who did not strike the first blow. He stripped no dead body of its clothing, touched nothing save the arms which he needed, and whatever could be made use of as food. In a second battle Critias fell, chief of the tyrants, and that, too,[1] just as he was fighting most valiantly, face to face with Thrasybulus.

3. When Critias had fallen, Pausanias, king of the Lacedaemonians,[2] came to the aid of the Athenians. He concluded a peace between Thrasybulus and the occupants of the city on the following terms: that except for the thirty tyrants and ten others who had been put in power later and had shown the same cruelty as their predecessors, no one should be punished with exile or confiscation of property; and

403 B.C.

carentur; rei publicae procuratio populo redderetur.
2 Praeclarum hoc quoque Thrasybuli, quod reconciliata
pace, cum plurimum in civitate posset, legem tulit
ne quis ante actarum rerum accusaretur neve multa-
3 retur, eamque illi oblivionis appellarunt. Neque
vero hanc tantum ferendam curavit, sed etiam ut
valeret effecit. Nam cum quidam ex iis qui simul
cum eo in exsilio fuerant caedem facere eorum
vellent cum quibus in gratiam reditum erat publice,
prohibuit et id quod pollicitus erat praestitit.

4. Huic pro tantis meritis honoris[1] corona a
populo data est, facta duabus virgulis oleaginis;
quam quod amor civium et non vis expresserat,
nullam habuit invidiam magnaque fuit gloria.[2]
2 Bene ergo Pittacus ille, qui in[3] septem sapientum
numero est habitus, cum Mytilenaei multa milia
iugerum agri ei muneri[4] darent, "Nolite, oro vos,"
inquit, "id mihi dare, quod multi invideant, plures
etiam concupiscant. Qua re ex istis nolo amplius
quam centum iugera, quae et meam animi aequita-
tem et vestram voluntatem indicent"; nam parva
munera diutina, locupletia non propria esse consue-
3 runt. Illa igitur corona contentus, Thrasybulus
neque amplius requisivit neque quemquam honore

---

[1] honoris causa, $\theta\,\pi\,\mu$ **V** Σ *and u in margin.*
[2] cum magnaeque, *Guill.*; magnaeque gloriae, *u.*
[3] in, *added by Nipp.*
[4] Mitileni ei (mut-, *P*; ei mitylenei, *R*; ei myt-, *M*) m.
milia iugerum et agri (agri et, *M R u*) munera, *Dan. A B M P R*;
corrected by Fleck.

---

[1] Cf. Val. Max. iv. 1. ext. 4, *haec oblivio quam Athenienses
amnestian vocant.*

that the administration of the government should be restored to the people. Another noble action of Thrasybulus was this: when peace was made and he held the chief power at Athens, he proposed a law providing that with reference to what had been done in the past no one should be accused or punished; and they called that law " the law of amnesty." [1] And he not only saw to it that the law was passed, but also that it was enforced; for whenever anyone of those who had been in exile with him wished to put to death those who had been officially pardoned, he prevented it and remained true to what he had promised.

4. In recognition of these great services he was presented by the people with an honorary crown made of two olive-branches. And since that crown was a token of the love of his fellow-citizens and was not wrung from them by force, it excited no envy, but brought him great glory. For Pittacus, who was numbered among the Seven Sages, well said, when the people of Mytilene wished to make him a present of many thousand acres of land: " Do not, I beg of you, give me a gift that may excite the jealousy of many and the cupidity of still more. But out of what you offer I desire no more than one hundred acres,[2] which will be a token of my moderation and your good-will." And indeed, as a rule, small gifts are lasting, lavish ones are not permanent. So with that crown Thrasybulus was content; he asked for nothing more, and he thought that no one was more

---

[2] The *iugerum* was a Roman measure equal to about two-thirds of an acre; according to Plutarch, Pittacus measured the amount which he would accept by the distance that he could hurl a spear.

se antecessisse existimavit. Hic sequenti tempore,
cum praetor classem ad Ciliciam [1] appulisset neque
satis diligenter in castris eius agerentur vigiliae, a
barbaris, ex oppido noctu eruptione facta, in taber-
naculo interfectus est.

IX. CONON

1. Conon Atheniensis Peloponnesio bello accessit
ad rem publicam, in eoque eius opera magni fuit;
nam et praetor pedestribus exercitibus praefuit et
praefectus classis res [2] magnas mari gessit. Quas ob
causas praecipuus ei honos habitus est. Namque
omnibus unus insulis praefuit, in qua potestate Pheras
2 cepit, coloniam Lacedaemoniorum. Fuit etiam extremo Peloponnesio bello praetor, cum apud Aegos
flumen copiae Atheniensium ab Lysandro sunt de-
victae. Sed tum afuit, eoque peius res administrata
est; nam et prudens rei militaris et diligens erat
3 imperator. Itaque nemini erat iis [3] temporibus
dubium, si adfuisset, illam Athenienses calamitatem
accepturos non fuisse.

2. Rebus autem adflictis, cum patriam obsideri
audisset, non quaesivit ubi ipse tuto viveret, sed

---

[1] Ciliciam, *Longueil*; Siciliam, *MSS.*
[2] magnas mari victorias, *P*; magnas mari res, *Nipp.*
[3] his, *MSS.*

---

[1] He was slain by the inhabitants of Aspendus in Pamphylia, who were exasperated at the riotous conduct of his
soldiers.

highly honoured than he. At a later time, as commander of a fleet, he landed in Cilicia; there his camp was not guarded with sufficient care, and when the barbarians had made a sortie by night from one of their towns, he was killed in his tent.[1]

388 B.C.

IX. CONON

1. Conon the Athenian began his public career at the time of the Peloponnesian war, and in that war he rendered important service; for he commanded the land forces with the rank of general, and as admiral of the fleet he did great deeds on the sea. In recognition of this an unusual honour was conferred upon him; he was given sole charge of all the islands, and while holding that commission[2] he took Pherae, a colony[3] of the Lacedaemonians. He was also commander-in-chief at the close of the Peloponnesian war, when the Athenian forces were defeated by Lysander at Aegospotamoi; but he was absent at the time, and in consequence the affair was badly managed; for he was skilled in military science and a careful commander. Hence no one who lived in those times doubted that, if he had been present, the Athenians would not have suffered that disaster.

413 B.C.

2. But when the calamity came and he heard that his native city was in a state of siege, he looked about for a place, not where he could himself live in

---

[2] The islands between Greece and Asia Minor are meant. Conon never had such a commission. He took Pherae in 393 B.C., when he was in the service of the Persian king; see 4. 2 ff.

[3] "Colony" is used in the Roman, not the Greek, sense; Pherae had been made subject to Sparta.

unde praesidio posset esse civibus suis. Itaque contulit se ad Pharnabazum, satrapem Ioniae et Lydiae eundemque generum regis et propinquum; apud quem ut multum gratia valeret multo labore multisque
2 effecit periculis. Nam cum Lacedaemonii, Atheniensibus devictis, in societate non manerent quam cum Artaxerxe fecerant, Agesilaumque bellatum misissent in Asiam, maxime impulsi a Tissapherne, qui ex intimis regis ab amicitia eius defecerat et cum Lacedaemoniis coierat societatem, hunc adversus Pharnabazus habitus est imperator, re quidem vera exercitui praefuit Conon eiusque omnia arbitrio gesta
3 sunt. Hic multum ducem summum Agesilaum impedivit saepeque eius consiliis obstitit, neque vero non fuit apertum, si ille non fuisset, Agesilaum
4 Asiam Tauro tenus regi fuisse erepturum. Qui postea quam domum a suis civibus revocatus est, quod Boeoti et Athenienses Lacedaemoniis bellum indixerant, Conon nihilo setius apud praefectos regis versabatur iisque omnibus magno erat usui.

3. Defecerat a rege Tissaphernes, neque id tam Artaxerxi quam ceteris erat apertum; multis enim magnisque meritis apud regem, etiam cum in officio non maneret, valebat. Neque id erat mirandum, si non facile ad credendum adducebatur, reminiscens
2 eius se opera Cyrum fratrem superasse. Huius

---

1 The so-called Corinthian war, 395–387 B.C.
2 At Cunaxa, 401 B.C.; see vii. 9. 5, above.

safety, but from which he could be a defence to his fellow-citizens. So he went to Pharnabazus, satrap of Ionia and Lydia, who was also son-in-law of the king and his near relative, with whom he succeeded in winning great influence by hard toil and many dangers. For the Lacedaemonians, after vanquishing the Athenians, did not remain true to the alliance which they had concluded with Artaxerxes, but sent Agesilaus to Asia to make war, being especially influenced by Tissaphernes, one of Artaxerxes' intimate friends, who, however, had betrayed his king's friendship and come to an understanding with the Lacedaemonians. Against him Pharnabazus was nominally commander-in-chief, but in reality Conon headed the army and everything was done as he directed. He proved a serious obstacle to that great general Agesilaus and often thwarted him by his strategy; in fact, it was evident that if it had not been for Conon, Agesilaus would have deprived the king of all Asia as far as the Taurus. Even after the Spartan was summoned home by his countrymen, because the Boeotians and Athenians had declared war[1] upon the Lacedaemonians, Conon none the less continued his relations with the king's prefects and rendered them all great assistance.

3. Tissaphernes had revolted from the king, but that was not so clear to Artaxerxes as it was to all others; for because of many important services the satrap retained his influence with his sovereign, even after he had ceased to be faithful to him. And it is not surprising that the king was not easily led to believe in his treachery, remembering, as he did, that it was thanks to him that he had overcome his brother Cyrus.[2] In order to accuse the traitor,

accusandi gratia Conon a Pharnabazo ad regem
missus, posteaquam venit, primum ex more Persarum
ad chiliarchum, qui secundum gradum imperii tenebat, Tithrausten accessit seque ostendit cum rege
3 conloqui velle.   Nemo enim sine hoc admittitur.[1]

Huic ille, " Nulla," inquit, " mora est, sed tu deli-
bera, utrum conloqui malis an per litteras agere quae
cogitas.   Necesse est enim, si in conspectum veneris,
venerari te regem (quod προσκύνησιν illi vocant).[2]
Hoc si tibi grave est, per me nihilo setius editis
mandatis conficies quod studes."   Tum Conon " Mihi
vero," inquit, " non est grave quemvis honorem
habere regi, sed vereor ne civitati meae sit opprobrio,
si, cum ex ea sim profectus quae ceteris gentibus
imperare consuerit, potius barbarorum quam illius
more fungar."   Itaque quae huic volebat scripta
tradidit.

4. Quibus cognitis, rex tantum auctoritate eius
motus est, ut et Tissaphernem hostem iudicarit et
Lacedaemonios bello persequi iusserit et ei permiserit
quem vellet eligere ad dispensandam pecuniam.   Id
arbitrium Conon negavit sui esse consilii, sed ipsius,
qui optime suos nosse deberet;   sed se suadere,
2 Pharnabazo id negotii daret.   Hinc magnis muneri-

---

[1] nemo . . . admittitur, *put after* vocant *by Cobet; by
others after* regem, *omitting* quod . . . vocant.
[2] quod . . . vocant, *omitted by* Wölflinn.

---

[1] The king's bodyguard, the μηλοφόροι, so called because
the butts of their spears were adorned with golden apples.

Conon was sent to the king by Pharnabazus and as soon as he arrived, he went first, according to the Persian custom, to Tithraustes, chief of the Thou- 395 B.C. sand,[1] who held the highest power next to the king, and explained that he wished an interview with the monarch. As a matter of fact, no one is admitted to the royal presence without that formality.

Tithraustes replied to his request: "There is nothing to prevent, but do you consider whether you prefer a personal interview rather than to communicate what you have in mind by letter. For it is essential, if you come into his presence, to do homage to the king (which the Greeks call προσκύνησις). If that is repugnant to you, you may equally well accomplish what you wish through me, by instructing me as to your wishes." To this Conon answered: "To me personally it is not repugnant to pay any possible honour to the king, but I fear that my country may be shamed if, having come from a state which is accustomed to command the other nations, I should conform rather to the customs of barbarians than of Athens." Accordingly, he wrote out what he wished and handed it to the satrap.

4. When the king had read the communication, Conon's prestige had so much weight with him that he pronounced Tissaphernes an enemy and commissioned Conon to carry on the war with the Lacedaemonians, authorizing him to chose anyone he wished as his paymaster. To make that choice, Conon declared, was not his province, but that of the king, who ought to know his own subjects best; but his recommendation was that the position be given to Pharnabazus. Then, after receiving valu-

bus donatus ad mare est missus, ut Cypriis et Phoenicibus ceterisque maritimis civitatibus naves longas imperaret classemque, qua proxima aestate mare tueri posset, compararet, dato adiutore Pharna-3 bazo, sicut ipse voluerat. Id ut Lacedaemoniis est nuntiatum, non sine cura rem administrant, quod maius bellum imminere arbitrabantur quam si cum barbaro solum contenderent; nam ducem fortem, prudentem[1] regiis[2] opibus praefuturum ac secum dimicaturum videbant, quem neque consilio neque 4 copiis superare possent. Hac mente magnam contrahunt classem; proficiscuntur Pisandro duce. Hos Conon apud Cnidum adortus, magno proelio fugat, multas naves capit, complures deprimit. Qua victoria non solum Athenae, sed etiam cuncta Graecia quae sub Lacedaemoniorum fuerat imperio liberata 5 est. Conon cum parte navium in patriam venit, muros dirutos a Lysandro utrosque, et Piraei et Athenarum, reficiendos curat pecuniaeque quinquaginta talenta, quae a Pharnabazo acceperat, civibus suis donat.

5. Accidit huic quod ceteris mortalibus, ut inconsideratior in secunda quam in adversa esset fortuna. Nam classe Peloponnesiorum devicta, cum ultum se iniurias patriae putaret, plura concupivit quam efficere 2 potuit. Neque tamen ea non pia et probanda fuerunt,

---

[1] et prudentem, *Halm*; prudenter, *Weidner, Guill.*; prudentemque, *u.*   [2] regis, *MSS.*

---

[1] See n. 2, p. 101.
[2] Athens recovered its freedom in 403 B.C.; the Lacedaemonians now lost their hegemony over the islands and the Greek cities of Asia.

able presents, Conon was sent to the seacoast, to levy ships of war on the Cypriotes, Phoenicians and other maritime states,[1] and to fit out a fleet with which in the following summer he could make the sea safe; Pharnabazus was appointed to help him, as Conon himself had asked. When this was reported to the Lacedaemonians, they made their preparations with care, thinking that a more serious war threatened them than if the contest was merely with the barbarian alone; for they saw that a brave leader was going to direct the king's power with foresight, and that they would have an adversary who would be their equal both in skill and in power. Because of this conviction they got together a great fleet and set sail under the command of Pisander. But they were attacked by Conon off Cnidus and 394 B.C. put to flight in a great battle; many of their ships were taken, several were sunk. That victory secured the freedom, not only of Athens,[2] but of all the Greek states which were under the rule of the Lacedaemonians. Conon with a part of his ships went to his native city, saw to the rebuilding of the walls both of the Piraeus and of Athens, which had 393 B.C. been destroyed by Lysander, and gave to his fellow-citizens the sum of fifty talents, which he had received from Pharnabazus.

5. But Conon had the same experience as the rest of mankind, and showed less wisdom in good fortune than in adversity. For after his decisive victory over the fleet of the Peloponnesians, thinking that he had avenged his country's wrongs, he entertained ambitions beyond his powers. These, however, were both patriotic and commendable, since he desired to increase the strength of his native land at

quod potius patriae opes augeri quam regis maluit.
Nam cum magnam auctoritatem sibi pugna illa
navali quam apud Cnidum[1] fecerat constituisset non
solum inter barbaros, sed etiam omnes Graeciae
civitates, clam dare operam coepit, ut Ioniam et
Aeoliam restitueret Atheniensibus.

3   Id cum minus diligenter esset celatum, Tiribazus,
qui Sardibus praeerat, Cononem evocavit, simulans
ad regem eum se mittere velle magna de re. Huius
nuntio parens cum venisset, in vincla coniectus est,

4 in quibus aliquamdiu fuit. Inde nonnulli eum ad
regem abductum ibique eum perisse scriptum reliquerunt. Contra ea Dinon historicus, cui nos
plurimum de Persicis rebus credimus, effugisse
scripsit; illud addubitat, utrum Tiribazo sciente an
imprudente sit factum.

X. DION

1. Dion, Hipparini filius, Syracusanus, nobili genere
natus, utraque implicatus tyrannide Dionysiorum.
Namque ille superior Aristomachen, sororem Dionis,
habuit in matrimonio, ex qua duos filios, Hipparinum
et Nisaeum, procreavit totidemque filias, nomine
Sophrosynen et Areten, quarum priorem Dionysio
filio, eidem cui regnum reliquit, nuptum dedit,
alteram, Areten, Dioni.

2   Dion autem praeter nobilem[2] propinquitatem
generosamque[2] maiorum famam multa alia ab natura
habuit bona, in iis ingenium docile, come, aptum ad

---

[1] Gnidum, *MSS.*
[2] nobilem *and* generosam *transposed by Dederich.*

---

[1] The term applied by the Greeks to the King of Persia.

the expense of that of the great king.[1] For since the famous naval battle that he had fought off Cnidos had given him high standing, not only with the barbarians, but with all the Greek states as well, he began to plot the restoration of Ionia and Aeolia to the Athenians.

Since his design was not concealed with sufficient care, Tiribazus, governor of Sardis, summoned Conon, pretending that he wished to send him to the king on a mission of importance.   Conon obeyed the summons, but on his arrival he was thrown into prison and remained in confinement for some time. Then, as some writers say, he was taken to the king and there met his end; Dinon, on the contrary, an historian in whose account of Persian affairs we have the most confidence, has written that he made his escape; but he is in doubt whether it was with or without the connivance of Tiribazus.

X. DION

1. Dion, son of Hipparinus, of Syracuse, sprung from a noble family, was connected with the tyranny of both the Dionysii; for the elder Dionysius married Aristomache, Dion's sister; by her he had two sons, Hipparinus and Nisaeus, and the same number of daughters, Sophrosyne and Arete. Of these daughters he gave the former in marriage to Dionysius, the son to whom he left his throne, the latter, Arete, to Dion.

Dion, however, besides that illustrious relationship and the distinguished renown of his ancestors, possessed many natural advantages, including a receptive mind, affability, and aptitude for the

artes optimas, magnam corporis dignitatem, quae
non minimum commendat,[1] magnas praeterea divitias
a patre relictas, quas ipse tyranni muneribus auxerat.
3 Erat intimus Dionysio priori, neque minus propter
mores quam adfinitatem. Namque etsi Dionysii
crudelitas ei displicebat, tamen salvum propter
necessitudinem, magis etiam suorum causa studebat.
Aderat in magnis rebus, eiusque consilio multum
movebatur tyrannus, nisi qua in re maior ipsius cupi-
4 ditas intercesserat. Legationes vero omnes quae
essent illustriores per Dionem administrabantur;
quas quidem ille diligenter obeundo, fideliter ad-
ministrando crudelissimum nomen tyranni sua
5 humanitate leniebat.[2] Hunc a Dionysio missum
Karthaginienses suspexerunt,[3] ut neminem umquam
Graeca lingua loquentem magis sint admirati.

2. Neque vero haec Dionysium fugiebant; nam
quanto esset sibi ornamento, sentiebat. Quo fiebat
ut uni huic maxime indulgeret neque eum secus
2 diligeret ac filium; qui quidem, cum Platonem
Tarentum venisse fama in Siciliam esset perlata,
adulescenti negare non potuerit quin eum accerseret,
cum Dion eius audiendi cupiditate flagraret. Dedit
ergo huic veniam magnaque eum ambitione Syracusas
3 perduxit. Quem Dion adeo admiratus est atque
adamavit, ut se ei totum traderet. Neque vero
minus ipse Plato delectatus est Dione. Itaque cum a
Dionysio [4] crudeliter violatus esset, quippe qui eum [5]

---

[1] commendat, *Lambin*; commendatur, *MSS.*
[2] leniebat, *Lambin*; tenebat, *MSS.*; tegebat, $\pi \mu F u$.
[3] sic suspexerunt, *Fleck.*
[4] Dionysio, $P A^2 B R M$; Dionysio tyranno, $A^1 u$; tyranno, *Nipp.*
[5] qui eum, *Pluygers*; quem, *MSS.*

highest accomplishments; great personal dignity, which is not the least of recommendations; large means too, left him by his father, which he had himself increased through the gifts of the tyrant. He was intimate with the elder Dionysius as much because of his character as their relationship; for although he disapproved of the tyrant's cruelty, yet his safety was dear to him on account of their kinship, and still more so for the sake of his own family. He assisted Dionysius in important matters of business, and the tyrant was strongly influenced by his advice, except when some especially ardent desire of his own had turned the scale. In fact, all embassies of special distinction were conducted through Dion, and since he entered upon them with care and managed them scrupulously, he lessened the tyrant's reputation for cruelty by his own kindliness. When he was sent by Dionysius to Carthage, he was so honoured that no native of Greece ever excited greater admiration.

2. Now all this did not escape the notice of Dionysius, for he was aware of the honour conferred upon him by his relative. In consequence, he favoured Dion beyond all others and loved him like a son. So when the report made its way to Sicily that Plato had come to Tarentum, he could not refuse the young man's request to invite the philosopher to his court, since Dion had an ardent longing to hear him. Therefore he gratified the youth's desire and brought Plato to Syracuse in great state. Him Dion so admired and loved that he devoted himself to him heart and soul. And, indeed, Plato for his part was no less delighted with Dion; so much so that, although he had been cruelly wronged by Dionysius, who had ordered him to be sold as a

venumdari iussisset, tamen eodem rediit eiusdem
Dionis precibus adductus.

4 Interim in morbum incidit Dionysius. Quo cum
gravi[1] conflictaretur, quaesivit a medicis Dion, quem
ad modum se haberet, simulque ab iis petiit, si forte
in maiore esset periculo, ut sibi faterentur; nam
velle se cum eo conloqui de partiendo regno, quod
sororis suae filios ex illo natos partem regni putabat
5 debere habere. Id medici non tacuerunt et ad
Dionysium filium sermonem rettulerunt. Quo ille
commotus, ne agendi esset Dioni potestas, patri
soporem medicos dare coegit. Hoc aeger sumpto, ut
somno sopitus, diem obiit supremum.

3. Tale initium fuit Dionis et Dionysii simultatis,
eaque multis rebus aucta est. Sed-tamen primis
temporibus aliquamdiu simulata inter eos amicitia
mansit. Cum Dion non desisteret obsecrare Dionysium ut Platonem Athenis arcesseret et eius consiliis
uteretur, ille, qui in aliqua re vellet patrem imitari,
2 morem ei gessit. Eodemque tempore Philistum
historicum Syracusas reduxit, hominem amicum non
magis tyranno quam tyrannis.[2] Sed de hoc in eo
libro plura sunt exposita qui de historicis Graecis
3 conscriptus est. Plato autem tantum apud Dionysium
auctoritate potuit valuitque eloquentia, ut ei per-
suaserit tyrannidis facere finem libertatemque

---

[1] graviter vel gravius, *u in margin.*   [2] tyrannidi, *Ascensius.*

---

[1] He had been banished by the elder Dionysius; see
Plutarch, *Dion*, 13 ff.

slave, he nevertheless returned to that same land, led once more by the entreaties of Dion.

Meanwhile Dionysius had fallen ill, and as he grew 367 B.C. worse, Dion inquired of the physicians how he was, at the same time begging them, if the king chanced to be in greater danger, not to conceal it from him; for he said that he wished to confer with Dionysius about dividing the kingdom, believing that the sons of his own sister, as children of the king, ought to have a share in the realm. This request the physicians did not keep secret, but reported what had been said to the younger Dionysius. The latter, disquieted by the information, compelled the physicians to give his father a soporific, in order that Dion might have no opportunity for a conference; and when the patient had taken the drug, he seemed to fall asleep and died without awakening.

3. Such was the beginning of the hostility between Dion and Dionysius, and it was aggravated by many circumstances. At first, however, they remained friends outwardly for a time, and when Dion did not cease to beg Dionysius to summon Plato from Athens and avail himself of the philosopher's advice, the tyrant, who wished to follow his father's example in some particular, granted the request. At the same time he recalled[1] the historian Philistus to Syracuse, a man who was no more friendly to the tyrant than to tyrants in general. But about him I have given fuller particulars in the book which I wrote on the Greek historians. As for Plato, such was his influence over the tyrant, and so great was the effect of his eloquence, that he persuaded Dionysius to put an end to his tyranny and restore

reddere Syracusanis. A qua voluntate Philisti
consilio deterritus aliquanto crudelior esse coepit.

4. Qui quidem cum a Dione se superari videret
ingenio, auctoritate, amore populi, verens ne, si eum
secum haberet, aliquam occasionem sui daret opprimendi, navem ei triremem dedit, qua Corinthum
deveheretur, ostendens se id utriusque facere causa,
ne, cum inter se timerent, alteruter alterum prae-
2 occuparet. Id cum factum multi indignarentur
magnaeque esset invidiae tyranno, Dionysius omnia
quae moveri poterant Dionis in navis imposuit ad
eumque misit. Sic enim existimari volebat id se
non odio hominis, sed suae salutis fecisse causa.
3 Postea vero quam audivit eum in Peloponneso
manum comparare sibique bellum facere conari,
Areten, Dionis uxorem, alii nuptum dedit filiumque
eius sic educari iussit, ut indulgendo turpissimis
4 imbueretur cupiditatibus. Nam puero, priusquam
pubes esset, scorta adducebantur, vino epulisque
obruebatur, neque ullum tempus sobrio relinque-
5 batur. Is usque eo vitae statum commutatum ferre
non potuit, postquam in patriam rediit pater—
namque appositi erant custodes, qui eum a pristino
victu deducerent—ut se de superiore parte aedium
deiecerit atque ita interierit. Sed illuc revertor.

5. Postquam Corinthum pervenit Dion et eodem
perfugit Heraclides, ab eodem expulsus Dionysio,

their freedom to the Syracusans; but he was dissuaded by the advice of Philistus and began to show considerably greater cruelty than before.

4. Since Dionysius perceived that he was surpassed by Dion in ability, in influence, and in the affections of the people, he feared that, if he kept his rival near him, he might furnish an opportunity for his own downfall. Accordingly, he gave him a trireme in 366 B.C. which to sail to Corinth, explaining that he did so for both their sakes; for since they feared each other, there was danger that one might take advantage of the other. Since that action excited widespread indignation and great hatred of the tyrant, Dionysius loaded all Dion's movable property into ships and sent it to him, wishing to give the impression that he had been actuated, not by hatred of his rival, but by regard for his own safety. But when he learned that the exile was levying a force in the Peloponnesus and planning to make war upon him, Dionysius gave Dion's wife, Arete, in marriage to another, and caused his son to be brought up under such conditions that, as the result of indulgence, he developed the most shameful passions. For before he had grown up, the boy was supplied with courtesans, gorged with food and wine, and kept in a constant state of drunkenness. When his father returned to his native land, the youth found it so impossible to endure the changed conditions of his life—for guardians were appointed to wean him from his former habits—that he threw himself from the top of his house and so perished. But I return to my subject.

5. After Dion arrived in Corinth, he found that Heraclides also had taken refuge there; he too had

qui praefectus fuerat equitum, omni ratione bellum
2 comparare coeperunt. Sed non multum proficiebant,
quod multorum annorum tyrannis[1] magnarum opum
putabatur; quam ob causam pauci ad societatem
3 periculi perducebantur. Sed Dion, fretus non tam
suis copiis quam odio tyranni, maximo animo duabus
onerariis navibus quinquaginta annorum imperium,
munitum quingentis longis navibus, decem equitum
centumque peditum milibus, profectus oppugnatum
—quod omnibus gentibus admirabile est visum—adeo
facile perculit, ut post diem tertium, quam Siciliam
attigerat,[2] Syracusas introierit. Ex quo intellegi
potest nullum esse imperium tutum nisi benevolentia munitum.

4 Eo tempore aberat Dionysius et in Italia classem
opperiebatur adversariorum, ratus neminem sine
magnis copiis ad se venturum. Quae res eum
5 fefellit. Nam Dion iis ipsis qui sub adversarii
fuerant potestate regios spiritus repressit totiusque
eius partis Siciliae potitus est quae sub Dionysii
fuerat potestate parique modo urbis Syracusarum
6 praeter arcem et insulam adiunctam oppido, eoque
rem perduxit, ut talibus pactionibus pacem tyrannus
facere vellet: Siciliam Dion obtineret, Italiam
Dionysius, Syracusas Apollocrates, cui maximam
fidem uni habebat Dionysius.[3]

---

[1] tyrannis, *Lambin*; tyrannus, *MSS.*
[2] attigerat, *Aldus*; attigerit, *MSS.*
[3] Dionysius, *Lambin*; Dion, *MSS.* (*deleted by Heusinger*);
a lacuna before or after Dion *is suspected by many.*

---

[1] Dionysius I had reigned thirty-eight years, from 406 to
367 B.C., and his son, so far, ten years.
[2] That is, Ortygia. The citadel was on this island, which
was joined to the rest of the city by a mole.

been banished by Dionysius, whose cavalry he had formerly commanded. The two exiles began to make active preparations for war, but they did not accomplish much, since the rule of the tyrants was of so many years' standing [1] that it was regarded as very powerful, and consequently few could be induced to share in so dangerous an undertaking. Nevertheless Dion, relying less upon his own resources than on hatred of the tyrant, although he had but two transports, sallied forth with the greatest courage to attack a dynasty of fifty years' duration, defended by five hundred war-ships, ten thousand horsemen and a hundred thousand foot. And he so easily overthrew his opponents—a success which filled all nations with amazement—that two days after landing in Sicily he entered Syracuse; which goes to show that no rule is secure which is not founded upon the devotion of its subjects.

At that time Dionysius was away from home, awaiting the enemy's fleet in Italy; for he thought that no one would come against him without great forces. But he was mistaken; for Dion with those very people who had been under the heel of his opponent broke the king's pride and gained possession of all that part of Sicily which Dionysius had ruled, as well as of the city of Syracuse, except the citadel and island [2] that formed a part of the town. So successful was he, in fact, that the tyrant consented to make peace on the following terms: Sicily was to fall to Dion, Italy [3] to Dionysius, and Syracuse to Apollocrates, who was especially trusted by Dionysius. [4]

---

[3] That is, the part of southern Italy which had fallen into the power of the Dionysii.   [4] See the critical note.

6. Has tam prosperas tamque inopinatas res consecuta est subita commutatio, quod fortuna, sua
mobilitate, quem paulo ante extulerat demergere
2 est adorta. Primum in filio de quo commemoravi
supra suam vim exercuit. Nam cum uxorem
reduxisset, quae alii fuerat tradita, filiumque vellet
revocare ad virtutem a perdita luxuria, accepit
3 gravissimum parens vulnus morte filii. Deinde
orta dissensio est inter eum et Heraclidem, qui, quod
ei [1] principatum non concedebat, factionem comparavit. Neque is minus valebat apud optimates,
quorum consensu praeerat classi, cum Dion exercitum
4 pedestrem teneret. Non tulit hoc animo aequo
Dion, et versum illum Homeri rettulit ex secunda
rhapsodia, in quo haec sententia est: non posse
bene geri rem publicam multorum imperiis. Quod
dictum magna invidia consecuta est; namque
aperuisse videbatur omnia in sua potestate esse
5 velle. Hanc ille non lenire obsequio, sed acerbitate
opprimere studuit, Heraclidemque, cum Syracusas
venisset, interficiundum curavit.

7. Quod factum omnibus maximum timorem
iniecit; nemo enim illo interfecto se tutum putabat.
Ille autem, adversario remoto, licentius eorum bona
quos sciebat adversus se sensisse militibus dispertivit.
2 Quibus divisis, cum cotidiani maximi fierent sumptus, celeriter pecunia deesse coepit, neque quo

---

[1] qui quod ei, *Fleck.*; qui quod, *R*, *Nipp.*; qui quidem,
MSS.

---

[1] See 4. 3.
[2] That is, *Iliad* ii. 204: οὐκ ἀγαθὸν πολυκοιρανίη, εἶς κοίρανος
ἔστω, εἶς βασιλεύς. The word *rhapsodia* (ῥαψῳδία) meant
originally " a recital of Epic poetry," but was applied by the
Romans to the books of Homer.

6. This success, so great and so unexpected, was followed by a sudden change, since Fortune, with her usual fickleness, proceeded to bring down the man whom she had shortly before exalted. First, she showed her cruelty in connection with the son of whom I have previously spoken; for when Dion had recovered his wife, who had been handed over to another,[1] and was trying to recall his son from his abandoned wantonness to a life of virtue, he suffered in the death of that son the wound most painful for a father. Next, dissension arose between him and Heraclides, who, unwilling to yield the first place to Dion, formed a party against him. Heraclides had no less influence with the aristocrats than Dion, and by them he was unanimously chosen to command the fleet, while Dion retained the land forces. This situation Dion could not bear with patience, but quoted the well-known verse of Homer from his second book,[2] of which the purport is, that a state cannot be well governed when there are many in authority. This saying of his, since it seemed to show that he aimed at supreme power, excited great dissatisfaction, a dissatisfaction which he did not try to lessen by mildness, but to crush out by severity; and when Heraclides had come to Syracuse, he contrived to have him assassinated.

7. That act filled all men with extreme fear; for after Heraclides had been killed, no one felt safe. But Dion, having rid himself of his rival, with still greater lawlessness divided among his soldiers the property of those whom he knew to be opposed to him. After distributing that money, as his daily expenses were very great, he soon began to be in need of funds, and there was nothing on which he

manus porrigeret suppetebat, nisi in amicorum
possessiones. Id eius modi erat, ut, cum milites
3 reconciliasset, amitteret optimates. Quarum rerum
cura angebatur et, insuetus male audiendi, non
animo aequo ferebat de se ab iis male existimari
quorum paulo ante in caelum fuerat elatus laudibus.
Vulgus autem, offensa in eum militum voluntate,
liberius loquebatur et tyrannum non ferendum
dictitabat.

8. Haec ille intuens cum quem ad modum sedaret
nesciret, et quorsum evaderent timeret, Callicrates
quidam, civis Atheniensis, qui simul cum eo ex
Peloponneso in Siciliam venerat, homo et callidus et
ad fraudem acutus, sine ulla religione ac fide, adiit
2 ad Dionem et ait: eum magno in periculo esse
propter offensionem populi et odium militum, quod
nullo modo evitare posset, nisi alicui suorum negotium
daret qui se simularet illi inimicum. Quem si in-
venisset idoneum, facile omnium animos cogniturum
adversariosque sublaturum, quod inimici etus dissidenti[1] suos sensus aperturi forent.
3   Tali consilio probato, excepit has partes ipse
Callicrates et se armat imprudentia Dionis. Ad eum
interficiundum socios conquirit, adversarios eius
4 convenit, coniuratione confirmat. Res, multis consciis quae gereretur, elata defertur ad Aristomachen,
sororem Dionis, uxoremque Areten. Illae timore

---

[1] dissidenti, *Bremi, F* λ; dissidentis, *most MSS.*; dissidentes
π *B R u.*

---

[1] The man's name was really Callippus.

could lay his hands except the possessions of his friends. The result of his conduct was, that when he had won back the soldiers, he lost the support of the aristocracy. The anxiety caused by these difficulties broke him down, and since he was not accustomed to criticism, he could not endure being thought ill of by those who but a short time before had exalted him to the skies with their praises. The common people too, now that he had lost the good-will of the soldiers, spoke their minds more freely and insisted that a tyrant could not be tolerated.

8. Dion, aware of all this discontent, not knowing how to allay it, and fearing its possible result, was approached by one Callicrates,[1] a citizen of Athens, who had come with him to Sicily from the Peloponnesus, a man both clever and skilled in deceit, utterly without scruple or sense of honour. He went to Dion and said: "You are in great peril because of the ill-feeling of the people and the hostility of the soldiers. This you can escape in only one way, that is, by instructing some one of your friends to pretend to be your enemy. If you can hit upon the right man, it will be easy for him to acquaint himself with the feelings of the public and get rid of those who are hostile to you, since your foes will disclose their real sentiments to an enemy of yours."

This plan was approved, and Callicrates himself took the proposed part and armed himself at the expense of Dion's heedlessness. To bring about his death, he sought accomplices, addressed himself to Dion's enemies, and secured their loyalty by an oath. The plot, since many were implicated in it, was revealed and came to the ears of Aristomache, Dion's sister, and of his wife, Arete. The two

perterritae conveniunt cuius de periculo timebant.
At ille negat a Callicrate fieri sibi insidias, sed illa
5 quae agerentur fieri praecepto suo. Mulieres nihilo
setius Callicratem in aedem Proserpinae deducunt
ac iurare cogunt nihil ab illo periculi fore Dioni.
Ille hac religione non modo non est deterritus, sed
ad maturandum concitatus est, verens ne prius consilium aperiretur suum, quam cogitata perfecisset.

9. Hac mente proximo die festo, cum a conventu
se remotum Dion domi teneret atque in conclavi
edito recubuisset, consciis facinoris loca munitiora
oppidi tradit, domum custodiis saepit, a foribus qui
2 non discedant certos praeficit, navem triremem
armatis ornat Philostratoque, fratri suo, tradit
eamque in portu agitari iubet, ut si exercere remiges
vellet, cogitans, si forte consiliis obstitisset fortuna,
3 ut haberet qua fugeret ad salutem. Suorum autem
e numero Zacynthios [1] adulescentes quosdam eligit
cum audacissimos tum viribus maximis, iisque dat
negotium, ad Dionem eant inermes, sic ut con-
veniendi eius gratia viderentur venire. Ii propter
4 notitiam sunt intromissi. At illi ut limen eius [2]
intrarant, foribus obseratis, in lecto cubantem
invadunt, colligant; fit strepitus, adeo ut exaudiri
posset foris.
5 Hic, sicut ante saepe dictum est, quam invisa sit

---

[1] Zacynthios, *u, in margin*; Zaguntios, *etc., MSS.*
[2] aedis, *Wagner.*

---

[1] It was the festival of Proserpina, the goddess by whom
Callicrates had sworn.
[2] Cf. 5. 3. The other instances probably appeared in the
lost books *De Regibus.*

women, filled with terror, went to find the man for
whose safety they feared; but he said that Callicrates
was not plotting against him, but was acting in
accordance with his directions. In spite of that, the
women took Callicrates to the temple of Proserpina
and forced him to swear that Dion would be in no
danger from him. But the conspirator, far from
being turned from his purpose by such an oath, was
urged to greater haste, for fear that his design
should be disclosed before he had accomplished his
purpose.

9. With that end in view, on a holiday which soon
followed,[1] when Dion had remained at home to avoid
the crowd and had lain down in an upper room,
Callicrates delivered to his accomplices the more
strongly fortified parts of the town, surrounded the
palace with guards, and chose trusty men to keep
constant watch at the doors. He then equipped a
trireme with armed men and committed it to his
brother Philostratus, with orders to row up and down
in the harbour, as if he were engaged in training his
oarsmen, so that if by any chance Fortune thwarted
his purpose, he might have the means of saving
himself by flight. Then from the number of his
followers he chose some young men from Zacynthos,
who were both very daring and very strong, and
directed them to go to Dion unarmed, so that it
might appear that they were coming to pay him a
visit. The youths, since they were acquaintances,
were admitted; but no sooner had they crossed his
threshold than they locked the door, rushed upon
Dion as he lay in bed, and held him fast. The noise
that they made could be heard outside.

In this instance too, as has often been said before,[2]

singularis potentia et miseranda vita, qui se metui
6 quam amari malunt, cuivis facile intellectu fuit. Namque ipsius [1] custodes, si propitia [2] fuissent voluntate,
foribus effractis servare eum potuissent, quod illi
inermes telum foris flagitantes vivum tenebant. Cui
cum succurreret nemo, Lyco quidam Syracusanus
per fenestras gladium dedit, quo Dion interfectus
est.

10. Confecta caede, cum multitudo visendi gratia
introisset, nonnulli ab insciis pro noxiis conciduntur.
Nam celeri rumore dilato [3] Dioni vim adlatam, multi
concurrerant, quibus tale facinus displicebat. Ii
falsa suspicione ducti immerentes ut sceleratos
2 occidunt. Huius de morte ut palam factum est,
mirabiliter vulgi mutata est voluntas; nam qui vivum
eum tyrannum vocitarant, eidem liberatorem patriae
tyrannique expulsorem praedicabant. Sic subito
misericordia odio successerat, ut eum suo sanguine
3 ab Acherunte, si possent, cuperent redimere. Itaque
in urbe celeberrimo loco, elatus publice, sepulcri
monumento donatus est. Diem obiit circiter annos
quinquaginta quinque natus, quartum post annum
quam ex Peloponneso in Siciliam redierat.

[1] ipsius, *Halm*; illi ipsi, *MSS.*
[2] propitia, *R*; propria, *the other MSS.*; prompta, *Halm.*
[3] dilato, *Lambin*; delato, *MSS.*

---

[1] These guards are obviously not the same as those mentioned in 9. 1. That Dion had guards outside his door is
shown by the fact that the Zacynthian youths had to be
recognized before they were admitted.

the hatred of absolute power and the wretched life of those who prefer to be feared rather than loved was readily apparent to all; for Dion's own guards,[1] if they had been well disposed, might have broken open the door and saved him, since he was still alive in the hands of his assailants, who were unarmed and calling for a weapon from without But when no one came to his help, one Lyco, a Syracusan, passed a sword through the windows,[2] and with it the tyrant was slain.

10. After the murder had been committed and a crowd had flocked in to see the sight, several men were killed by mistake, in the belief that they had done the deed. For the rumour that violence had been offered to Dion quickly spread, and many hastened to the spot to whom such a crime was abhorrent. These it was who, misled by suspicion, slew the innocent in place of the guilty. No sooner was Dion's death made known than the sentiment of the people changed in a remarkable manner. For those who had called him a tyrant while he was alive now insisted that he had saved his country and freed it from a tyrant. Hence, on a sudden, pity succeeded to hatred, and the people would have redeemed him from Acheron, had it been possible, at the price of their own blood. And so he was buried in the most frequented part of the city at public expense, and the place of his burial was marked by a monument. He died at the age of about fifty-five, 353 B.C. three years after returning from the Peloponnesus to Sicily.

[2] Since Dion was in an upper room, the sword must have been passed from the window of an adjacent house; hence *fenestras,* instead of *fenestram.* It is true that the account of Plutarch (*Dion* 57) differs from that of Nepos.

XI. IPHICRATES

1. Iphicrates Atheniensis non tam magnitudine rerum gestarum quam disciplina militari nobilitatus est. Fuit enim talis dux, ut non solum aetatis suae cum primis compararetur, sed ne de maioribus natu 2 quidem quisquam anteponeretur. Multum vero in bello est versatus, saepe exercitibus praefuit, nusquam culpa male rem gessit; semper consilio vicit tantumque eo valuit, ut multa in re militari partim 3 nova attulerit, partim meliora fecerit. Namque ille pedestria arma mutavit. Cum ante illum imperatorem maximis clipeis, brevibus hastis, minutis gladiis 4 uterentur, ille e contrario peltam pro parma fecit— a quo postea peltastae pedites appellantur—ut ad motus concursusque essent leviores, hastae modum duplicavit, gladios longiores fecit. Idem genus loricarum mutavit[1] et pro sertis atque aeneis linteas dedit. Quo facto expeditiores milites reddidit; nam pondere detracto, quod aeque corpus tegeret et leve esset curavit.

2. Bellum cum Thraecibus gessit, Seuthem, socium Atheniensium, in regnum restituit. Apud Corinthum tanta severitate exercitui praefuit, ut nullae umquam in Graecia neque exercitatiores 2 copiae neque magis dicto audientes fuerint duci, in

[1] mutavit, *u*; *the MSS. omit.*

---

[1] The *clipeus* and *parma* were round shields; the *pelte*, a light, crescent-shaped shield. Nepos apparently uses *pro parma*, instead of *pro clipeo*, for the sake of the alliteration.
[2] In the Corinthian war, 393 to 391 B.C.

XI. IPHICRATES

1. Iphicrates, the Athenian, gained renown by his great deeds, but still more by his knowledge of the art of war; for not only was he a leader comparable with the greatest of his own time, but not even among the men of earlier days was there anyone who surpassed him. Indeed, a great part of his life was spent in warfare, he often commanded armies, and he never lost a battle through his own fault. It was always by knowledge of war that he gained his victories, and his knowledge was so great that he introduced many novelties in military equipment, as well as many improvements. For example, he changed the arms of the infantry. While before he became commander they used very large shields, short spears and little swords, he on the contrary exchanged *peltae*, or Thracian shields,[1] for the round ones (for which reason the infantry have since been called peltasts), in order that the soldiers might move and charge more easily when less burdened. He doubled the length of the spear and increased that of the swords; he changed the character of their breastplates, giving them linen ones in place of bronze cuirasses or chain armour. In that way he made the soldiers more active; for while he diminished the weight of their armour, he contrived to protect their bodies equally well without overloading them.

2. He waged war with the Thracians; he restored 389 B.C. Seuthes, an ally of the Athenians, to his throne. At Corinth[2] such was the strictness of his command of the army, that no troops in Greece were better drilled or more obedient to their leader; and he made them

eamque consuetudinem adduxit ut, cum proelii
signum ab imperatore esset datum, sine ducis opera
sic ordinatae consisterent, ut singuli peritissimo ab
3 imperatore dispositi viderentur.   Hoc exercitu moram
Lacedaemoniorum interfecit, quod maxime tota
celebratum est Graecia.   Iterum eodem bello omnes
copias eorum fugavit, quo facto magnam adeptus est
4 gloriam.   Cum Artaxerxes Aegyptio regi bellum
inferre voluit, Iphicraten ab Atheniensibus ducem
petivit, quem praeficeret exercitui conducticio, cuius
numerus duodecim milium fuit.   Quem quidem sic
omni disciplina militari erudivit, ut quemadmodum
quondam Fabiani milites vere[1] Romani appellati
sunt, sic Iphicratenses apud Graecos in summa
5 laude fuerint.   Idem subsidio Lacedaemoniis profectus, Epaminondae retardavit impetus; nam nisi
eius adventus appropinquasset, non prius Thebani
Sparta abscessissent, quam captam incendio deles-
sent.

3. Fuit autem et animo magno et corpore im-
peratoriaque forma, ut ipso aspectu cuivis iniceret
2 admirationem sui, sed in labore nimis remissus
parumque patiens, ut Theopompus memoriae prodidit; bonus vero civis fideque magna.   Quod cum
in aliis rebus declaravit, tum maxime in Amyntae
Macedonis liberis tuendis.   Namque Eurydice, mater
Perdiccae et Philippi, cum his duobus pueris, Amynta

---

[1] vere, *added by Wagner.*

---

[1] A *mora* consisted of from 400 to 900 men.
[2] Doubtless referring to Q. Fabius Maximus Cunctator,
the opponent of Hannibal.   Wagner cites Livy XXII. 14. 11,
vir ac vere Romanus.   Romani alone sometimes has the same
force; *e.g.* Livy VII. 13. 9, etc.

form the habit, when the signal for battle had been given by the commander, without waiting for an officer's command to take their places in such good order that each man seemed to have been assigned his position by a most skilful general. It was with that army that he annihilated a regiment[1] of the Lacedaemonians, a feat which was highly praised all over Greece. On another occasion in that same war he put all their forces to flight, an exploit by which he gained great glory. When Artaxerxes wished to make war on the king of Egypt, he asked the Athenians for Iphicrates as one of his generals, to command an army of twelve thousand mercenaries. That army the Athenian trained so thoroughly in all varieties of military discipline, that just as in days of old the soldiers of Fabius[2] were called true Romans, so "soldiers of Iphicrates" became a title of the greatest honour among the Greeks. Again, having gone to the aid of the Lacedaemonians, he thwarted 369 B.C. the designs of Epaminondas; for if his arrival had not been imminent, the Thebans would not have left Sparta until they had taken and burned the city.[3]

3. He had, in addition to nobility of soul and great size of body, the aspect of one born to command, so that his appearance alone inspired admiration in all men; but, as Theopompus has recorded, he was not steadfast enough in effort and he lacked endurance: nevertheless, he was a good citizen and the soul of honour. This was manifest both on other occasions and especially in protecting the children of Amyntas, 368 B.C. the Macedonian; for after his death Eurydice, the mother of Perdiccas and Philippus, took refuge

---

[3] Cf. xvii. 6. 1, where Agesilaus, more justly, has credit for this.

mortuo, ad Iphicraten confugit eiusque opibus
3 defensa est. Vixit ad senectutem, placatis in se
suorum civium animis. Causam capitis semel dixit,
bello sociali, simul cum Timotheo, eoque iudicio est
absolutus.

4 Menesthea filium reliquit ex Thraessa natum, Coti
regis filia. Is cum interrogaretur utrum pluris,
patrem matremne, faceret, " Matrem," inquit. Id
cum omnibus mirum videretur, at ille " Merito,"
inquit, " facio; nam pater, quantum in se fuit,
Thraecem me genuit, contra ea mater Atheniensem."

XII. CHABRIAS

1. Chabrias Atheniensis. Hic quoque in summis
habitus est ducibus resque multas memoria dignas
gessit. Sed ex iis elucet maxime inventum eius in
proelio quod apud Thebas fecit, cum Boeotis subsidio
2 venisset. Namque in eo victoria fidentem summum
ducem Agesilaum fugatis iam ab eo conducticiis
catervis coercuit,[1] reliquam phalangem loco vetuit
cedere obnixoque genu scuto, proiecta hasta impetum excipere hostium docuit. Id novum Agesilaus
contuens progredi non est ausus suosque iam in-

---

[1] coercuit, *added by Wagner.*

---

[1] The so-called Social War, 357–355 B.C. See xiii. 3. 1.
[2] Cotys (Cotyis) is the proper form of the name.
[3] *Reliquam phalangem* obviously does not mean " the rest
of the phalanx," but the " rest (of the army, namely) the

with Iphicrates with these two boys, and was defended with all his power. He lived to a good old
age, enjoying the devotion of his fellow-citizens.
Only once did he have occasion to defend himself
against a capital charge; that was during the war
with the allies,[1] in company with Timotheus, and
he was acquitted.

He left a son Mnestheus, the offspring of a Thracian
woman, the daughter of King Cotus.[2] When
Mnestheus was once asked whether he thought more
of his father or of his mother, he answered: "My
mother." When everyone expressed surprise at his
reply, he added: "I have good reason for that; for
my father did everything in his power to make me a
Thracian; my mother, on the contrary, made me an
Athenian."

XII. CHABRIAS

1. Chabrias, the Athenian. This man also was
rated as one of the greatest of commanders and did
many deeds worthy of record. But especially
brilliant among these was his device in the battle
which he fought near Thebes, when he came to
the aid of the Boeotians. On that occasion, though 378 B.C.
the consummate leader Agesilaus felt sure of victory,
since he had already put to flight the throngs of
mercenaries, Chabrias checked him, forbade the
phalanx, which was left[3] unsupported, to abandon
its position, and instructed the soldiers to receive
the enemy's onset with buckler on knee and lance
advanced. On seeing these novel tactics, Agesilaus
did not dare to attack, but although his forces had

phalanx "; cf. *reliquos Pisidas*, xiv. 6. 7. *Alius* is sometimes
used in the same way; see *Class. Phil.* xxiii. pp. 60 ff.

3 currentes tuba revocavit. Hoc usque eo tota
Graecia fama celebratum est, ut illo statu Chabrias
sibi statuam fieri voluerit, quae publice ei ab
Atheniensibus in foro constituta est. Ex quo factum
est ut postea athletae ceterique artifices suis[1] stati-
bus in[2] statuis ponendis uterentur, cum victoriam
essent adepti.

2. Chabrias autem multa in Europa bella administravit, cum dux Atheniensium esset; in Aegypto
sua sponte gessit. Nam Nectenebin adiutum
2 profectus, regnum ei constituit. Fecit idem Cypri,
sed publice ab Atheniensibus Euagorae adiutor datus,
neque prius inde discessit, quam totam insulam bello
devinceret; qua ex re Athenienses magnam gloriam
3 sunt adepti. Interim bellum inter Aegyptios et
Persas conflatum est. Athenienses cum Artaxerxe
societatem habebant, Lacedaemonii cum Aegyptiis,
a quibus magnas praedas Agesilaus, rex eorum,
faciebat. Id intuens Chabrias, cum in re nulla
Agesilao cederet, sua sponte eos adiutum profectus,
Aegyptiae classi praefuit, pedestribus copiis Agesilaus.

3. Tum praefecti regis Persae legatos miserunt
Athenas, questum quod Chabrias adversum regem
bellum gereret cum Aegyptiis. Athenienses diem
certam Chabriae praestituerunt, quam ante domum
nisi redisset, capitis se illum damnaturos denuntia-
runt. Hoc ille nuntio Athenas rediit, neque ibi

---

[1] suis, *MacMichael and Rubner* ; iis, *MSS.*
[2] in, *added in u.*

---

[1] See xvii. 7. 2 and 8. 6. The narration of events in 2 and
3. 1 is confused and inexact.

already begun the charge, he sounded the recall. This manœuvre became so famous all over Greece that, when a statue was publicly erected to Chabrias in the agora at Athens, he chose to be represented in that position. The result was that after that time athletes, and artists as well, adopted appropriate attitudes for the statues which were set up in their honour when they had won victories.

2. Now Chabrias carried on many wars in Europe as general of the Athenians; in Egypt he made war on his own responsibility. For having gone to the aid of Nectenebis, he secured for him the possession of his throne. He did the same thing in Cyprus, but in that case he was officially appointed by the Athenians to aid Euagoras; and he did not leave the island until he had completely conquered it, an exploit by which the Athenians gained great fame. In the meantime war broke out between the Egyptians and the Persians. The Athenians had an alliance with Artaxerxes; the Lacedaemonians sided with the Egyptians, from whom their king Agesilaus was making large sums of money.[1] Chabrias, seeing this, and not wishing to yield the palm to Agesilaus in anything, went on his own responsibility to the aid of the Egyptians and was made commander of their fleet, while Agesilaus led the land forces.

3. Then the prefects of the Persian king sent envoys to Athens, to remonstrate because Chabrias was warring against their king, acting as an ally of the Egyptians. The Athenians appointed a fixed time for Chabrias to return home, declaring that if he did not obey, they would condemn him to death. In consequence of this threat he returned to Athens,

2 diutius est moratus quam fuit necesse. Non enim
libenter erat ante oculos suorum civium, quod et
vivebat laute et indulgebat sibi liberalius quam ut
3 invidiam vulgi posset effugere. Est enim hoc commune vitium in magnis liberisque civitatibus, ut invidia gloriae comes sit; et libenter de iis detrahunt
quos eminere videant altius, neque animo aequo
pauperes alienam opulentium intuuntur fortunam.
Itaque Chabrias, quoad ei licebat, plurimum aberat.
4 Neque vero solus ille aberat Athenis libenter, sed
omnes fere principes fecerunt idem, quod tantum se
ab invidia putabant afuturos,[1] quantum a conspectu
suorum recesserint. Itaque Conon plurimum Cypri
vixit, Iphicrates in Thraecia, Timotheus Lesbo,
Chares Sigeo, dissimilis quidem Chares horum et
factis et moribus, sed tamen Athenis et honoratus et
potens.

4. Chabrias autem periit bello sociali tali modo.
Oppugnabant Athenienses Chium. Erat in classe
Chabrias privatus, sed omnes qui in magistratu erant
auctoritate anteibat, eumque magis milites quam qui
2 praeerant aspiciebant. Quae res ei maturavit
mortem. Nam dum primus studet portum intrare
gubernatoremque iubet eo derigere navem, ipse sibi
perniciei fuit; cum enim eo penetrasset, ceterae non

---

[1] afuturos, *Fleck*; futuros, *most MSS*.; abfuturos, *u V*.

---

[1] In 356 B.C.: see n. 1, p. 130.
[2] That is, he was not commander-in-chief; he seems to
have commanded a trireme.

but remained there no longer than was absolutely necessary. For he did not care to be under the eyes of his fellow-citizens, because he was living elegantly and indulging himself too generously to be able to avoid the distrust of the common people. In fact, it is a common fault of great states which enjoy freedom that jealousy waits upon glory and that the people take pleasure in humbling those whom they see rising above the level of their fellows. Those of moderate means cannot regard with patience the good fortune of others who are rich. And it was for that reason that Chabrias, as long as he was able to do so, frequently absented himself.

And Chabrias was not the only one who was glad to leave Athens, but almost all the leading men felt as he did, believing that they would be free from suspicion to the extent that they withdrew from the sight of their countrymen. Accordingly, Conon spent a good part of his life in Cyprus, Iphicrates in Thrace, Timotheus in Lesbos, and Chares at Sigeum; it is true that Chares differed from the others in actions and character, but nevertheless he was both honoured and influential in Athens.

4. Now Chabrias lost his life during the Social War[1] in the following manner. The Athenians were attacking Chios. With the fleet was Chabrias in a private capacity,[2] but his influence was greater than that of all who held command, and the soldiers looked to him rather than to their chiefs. That position of influence hastened his death; for desiring to be the first to enter the port, he ordered his steersman to direct his ship to that point. In that way he brought about his own destruction; for when he had forced his way in, the rest of the ships did not

sunt secutae. Quo facto circumfusus hostium concursu cum fortissime pugnaret, navis rostro percussa
3 coepit sidere. Hinc refugere cum posset, si se in mare deiecisset, quod suberat classis Atheniensium quae exciperet natantes, perire maluit quam armis abiectis navem relinquere, in qua fuerat vectus. Id ceteri facere noluerunt, qui nando in tutum pervenerunt. At ille, praestare honestam mortem existimans turpi vitae, comminus pugnans telis hostium interfectus est.

XIII. TIMOTHEUS

1. Timotheus, Cononis filius, Atheniensis. Hic a patre acceptam gloriam multis auxit virtutibus; fuit enim disertus, impiger, laboriosus, rei militaris peritus
2 neque minus civitatis regendae. Multa huius sunt praeclare facta, sed haec maxime illustria. Olynthios et Byzantios bello subegit. Samum cepit; in quo oppugnando superiore bello Athenienses mille et ducenta talenta consumpserant, id ille sine ulla publica impensa populo restituit. Adversus Cotum bella gessit ab eoque mille et ducenta talenta praedae
3 in publicum rettulit. Cyzicum obsidione liberavit. Ariobarzani simul cum Agesilao auxilio profectus est, a quo cum Laco pecuniam numeratam accepisset, ille cives suos agro atque urbibus augeri maluit quam

---

[1] In 444–439 B.C., when Samos, which had revolted from Athens, was reduced by Pericles.
[2] See note 2, p. 130. [3] Cf. xvii. 7. 2.

follow. Consequently he was surrounded by the enemy coming from all sides, and although he fought valiantly, his ship was rammed and began to sink. Even then Chabrias might have escaped by throwing himself into the sea, since the Athenian fleet was at hand to pick up swimmers; but he preferred to die rather than throw away his arms and abandon the ship in which he had sailed. The rest did not share that feeling, but saved themselves by swimming. He, however, thinking an honourable death preferable to a shameful life, was slain by the enemy's weapons in hand-to-hand-combat.

XIII. TIMOTHEUS

1. Timotheus, the Athenian, son of Conon. This man increased by his many accomplishments the glory which he had inherited from his father; for he was eloquent, energetic and industrious; he was skilled in the art of war and equally so in statesmanship. Many are his illustrious deeds, but the following are the most celebrated; his arms were victorious over the Olynthians and the Byzantines; he took Samos, and although in a former war the Athenians had spent twelve hundred talents in the siege of that town,[1] he restored it to the people without any expense to the state. He waged war against Cotus [2] and gained booty to the value of twelve hundred talents, which he paid into the public treasury. He freed Cyzicus from a blockade. With Agesilaus he went to the aid of Ariobarzanes, and while the Laconian accepted a cash payment for his services,[3] Timotheus preferred that his fellow-citizens should have additional territory and cities, rather than that he should receive a recom-

365 B.C.

id sumere cuius partem domum suam ferre posset.
Itaque accepit Crithoten[1] et Sestum.

2. Idem classi praefectus circumvehens Peloponnesum, Laconicen populatus, classem eorum
fugavit, Corcyram sub imperium Atheniensium redegit sociosque idem adiunxit Epirotas, Athamanas,
Chaonas omnesque eas gentes, quae mare illud
2 adiacent. Quo facto Lacedaemonii de diutina contentione destiterunt et sua sponte Atheniensibus
imperii maritimi principatum concesserunt, pacemque his legibus constituerunt, ut Athenienses mari
duces essent. Quae victoria tantae fuit Atticis
laetitiae, ut tum primum arae Paci publice sint
3 factae eique deae pulvinar sit institutum. Cuius laudis
ut memoria maneret, Timotheo publice statuam in
foro posuerunt. Qui honos huic uni ante id tempus
contigit, ut, cum patri populus statuam posuisset,
filio quoque daret. Sic iuxta posita recens filii
veterem patris renovavit memoriam.

3. Hic cum esset magno natu et magistratus gerere
desisset, bello Athenienses undique premi sunt coepti.
Defecerat Samus, descierat Hellespontus, Philippus
iam tum valens, Macedo,[2] multa moliebatur; cui
oppositus Chares cum esset, non satis in eo praesidii

---

[1] Crithoten, *Gebhard*; Crithonem, etc., *MSS.*
[2] Macedo, *omitted by Bosius*; *put after* Philippus *by Lupus*;
Guill. omits Philippus.

---

[1] *Pulvinar* is the cushion on which the image of the goddess
was placed, in order that offerings might be set before her.
Altars to Peace had existed earlier, the new departure was the
annual offering.
[2] According to Dèmosthenes (xx. 70), Conon was the first to
be honoured with a statue, after Harmodius and Aristogeiton.
[3] The reference is to the Social War of 357–355 B.C. Nepos
is inaccurate in the details.

pense of which he could bear a part home with
him. Accordingly, he was given Crithote and
Sestus.

2. Again put in command of the fleet, he sailed 375 B.C.
around the Peloponnesus and pillaged the land of
the Laconians, put their fleet to flight, and brought
Corcyra under the sway of Athens; he also joined to
Athens as allies the Epirotes, Athamanes, Chaones,
and all the peoples bordering on that part of the sea.
Thereupon the Lacedaemonians gave up a long-
continued contest, and voluntarily yielded to the 374 B.C.
Athenians the first place in maritime power, making
peace on terms which acknowledged the supremacy
of Athens on the sea. That victory filled the people
of Attica with such great joy that then for the first
time an altar was publicly consecrated to Peace and
a feast established in her honour.[1] In order to perpetuate the memory of so glorious a deed, the
Athenians set up a statue of Timotheus in the agora,
at the cost of the state. This was an honour which
had fallen to him alone of all men up to that time,
namely, that when the state had erected a statue to a
father, a son received the same tribute.[2] Thus the
new statue of the son, placed beside that of the father,
revived the memory of the latter, which had now
grown old.

3. When Timotheus was advanced in years and
had ceased to hold office, war began to threaten the
Athenians from every quarter: Samos had revolted,
the Hellespont had seceded,[3] Philip of Macedon, who
was even then powerful, was making many plots.
Against the last-named Chares [4] had been sent, but
was not thought capable of defending the country.

---

[4] He is mentioned also in xii. 3. 4. and xix. 2. 3.

2 putabatur. Fit Menestheus praetor, filius Iphicratis,
gener Timothei, et ut ad bellum proficiscatur decerni-
tur. Huic in consilium dantur duo, usu sapientiaque
praestantes,[1] pater et socer, quod in his tanta erat
auctoritas, ut magna spes esset per eos amissa posse
3 recuperari. Hi cum Samum profecti essent et
eodem Chares, illorum adventu cognito, cum suis
copiis proficisceretur, ne quid absente se gestum
videretur, accidit, cum ad insulam appropinquarent,
ut magna tempestas oriretur; quam evitare duo
veteres imperatores utile arbitrati, suam classem
4 suppresserunt. At ille temeraria usus ratione non
cessit maiorum natu auctoritati, velut[2] in sua manu
esset fortuna. Quo contenderat pervenit, eodemque
ut sequerentur ad Timotheum et Iphicraten nuntium
misit.

Hinc male re gesta, compluribus amissis navibus, eo
unde erat profectus se recepit litterasque Athenas
publice misit, sibi proclive fuisse Samum capere, nisi
5 a Timotheo et Iphicrate desertus esset. Populus
acer, suspicax ob eamque rem mobilis, adversarius[3]
invidus—etiam potentiae in crimen vocabantur[4]
—domum revocat; accusantur proditionis. Hoc
iudicio damnatur Timotheus lisque eius aestimatur
centum talentis. Ille odio ingratae civitatis coactus,
Chalcidem se contulit.

---

[1] *After* praestantes *the MSS. have* quorum consilium
uteretur; *deleted by Halm.*

[2] velut, *Heusinger;* et ut *and* et, *MSS.;* et ut si, *u.*

[3] adversariis, *Wagner.*

[4] etiam . . . vocabantur, *omitted by Halm;* etenim potentia . . . vocabatur, *Andresen (Gitlbauer).*

---

[1] This sentence is difficult and probably corrupt; see the
crit. notes. On *potentiae . . . vocabantur* cf. i. 8. 1; ii. 8. 1.

Menestheus, son of Iphicrates and son-in-law of Timotheus, was made general, and it was decided that he should undertake that war. He was given as advisers two men eminent for their experience and wisdom, his father and his father-in-law, since they had such high standing as to inspire strong hopes that through them what had been lost might be recovered. The three then sailed for Samos, and Chares, who had been advised of their coming, went with his forces to the same place, in order that nothing might seem to have been done without his presence. As they were drawing near to the island, it chanced that a great storm arose, and the two old generals, thinking it best to avoid it, anchored their fleet. But Chares, adopting a bold course, did not heed the advice of his elders, believing that he was the master of fortune. He arrived at his destination, and sent word to Timotheus and Iphicrates to join him.

Then, having suffered defeat and lost a number of his ships, he returned to the place from which he had set out and sent an official report to Athens, alleging that he could easily have taken Samos if he had not been left in the lurch by Timotheus and Iphicrates. The Athenians, being impulsive, distrustful and therefore changeable, hostile and envious (moreover, the men who were accused were powerful), summoned them all back home.[1] They were cited to appear in court and accused of treason. Timotheus was found guilty and his fine was fixed at one hundred talents. Whereupon, driven by indignation at his country's ingratitude, he withdrew to Chalcis.[2]

[2] In 355 B.C.; he died the same year.

4. Huius post mortem cum populum iudicii sui paeniteret, multae novem partes detraxit et decem talenta Cononem, filium eius, ad muri quandam partem reficiendam iussit dare. In quo fortunae varietas est animadversa. Nam quos avus muros ex hostium praeda patriae restituerat, eosdem nepos cum summa ignominia familiae ex sua re familiari

2 reficere coactus est. Timothei autem moderatae sapientisque vitae cum pleraque possimus proferre testimonia, uno erimus contenti, quod ex eo facile conici poterit quam carus suis fuerit. Cum Athenis adulescentulus causam diceret, non solum amici privatique hospites ad eum defendendum convenerunt, sed etiam in iis Iason, tyrannus Thessaliae, qui

3 illo tempore fuit omnium potentissimus. Hic cum in patria sine satellitibus se tutum non arbitraretur, Athenas sine ullo praesidio venit tantique hospitem fecit, ut mallet ipse[1] capitis periculum adire quam Timotheo de fama dimicanti deesse. Hunc adversus tamen Timotheus postea populi iussu bellum gessit, patriae sanctiora iura quam hospitii esse duxit.

4 Haec extrema fuit aetas imperatorum Atheniensium, Iphicratis, Chabriae, Timothei, neque post illorum obitum quisquam dux in illa urbe fuit dignus memoria.

5 Venio nunc ad fortissimum virum maximique consilii omnium barbarorum, exceptis duobus

---

[1] ipse, *Wölfflin*; se, *MSS.*

---

[1] This was in 373 B.C.; as Timotheus was then forty years of age, *adulescentulus* is used without diminutive force, as is not unusual in colloquial speech.

[2] *Hospites* were those in other states with whom he had relations of guest-friendship; see note 1, p. 36.

4. After his death the people repented of the sentence they had passed upon Timotheus, remitted nine-tenths of the fine, and required his son Conon to pay, for repairing a part of the city wall, only ten talents. In this event we see the inconsistency of Fortune; for the very walls which his grandfather had restored to his country from booty taken from the enemy the younger Conon was compelled to repair from his own estate with great dishonour to his family. Now Timotheus lived a well-regulated and wise life; although I might give many proofs of this, I shall content myself with one, from which it may easily be imagined how dear he was to his friends. When he was a young man[1] and was involved in a law-suit at Athens, not only did his friends at home and those abroad[2] in private station flock to his defence, but among the latter was none other than Jason, tyrant of Thessaly, at that time the most powerful of all such rulers. That great man, although he did not think himself safe even in his own country without guards, came to Athens without a single attendant, being so devoted to his guest-friend that he preferred to risk his own life rather than fail Timotheus when he was defending his honour. Yet Timotheus afterwards, by order of the people, made war upon this very Jason, regarding the rights of his country as more sacred than those of hospitality.

The era of Athenian generals came to an end with Iphicrates, Chabrias and Timotheus, and after the death of those eminent men no general in that city was worthy of notice.

I now pass to the bravest and ablest man of all the barbarians, with the exception of the two Car-

6 Karthaginiensibus, Hamilcare et Hannibale. De quo hoc plura referemus, quod et obscuriora sunt eius gesta pleraque et ea quae prospere ei cesserunt, non magnitudine copiarum, sed consilii, quo tum omnes superabat, acciderunt; quorum nisi ratio explicata fuerit, res apparere non poterunt.

XIV. DATAMES

1. Datames, patre Camisare, natione Care, matre Scythissa natus, primum militum in[1] numero fuit apud Artaxerxen eorum qui regiam tuebantur. Pater eius Camisares, quod et manu fortis et bello strenuus et regi multis locis fidelis erat repertus, habuit provinciam partem Ciliciae iuxta Cappadociam, quam in-
2 colunt Leucosyri. Datames, militare munus fungens, primum qualis esset aperuit in bello quod rex adversus Cadusios gessit. Namque hic, multis milibus regiorum interfectis,[2] magni fuit eius opera. Quo factum est, cum in eo bello cecidisset Camisares, ut[3] paterna ei traderetur provincia.

2. Pari se virtute postea praebuit, cum Autophrodates iussu regis bello persequeretur eos qui defecerant. Namque huius opera hostes, cum castra iam intrassent, profligati sunt exercitusque reliquus conservatus regis est; qua ex re maioribus rebus praeesse

[1] in, *added by Fleck.*; in *before* militum, *Nipp.*
[2] multis . . . interfectis, *put after* intrassent (2. 1) *by Cobet, followed with variations by Guill.*
[3] ut, *added by Heusinger.*

---

[1] Since 2. 4 seems to indicate that the mother of Datames was a Paphlagonian, some take Scythissa as her name.

thaginians, Hamilcar and Hannibal. About him I shall give the more details, because the greater number of his exploits are less familiar and because his successes were due, not to the greatness of his forces, but to his strategy, in which he excelled all the men of his day. And unless the true inwardness of these successes be explained, his career cannot be understood.

XIV. DATAMES

1. Datames, son of Camisares, a Carian by nationality, born of a Scythian mother,[1] began his career as one of the corps of soldiers who guarded the palace of Artaxerxes.[2] His father Camisares, because of his personal bravery and valour in war, and because he had on many occasions proved his loyalty to the king, governed that part of Cilicia which adjoins Cappadocia and is inhabited by the Leucosyri, or "White Syrians." Datames, while serving as a soldier, first showed his quality in the war which the king waged against the Cadusii, in which, although many thousands of the king's troops were slain, his *c.* 380 services were of great value. The consequence was, that since Camisares had fallen in the course of that war, Datames became governor of his father's province.

2. He later showed himself equally valiant when Autophrodates, at the king's command, was making war upon the peoples that had revolted. For when the enemy had already entered the Persian camp, it was owing to Datames that they were routed and the rest of the king's army was saved. And because of that exploit he began to be entrusted with more

[1] Artaxerxes Mnemon, as everywhere in xiv.

2 coepit. Erat eo tempore Thuys dynastes Paphla-
goniae, antiquo genere, ortus a Pylaemene [1] illo quem
Homerus Troico bello a Patroclo interfectum ait.
3 Is regi dicto audiens non erat. Quam ob causam bello
eum persequi constituit eique rei praefecit Datamen,
propinquum Paphlagonis; namque ex fratre et sorore
erant nati. Quam ob causam Datames primum
experiri voluit ut sine armis propinquum ad officium
reduceret. Ad quem cum venisset sine praesidio,
quod ab amico nullas vereretur insidias, paene
interiit; nam Thuys eum clam interficere voluit.
4 Erat mater cum Datame, amita Paphlagonis. Ea
5 quid ageretur resciit, filiumque monuit. Ille fuga
periculum evitavit bellumque indixit Thuyni. In
quo cum ab Ariobarzane, praefecto Lydiae et Ioniae
totiusque Phrygiae, desertus esset, nihilo segnius
perseveravit vivumque Thuyn cepit cum uxore et
liberis.

3. Cuius facti ne prius fama ad regem quam ipse
perveniret, dedit operam. Itaque omnibus insciis
eo ubi erat rex venit posteroque die Thuyn, hominem
maximi corporis terribilique facie, quod et niger et
capillo longo barbaque erat promissa, optima veste
texit, quam satrapae regii gerere consuerant, ornavit
etiam torque atque armillis aureis ceteroque regio
2 cultu; ipse agresti duplici amiculo circumdatus

---

[1] Pylaemene, *Aldus.*

---

[1] In *Iliad* v. 576 he is said to have been slain by Menelaus.

important commands. At that time there was a prince of Paphlagonia called Thuys, of an old family, being a descendant of that Pylaemenes who, according to Homer, was slain by Patroclus in the Trojan war.[1] He did not own obedience to the king, who for that reason determined to make war upon him. He gave the management of the campaign to Datames, who was a near relative of the Paphlagonian; for the father of the one and the mother of the other were brother and sister. That being the case, Datames wished first to try to recall his kinsman to his duty without resort to arms. But having come to him without an escort, because he feared no treachery from a friend, Datames all but lost his life; for Thuys tried to kill him secretly. Datames was accompanied by his mother, who was the maternal aunt of the Paphlagonian; she learned of the plot and warned her son, who escaped the danger by flight and declared war upon Thuys. Although in the course of that war Datames was deserted by Ariobarzanes, governor of Lydia, Ionia and all Phrygia, he kept on with undiminished vigour and took Thuys alive, along with his wife and children.

3. Datames took pains to prevent the news of his success from reaching the king before his own arrival. Therefore, without the knowledge of anyone, he came to the place where the king was, and on the following day, he dressed up Thuys—who was a man of huge size and fearful aspect, being very dark, with long hair and flowing beard—putting on him the fine raiment which the king's satraps are accustomed to wear, adorning him too with a neck-chain and bracelets of gold and the other habiliments of a king. Datames himself, wearing a peasant's double

hirtaque tunica, gerens in capite galeam venatoriam, dextra manu clavam, sinistra copulam, qua vinctum ante se Thuynem agebat, ut si feram bestiam captam duceret.

3 Quem cum omnes conspicerent propter novitatem ornatus ignotamque formam ob eamque rem magnus esset concursus, fuit non nemo qui agnosceret 4 Thuyn regique nuntiaret. Primo non accredidit itaque Pharnabazum misit exploratum. A quo ut rem gestam comperit, statim admitti iussit, magno opere delectatus cum facto tum ornatu, imprimis quod nobilis rex in potestatem inopinanti venerat. 5 Itaque magnifice Datamen donatum ad exercitum misit, qui tum contrahebatur duce Pharnabazo et Tithrauste ad bellum Aegyptium, parique eum atque illos imperio esse iussit. Postea vero quam Pharnabazum rex revocavit, illi summa imperii tradita est.[1]

4. Hic cum maximo studio compararet exercitum Aegyptumque proficisci pararet, subito a rege litterae sunt ei missae, ut Aspim aggrederetur, qui Cataoniam tenebat; quae gens iacet supra Ciliciam, 2 confinis Cappadociae. Namque Aspis, saltuosam regionem castellisque munitam incolens, non solum imperio regis non parebat, sed etiam finitimas regiones 3 vexabat et quae regi portarentur abripiebat. Datames etsi longe aberat ab eis regionibus et a maiore re abstrahebatur, tamen regis voluntati morem

---

[1] tradita sunt, *Dan. A B P.*

cloak and a shaggy tunic, with a hunter's cap on his head, in his right hand a club and in the left a leash to which Thuys was attached, drove the Paphlagonian before him as if he were bringing in a wild beast that he had captured.

When their strange garb and the unusual appearance of the captive had attracted all eyes, and in consequence a great crowd had gathered, someone recognized Thuys and informed the king. At first, Artaxerxes was incredulous and so sent Pharnabazus to investigate. Having learned the truth from him, he at once ordered the two to be admitted, greatly pleased with the capture and the masquerade, in particular because the notorious king had come into his power sooner than he expected. Accordingly, he rewarded Datames munificently and sent him to the army which was then being mustered under Pharnabazus and Tithraustes for the war in Egypt, *c. 378* giving him equal authority with the two Persians. *B.C.* In fact, when the king later recalled Pharnabazus, the chief command passed to Datames.

4. While Datames was busily engaged in organizing this army and preparing to embark for Egypt, suddenly a letter was sent to him by the king, ordering him to attack Aspis, the ruler of Cataonia; that country lies beyond Cilicia, next to Cappadocia. The reason for the attack was, that Aspis, dwelling in a region that was wooded and fortified with strongholds, far from acknowledging allegiance to Artaxerxes, even overran the regions neighbouring to Persia and carried off what was being brought to the king. Datames was far distant from the regions in question and was drawn in the opposite direction by a more important enterprise; but nevertheless he

gerendum putavit. Itaque cum paucis, sed viris
fortibus navem conscendit, existimans, quod accidit,
facilius se imprudentem parva manu oppressurum
quam paratum quamvis magno exercitu.

4   Hac delatus in Ciliciam, egressus inde, dies noctes-
que iter faciens Taurum transit eoque quo studuerat
venit. Quaerit quibus locis sit Aspis; cognoscit haud
longe abesse profectumque eum venatum. Quae dum
speculatur, adventus eius causa cognoscitur. Pisidas
cum iis quos secum habebat ad resistendum Aspis
5 comparat. Id Datames ubi audivit, arma sumit, suos
sequi iubet; ipse equo concitato ad hostem vehitur.
Quem procul Aspis conspiciens ad se ferentem
pertimescit atque a conatu resistendi deterritus
sese dedidit. Hunc Datames vinctum ad regem
ducendum tradit Mithridati.

5. Haec dum geruntur, Artaxerxes, reminiscens a
quanto bello ad quam parvam rem principem ducum
misisset, se ipse reprehendit et nuntium ad exercitum
Acen misit, quod nondum Datamen profectum
putabat, qui diceret ne ab exercitu discederet. Hic
priusquam perveniret quo erat profectus, in itinere
2 convenit qui Aspim ducebant. Qua celeritate cum
magnam benevolentiam regis Datames consecutus
esset, non minorem invidiam aulicorum excepit,
quod illum unum pluris quam se omnes fieri videbant.

---

[1] A warlike and independent people of that region, who
served as mercenaries.
[2] Son of Artaxerxes; see 10. 1.

thought that he ought to do what the king desired. He therefore embarked upon a ship, taking with him only a few, but brave, soldiers, believing—as turned out to be the case—that it would be easier to crush his enemy with a small force by taking him off his guard, than with any possible numbers when he was ready to defend himself.

Sailing to Cilicia and disembarking there, Datames marched day and night, crossed the Taurus, and arrived at his destination. On inquiring where Aspis was, he learned that he was not far off, and that he had gone a-hunting. While Datames was considering what to do, the reason for his arrival became known, and Aspis prepared to resist him with the Pisidians [1] in addition to the soldiers that he had with him. When Datames heard of this, he took up arms, ordered his men to follow; he himself rode at full speed to meet the enemy. Aspis, catching sight of him afar off, as he rushed upon him, was seized with fear, and abandoning any thought of resistance, gave himself up. Datames put him in irons and delivered him to Mithridates [2] to be taken to the king.

5. While all this was going on, Artaxerxes, remembering from how important a war he had sent his leading general on so insignificant an errand, thinking that Datames had not yet started, sent a messenger to the army at Ace, telling him not to leave the army; but before the messenger arrived at his destination, he met on the way those that were bringing Aspis to the king. Although by that rapid action Datames gained high favour with Artaxerxes, he incurred equally great jealousy from the courtiers, because they realized that he was more highly esteemed

Quo facto, cuncti ad eum opprimendum consenserunt.
3 Haec Pandantes, gazae custos regiae, amicus Datami,
perscripta ei mittit, in quibus docet eum in magno
fore periculo, si quid illo imperante adversi in
4 Aegypto accidisset. Namque eam esse consuetudinem regiam, ut casus adversos hominibus tribuant,
secundos fortunae suae. Quo fieri ut facile im-
pellantur ad eorum perniciem quorum ductu res male
gestae nuntientur. Illum hoc maiore fore in discrimine, quod, quibus rex maxime oboediat, eos
habeat inimicissimos.

5   Talibus ille litteris cognitis, cum iam ad exercitum
Acen venisset, quod non ignorabat ea vere scripta,
desciscere a rege constituit. Neque tamen quic-
6 quam fecit quod fide sua esset indignum. Nam
Mandroclem Magnetem exercitui praefecit; ipse
cum suis in Cappadociam discedit coniunctamque
huic Paphlagoniam occupat, celans qua voluntate
esset in regem. Clam cum Ariobarzane facit
amicitiam, manum comparat, urbes munitas suis
tuendas tradit.

   6. Sed haec propter hiemale tempus minus
prospere procedebant. Audit Pisidas quosdam [1]
copias adversus se parare. Filium eo Arsidaeum
cum exercitu mittit; cadit in proelio adulescens.
Proficiscitur eo pater non ita cum magna manu,
celans quantum vulnus accepisset, quod prius ad
hostem pervenire cupiebat, quam de male re gesta

---

[1] quosdam, *Lupus*; quasdam, *MSS.*

than any of them. Because of that they all united in a conspiracy to ruin him. Of this plot Pandantes, keeper of the royal treasure, who was a friend of Datames, gave him full information in a letter, telling him that he would be in great danger if he suffered any check during his command in Egypt. He added that it was the habit of kings to attribute disasters to men, but success to their own good fortune; that consequently they were easily led to bring about the ruin of those who were reported to have suffered defeat; and that Datames would be in the greater peril because he had the bitter enmity of those who had special influence with the king.

When Datames had read that letter, although he had already reached the army at Ace, knowing that what had been written him was true, he determined to leave the king's service. Yet he did nothing to stain his honour; for he put Mandrocles of Magnesia in command of the army, and he himself with his own men went off to Cappadocia and took possession of the neighbouring district of Paphlagonia, concealing his feelings towards the king. Then he secretly came to an understanding with Ariobarzanes, gathered a band of soldiers, and entrusted the fortified cities to the protection of his friends.

6. But because of the winter season these preparations did not advance rapidly. Hearing that some of the Pisidians were arming troops against him, he sent his son Arsidaeus with an army to meet them, and the young man fell in the battle that followed. Then the father set out against them with not so very large a force, concealing the severe wound that he had suffered, because he wished to encounter the enemy before the report of the defeat came to his

fama ad suos perveniret, ne cognita filii morte animi
2 debilitarentur militum. Quo contenderat pervenit
iisque locis castra ponit, ut neque circumiri multitudine adversariorum posset neque impediri quominus
ipse ad dimicandum manum haberet expeditam.

3 Erat cum eo Mithrobarzanes, socer eius, praefectus
equitum. Is, desperatis generi rebus, ad hostes
transfugit. Id Datames ut audivit, sensit si in
turbam exisset ab homine tam necessario se relictum,
4 futurum ut ceteri consilium sequerentur. In vulgus
edit suo iussu Mithrobarzanem profectum pro
perfuga, quo facilius receptus interficeret hostes; qua
re relinqui eum par non esse et omnes confestim
sequi. Quod si animo strenuo fecissent, futurum ut
adversarii non possent resistere, cum et intra vallum
5 et foris caederentur. Hac re probata exercitum
educit, Mithrobarzanem persequitur, qui cum ad
6 hostes pervenerat, Datames signa inferri iubet. Pisidae, nova re commoti, in opinionem adducuntur
perfugas mala fide compositoque fecisse, ut recepti
maiori essent calamitati. Primum eos adoriuntur.
Illi cum quid ageretur aut qua re fieret ignorarent,
coacti sunt cum iis pugnare ad quos transierant, ab
iisque stare quos reliquerant; quibus cum neutri

men, for fear that the news of his son's death might affect the soldiers' spirits. He arrived at his destination and pitched his camp in such a position that he could not be surrounded by the superior numbers of his adversaries nor prevented from having his own force ready for battle.

He had with him Mithrobarzanes, his father-in-law, as commander of his cavalry, but he, regarding the position of his son-in-law as desperate, deserted to the enemy. When Datames heard of this, he knew that if it was bruited about that he had been forsaken by a man so nearly related to him, all the rest would follow the example. He therefore circulated the report that it was by his command that Mithrobarzanes had gone, under pretence of deserting, in order that he might, once received by the enemy, destroy them the more easily; therefore it would not be right to abandon him, but all ought to follow him at once. If they would act vigorously, the enemy would be unable to resist, since they would be assailed inside and outside of their intrenchments. When this idea met with favour, he led out his army and pursued Mithrobarzanes; and when the deserter had reached the enemy, Datames gave the order to attack. The Pisidians, surprised by this strange manœuvre, were led to believe that the deserters had acted in bad faith and by prearrangement, in order that when received among the enemy they might cause a greater disaster. First they attacked the deserters, and since the latter did not understand what was going on or why it was done, they were forced to fight against those to whom they had deserted and side with those whom they had abandoned; and since neither army showed them any

7 parcerent, celeriter sunt concisi. Reliquos Pisidas resistentes Datames invadit; primo impetu pellit, fugientis persequitur, multos interficit, castra hostium capit.

8 Tali consilio uno tempore et proditores perculit et hostes profligavit et, quod ad perniciem suam fuerat cogitatum, id ad salutem convertit. Quo neque acutius ullius imperatoris cogitatum neque celerius factum usquam legimus.

7. Ab hoc tamen viro Sysinas, maximo natu filius, desciit ad regemque transiit et de defectione patris detulit. Quo nuntio Artaxerxes commotus, quod intellegebat sibi cum viro forti ac strenuo negotium esse, qui cum cogitasset, facere auderet [1] et prius cogitare quam conari consuesset, Autophrodatem in
2 Cappadociam mittit. Hic ne intrare posset, saltum in quo Ciliciae portae sunt sitae Datames prae-
3 occupare studuit. Sed tam subito copias contrahere non potuit. A qua re depulsus cum ea manu, quam contraxerat, locum deligit talem, ut neque circumiretur ab hostibus neque praeteriret adversarius quin ancipitibus locis premeretur, et, si dimicare eo vellet, non multum obesse multitudo hostium suae paucitati posset.

8. Haec etsi Autophrodates videbat, tamen statuit congredi quam cum tantis copiis refugere aut tam diu
2 uno loco sedere. Habebat barbarorum equitum

---

[1] et cum cogitasset, facere auderet, *put after* consuesset *by Andresen and others.*

---

[1] See note on *reliquam phalangem* xii. 1. 2 (p. 130)

mercy, they were quickly cut to pieces. The Pisidians, who remained,[1] continued to resist, but Datames fell upon them, routed them at the first onset, pursued the fugitives, killing many of them, and captured the enemy's camp.

By this stratagem Datames at the same time punished the traitors and vanquished the enemy, thus making the plot which had been devised for his ruin the means of his safety. Never have I read anywhere of a cleverer stratagem of any commander, or one which was more speedily executed.

7. Yet this man was deserted by Sysinas, his eldest son, who went over to the king and reported to him his father's defection. The news of this disturbed Artaxerxes, since he knew that he had to do with a brave and energetic man, who, when he had reflected, had the courage to carry out his plan, and was in the habit of reflecting before acting. Accordingly, he sent Autophrodates to Cappadocia. To prevent him from entering the country, Datames wished to occupy the wooded gorge in which the Cilician Gates are situated; but he could not muster his forces with sufficient speed. Thwarted in that, with the band which he had assembled he chose a position where he could not be surrounded by the enemy, one which his opponent could not pass without being caught in an unfavourable situation; and if the latter decided to fight there, the enemy's great numbers would not have much advantage over his own small force. 368-7 B.C.

8. Although Autophrodates realized the situation, he nevertheless determined to engage rather than retreat with so great a force or linger for so long a time in one spot. Of barbarians he had twenty thousand

$\overline{XX}$, peditum $\overline{C}$, quos illi Cardacas appellant, eiusdemque generis $\overline{III}$ funditorum, praeterea Cappadocum $\overline{VIII}$, Armeniorum $\overline{X}$, Paphlagonum $\overline{V}$, Phrygum $\overline{X}$, Lydorum $\overline{V}$, Aspendiorum et Pisidarum circiter $\overline{III}$, Cilicum $\overline{II}$, Captianorum totidem, ex Graecia conductorum $\overline{III}$, levis armaturae maximum numerum.

3   Has adversus copias spes omnis consistebat Datami in se locique natura; namque huius partem non habebat vicesimam militum. Quibus fretus conflixit adversariorumque multa milia concidit, cum de ipsius exercitu non amplius hominum mille cecidisset. Quam ob causam postero die tropaeum posuit, quo
4 loco pridie pugnatum erat.   Hinc cum castra movisset semperque inferior copiis superior omnibus proeliis discederet, quod numquam manum consereret, nisi cum adversarios locorum angustiis clausisset, quod perito regionum callideque cogitanti saepe accidebat,
5 Autophrodates, cum bellum duci maiore regis calamitate quam adversariorum videret, pacem amicitiamque hortatus est, ut cum rege in gratiam
6 rediret.   Quam ille etsi fidam non fore putabat, tamen condicionem accepit seque ad Artaxerxem legatos missurum dixit. Sic bellum quod rex adversus Datamen susceperat sedatum est. Autophrodates in Phrygiam se recepit.

   9. At rex, quod implacabile odium in Datamen

---

[1] A Greek word κάρδακες, a translation of the term applied by the Persians to mercenary soldiers belonging to the barbarian tribes of the Persian empire.

horse and a hundred thousand foot, of the troops that the Persians call Cardaces,[1] besides three thousand slingers of the same nationality; and in addition, eight thousand Cappadocians, ten thousand Armenians, five thousand Paphlagonians, ten thousand Phrygians, five thousand Lydians, about three thousand Aspendians and Pisidians, two thousand Cilicians, the same number of Captiani, and three thousand Greek mercenaries, along with an enormous number of light-armed troops.

For encountering these forces Datames' sole hope lay in himself and in the nature of his position; for he had not a twentieth part as many men. Relying upon such forces as he had, he accepted battle and slew many thousands of his adversaries, while of his own army he lost not more than a thousand men. To commemorate his victory, he erected a trophy on the following day on the spot where he had fought the day before. Then he moved his camp and departed, having come off victor in all his engagements, although always outnumbered, since he never joined battle except when he had shut his foes in some narrow defile; which often happened, owing to his knowledge of the country and his skilful strategy. Then Autophrodates, seeing that to prolong the war was more disastrous to the king than to his adversaries, urged peace and friendship, and reconciliation with the king. And although Datames had no faith in the king's sincerity, he nevertheless accepted the proposal and promised to send envoys to Artaxerxes. Thus the war which the king had made upon Datames came to an end. Autophrodates withdrew into Phrygia.

9. The king, however, having conceived im-

susceperat, postquam bello eum opprimi non posse
animadvertit, insidiis interficere studuit; quas ille
2 plerasque evitavit.[1] Sicut, cum ei nuntiatum esset
quosdam sibi insidiari, qui in amicorum erant numero,
—de quibus, quod inimici detulerant, neque credendum neque neglegendum putavit,—experiri voluit
3 verum falsumne sibi esset relatum. Itaque eo
profectus est, in quo itinere futuras insidias dixerant.
Sed elegit corpore ac statura simillimum sui eique
vestitum suum dedit atque eo loco ire quo ipse consuerat iussit; ipse autem ornatu vestituque militari
inter corporis custodes iter facere coepit.

4   At insidiatores, postquam in eum locum agmen
pervenit, decepti ordine atque vestitu, impetum in
eum faciunt qui suppositus erat. Praedixerat autem
iis Datames cum quibus iter faciebat ut parati essent
5 facere quod ipsum vidissent. Ipse, ut concurrentes
insidiatores animum advertit, tela in eos coniecit.
Hoc idem cum universi fecissent, priusquam per-
venirent ad eum quem aggredi volebant, confixi
conciderunt.

   10. Hic tamen tam callidus vir extremo tempore
captus est Mithridatis, Ariobarzanis filii, dolo.
Namque is pollicitus est regi se eum interfecturum,
si sibi[2] rex permitteret ut quodcumque vellet liceret

---

¹ evitavit, *Nipp.* (vitavit, *ed.* 11, *Witte*); vitavit, *MSS.*
² sibi, *Ortmann*; ei, *MSS.*

placable hatred of Datames and finding that he could not get the better of him in war, tried to kill him by treachery; but Datames escaped many of his plots. For example, when it was reported to him that certain men were conspiring against him who were included among his friends, he thought that charges against friends, made by their personal enemies, ought neither to be believed nor disregarded; but he wished to find out whether what had been reported to him was true or false. Accordingly, he set out for the place on the road to which it was reported that the ambuscade would be laid. But he selected a man who closely resembled him in figure and stature, dressed him in his own costume, and directed him to take the place in the line which he himself usually occupied. Then Datames, equipped and dressed like a common soldier, began the march among his body-guard.

Now the traitors, when the army reached the appointed place, misled by his place in the line and his costume, made their attack upon the man who had taken Datames' place. But Datames had ordered those with whom he was marching to be ready to do what they saw him doing, and he, as soon as he saw the traitors rushing forward, hurled weapons at them; and since the whole troop did the same, before the assassins could reach the man whom they wished to attack they all fell, pierced with wounds.

10. Yet this man, cunning as he was, finally fell victim to the craft of Mithridates, the son of Ariobarzanes; for he had promised the king to kill Datames, provided the king would allow him to do with impunity anything that he chose, and would give

impune facere fidemque de ea re more Persarum
2 dextra dedisset. Hanc ut accepit a rege missam,
copias parat et absens amicitiam cum Datame facit,
regis provincias vexat, castella expugnat, magnas
praedas capit, quarum partim suis dispertit, partim
ad Datamen mittit; pari modo complura castella ei
3 tradit. Haec diu faciundo persuasit homini se
infinitum adversus regem suscepisse bellum, cum
nihilo magis, ne quam suspicionem illi praeberet
insidiarum, neque colloquium eius petivit neque in
conspectum venire studuit. Sic absens amicitiam
gerebat, ut non beneficiis mutuis, sed communi odio
quod erga regem susceperant contineri viderentur.

11. Id cum satis se confirmasse arbitratus est,
certiorem facit Datamen tempus esse maiores res
parari et bellum cum ipso rege suscipi, deque ea re,
si ei videretur, quo loco vellet in colloquium veniret.
Probata re, colloquendi tempus sumitur locusque quo
2 conveniretur. Huc Mithridates cum uno cui maxime
habebat fidem ante aliquot dies venit compluri-
busque locis separatim gladios obruit eaque loca
diligenter notat. Ipso autem colloquii die utrique
locum qui explorarent atque ipsos scrutarentur
mittunt; deinde ipsi sunt congressi.

---

[1] The messenger gave his right hand to Datames as the
king's representative; cf. Justin. xi. 15. 3, dextram fert;
Xen. *Cyrop.* iv. 2. 7, φέρει δεξιάν; etc. The custom of
sending a representation of a hand as a token (Tac. *Hist.* i.
54; ii. 8) is a later one.

him a pledge to that effect in the Persian fashion with his right hand. When he had received that pledge from the king's messenger,[1] Mithridates prepared his forces and made friends with Datames without meeting him. He then began to raid the king's provinces and storm his fortresses, gaining a great amount of booty, of which he divided a part among his soldiers and sent a part to Datames; he likewise handed over several fortresses to the Carian. By continuing this conduct for a long time he convinced Datames that he was engaged in implacable war against the king, while nevertheless, to avoid exciting any suspicion of treachery, he neither sought an interview with his intended victim, nor did he try to meet him face to face. From a distance he played the part of a friend, in such a way that they seemed to be united, not by mutual services, but by the common hatred which they felt for the king.

11. When Mithridates thought that he had made his enmity to the king sufficiently evident, he informed Datames that it was time to raise greater armies and make war directly on Artaxerxes; and he invited him to hold a conference about that matter, if he approved, in any place that he wished. The proposition was accepted, and a time and place appointed for their meeting. Mithridates went to the spot several days in advance, with a single companion in whom he had the greatest confidence; and in several different places, which he carefully marked, he buried swords. And on the very day of the meeting both parties sent men to examine the place and search the generals themselves; then the two met.

3   His cum aliquamdiu in colloquio fuissent et diversi discessissent iamque procul Datames abesset, Mithridates, priusquam ad suos perveniret, ne quam suspicionem pareret, in eundem locum revertitur atque ibi ubi telum erat infossum resedit,[1] ut si lassitudine cuperet adquiescere, Datamenque revocavit, simulans se quiddam in colloquio esse ob-

4 litum.   Interim telum quod latebat protulit nudatumque vagina veste texit ac Datami venienti ait digredientem se animadvertisse locum quendam, qui erat in conspectu, ad castra ponenda esse idoneum.

5 Quem cum digito demonstraret et ille respiceret, aversum ferro transfixit priusque quam quisquam posset succurrere, interfecit.   Ita ille vir, qui multos consilio, neminem perfidia ceperat, simulata captus est amicitia.

XV. EPAMINONDAS

1. Epaminondas, Polymnidis[2] filius, Thebanus. De hoc priusquam scribimus, haec praecipienda videntur lectoribus, ne alienos mores ad suos referant, neve ea quae ipsis leviora sunt pari modo apud ceteros fuisse

2 arbitrentur.   Scimus enim musicen nostris moribus abesse a principis persona, saltare vero etiam in vitiis poni; quae omnia apud Graecos et grata et

---

[1] infossum resedit, *Heusinger*; repostum insedit, *Can.*; impostum resedit, *Dan. A P*; impostum resedit, *the other MSS.*
[2] Polymnidis, *Heusinger*; Polymni, *MSS.*

---

[1] On the form of this Life see Introd., p. xii.
[2] Cf. Praef. 2.   [3] See Cic. *pro Mur.* 13.

After they had conferred there for some time, they departed in opposite directions; but when Datames was already a considerable distance away, Mithridates, in order not to arouse any suspicion, returned to the place of meeting before joining his attendants, and sat down at a spot where a weapon had been buried, as if he were tired and wished to rest; then he called Datames back, pretending that he had overlooked something in the course of the conference. In the meantime he took out the hidden sword, drew it from its sheath, and concealed it under his cloak. When Datames came, Mithridates said to him that just as he was leaving he had noticed a spot, visible from where they sat, which was suitable for pitching a camp. He pointed out the place, and as Datames turned to look at it, the traitor plunged the sword into his back and killed him before anyone could come to his help. Thus that 362 B.C. great man, who had triumphed over many by strategy, but never by treachery, fell a victim to feigned friendship.

XV. EPAMINONDAS

1. Epaminondas, the Theban, son of Polymnis.[1] Before writing about this man, I think I ought to warn my readers not to judge the customs of other nations by their own,[2] and not to consider conduct which in their opinion is undignified as so regarded by other peoples. We know, for example, that according to our ideas music is unsuited to a personage of importance, while dancing is even numbered among the vices;[3] but with the Greeks all such accomplishments were regarded as becoming and

3 laude digna ducuntur. Cum autem exprimere imaginem consuetudinis atque vitae velimus Epaminondae, nihil videmur debere praetermittere
4 quod pertineat ad eam declarandam. Qua re dicemus primum de genere eius, deinde quibus disciplinis et a quibus sit eruditus, tum de moribus ingeniique facultatibus et si qua alia memoria digna erunt, postremo de rebus gestis, quae a plurimis animi [1] anteponuntur virtutibus.

2. Natus igitur patre quo diximus, genere honesto, pauper iam a maioribus relictus est,[2] eruditus autem sic ut nemo Thebanus magis. Nam et citharizare et cantare ad chordarum sonum doctus est a Dionysio, qui non minore fuit in musicis gloria quam Damon aut Lamprus, quorum pervulgata sunt nomina, cantare tibiis ab Olympiodoro, saltare a Calliphrone.
2 At philosophiae praeceptorem habuit Lysim Tarentinum, Pythagoreum; cui quidem sic fuit deditus, ut adulescens tristem ac severum senem omnibus aequalibus suis in familiaritate anteposuerit; neque prius eum a se dimisit,[3] quam in doctrinis tanto antecessit condiscipulos, ut facile intellegi posset pari modo superaturum omnes in ceteris artibus.
3 Atque haec ad nostram consuetudinem sunt levia et potius contemnenda; at in Graecia, utique olim, magnae laudi erant.
4 Postquam ephebus est factus et palaestrae dare operam coepit, non tam magnitudini virium servivit

---

[1] animi, *Koene*; omnium, *MSS.*
[2] est, *added by Hahn, Fleck.*; *after* natus, *Nipp.*
[3] dimisit, *Nipp.*; dimiserit, *MSS.*

even praiseworthy. Since, then, I wish to portray
the life and habits of Epaminondas, it seems to me
that I ought to omit nothing which contributes to
that end. Therefore I shall speak first of his family,
then of the subjects which he studied and his
teachers, next of his character, his natural qualities,
and anything else that is worthy of record. Finally,
I shall give an account of his exploits, which many
writers consider more important than mental
excellence.

2. Well then, he was born of the father whom I
have mentioned; his family was an honourable one,
but had been in moderate circumstances for some
time; yet in spite of that he received as good an
education as any Theban. Thus he was taught to
play the lyre, and to sing with an instrumental
accompaniment, by Dionysius, who in the musical
world was equal in reputation to Damon or Lamprus,
whose names are known everywhere. He learned
to play the pipes from Olympiodorus and to dance
from Calliphron. In philosophy he had as his master
Lysis of Tarentum, the Pythagorean, and to him he
was so attached that in his youth he was more
intimate with that grave and austere old man than
with any of the young people of his own age; and he
would not allow his teacher to leave him until he so
far surpassed his fellow-students in learning, that it
could readily be understood that in a similar way he
would surpass all men in all other accomplishments.
Now these last, according to our views, are trivial, or
rather, contemptible; but in Greece, especially in
bygone days, they were highly esteemed.

As soon as Epaminondas attained military age and
began to interest himself in physical exercise, he

quam velocitati; illam enim ad athletarum usum, hanc ad belli existimabat utilitatem pertinere.

5 Itaque exercebatur plurimum currendo et luctando ad eum finem, quoad stans[1] complecti posset atque contendere. In armis vero plurimum studii consumebat.

3. ·Ad hanc corporis firmitatem plura etiam animi bona accesserant. Erat enim modestus, prudens, gravis, temporibus sapienter utens, peritus belli, fortis manu, animo maximo, adeo veritatis diligens,

2 ut ne ioco quidem mentiretur. Idem continens, clemens patiensque admirandum in modum, non solum populi, sed etiam amicorum ferens iniurias; in primis commissa celans, quod[2] interdum non minus prodest quam diserte dicere, studiosus audiendi;

3 ex hoc enim facillime disci arbitrabatur. Itaque cum in circulum venisset in quo aut de re publica disputaretur aut de philosophia sermo haberetur, numquam inde prius discessit, quam ad finem sermo esset adductus.

4 Paupertatem adeo facile perpessus est, ut de re publica nihil praeter gloriam ceperit. Amicorum in se tuendo caruit facultatibus, fide[3] ad alios sublevandos saepe sic usus est, ut iudicari possit

5 omnia ei cum amicis fuisse communia. Nam cum aut civium suorum aliquis ab hostibus esset captus aut virgo amici nubilis, quae propter paupertatem

---

[1] quoad stans, *u*; quo adstans, *MSS.*
[2] quodque, *Eussner.*
[3] isdem, *M. Haupt*; idem, *Nipp.*

---

[1] See crit. note.
[2] After the manner of the Pythagoreans; see Gell. i. 9. 12.

aimed less at great strength than at agility; for he thought that the former was necessary for athletes, but that the latter would be helpful in warfare. Accordingly, he trained himself thoroughly in running and wrestling, but in the latter only to the extent of being able, while still standing, to seize his opponent and contend with him. But it was to the use of arms that he devoted his greatest efforts.

3. To the bodily strength that he thus acquired there were added still greater mental gifts; for he was temperate, prudent, serious, and skilful in taking advantage of opportunities; practised in war, of great personal courage and of high spirit; such a lover of the truth that he never lied even in jest. Furthermore, he was self-controlled, kindly, and forbearing to a surprising degree, putting up with wrongs, not only from the people, but even from his friends; he was most particular in keeping secrets, a quality which is sometimes no less valuable than eloquence, and he was a good listener; for he thought that to be the easiest way of acquiring information. Therefore, whenever he was in a gathering where there was an argument about affairs of state or philosophical discussion, he never left until the conversation was ended.

He found it so easy to endure narrow means that from his public services he gained nothing but glory, and he declined to use the wealth of his friends for his own necessities. In aiding others, on the contrary, he made such use of their trust[1] in him that one might suppose that he and his friends shared all their possessions in common.[2] For if anyone of his fellow-citizens had been taken by the enemy, or if a friend's daughter was of marriageable age but

collocari non posset, amicorum consilium [1] habebat et
quantum quisque daret pro facultatibus imperabat.
6 Eamque summam cum confecerat,[2] priusquam [3] acciperet pecuniam, adducebat eum qui quaerebat ad
eos qui conferebant, eique ut ipsi numerarent faciebat,
ut ille ad quem ea res perveniebat sciret quantum
cuique deberet.

4. Temptata autem eius est abstinentia a Diome-
donte Cyziceno; namque is rogatu Artaxerxis regis
Epaminondam pecunia corrumpendum susceperat.
Hic magno cum pondere auri Thebas venit et
Micythum adulescentulum quinque talentis ad
suam perduxit voluntatem, quem tum Epaminondas plurimum diligebat.[4] Micythus Epaminondam convenit et causam adventus Diomedontis
2 ostendit. At ille Diomedonti coram " Nihil," inquit,
" opus pecunia est; nam si rex ea vult quae Thebanis
sunt utilia, gratiis facere sum paratus; sin autem
contraria, non habet auri atque argenti satis. Namque
orbis terrarum divitias accipere nolo pro patriae
3 caritate. Tu quod me incognitum temptasti tuique
similem existimasti non miror tibique ignosco; sed
egredere propere, ne alios corrumpas, cum me
non potueris. Et tu, Micythe, argentum huic redde,
aut, nisi id confestim facis, ego te tradam magis-
4 tratui." Hunc Diomedon cum rogaret, ut tuto exiret [5]
suaque quae attulerat liceret efferre, " Istud
quidem," inquit, " faciam, neque tua causa, sed mea,

---

[1] concilium, *Aldus*.   [2] confecerat, *Halm*; fecerat, *MSS.*
[3] potiusquam, *Halm*; *Fleck. added* ipse.
[4] quem ... diligebat, *put after* adulescentulum *by Pluygers.*
[5] exire, *ed. Briziana.*

---

[1] *Magistratui* is used collectively; cf. ii. 7. 4 and the note
(p. 34).

could not be wedded because of lack of means, he took counsel of his friends and fixed the amount of the contribution which each was to make, adapting the sum to the contributor's means. And having made up the necessary amount, before taking the money he presented the one who was in need to the contributors, in order that the man who received help might know how much he owed each one.

4. His integrity was tested by Diomedon, of 368 b.c. Cyzicus, who, at the request of King Artaxerxes, had undertaken to bribe Epaminondas. Diomedon came to Thebes with a great amount of gold, and with five talents won the support of a young man named Micythus, to whom Epaminondas was greatly attached at that time. Micythus went to Epaminondas and explained the reason for Diomedon's coming. But the great man dealt with the Persian face to face, saying: "There is no need of money; for if what the king wishes is to the interest of the Thebans, I am ready to do it free of charge; but if the contrary is true, he has not gold and silver enough; for I would not take all the riches in the world in exchange for my love of country. As for you, who do not know me, I am not surprised that you have tried to tempt me and believed me to be a man like yourself, and I forgive you; but leave here at once, so that you may not corrupt others, since you have failed with me. And you, Micythus, give this man back his money; and if you do not do so immediately, I shall hand you over to the magistrates."[1] When Diomedon asked that he might go away in safety and be allowed to take the money that he had brought with him, Epaminondas replied: "I will grant your request, not, however, for your sake,

ne, si tibi sit pecunia adempta, aliquis dicat id ad
me ereptum pervenisse, quod delatum accipere
noluissem."

5   A quo cum quaesisset quo se deduci vellet, et ille
Athenas dixisset, praesidium dedit, ut tuto perveniret.   Neque vero id satis habuit, sed etiam ut
inviolatus in navem escenderet per Chabriam
Atheniensem, de quo supra mentionem fecimus,
6 effecit.   Abstinentiae erit hoc satis testimonium.
Plurima quidem proferre possimus, sed modus adhi-
bendus est, quoniam uno hoc volumine vitam excellentium virorum complurium concludere consti-
tuimus, quorum res[1] separatim multis milibus
versuum complures scriptores ante nos explicarunt.

   5. Fuit etiam disertus ut nemo ei Thebanus par
esset eloquentia, neque minus concinnus in brevitate
respondendi quam in perpetua oratione ornatus.
2 Habuit obtrectatorem Menecliden quendam, indidem
Thebis, et adversarium in administranda re publica,
satis exercitatum in dicendo, ut Thebanum scilicet;
3 namque illi genti plus inest virium quam ingenii.   Is
quod in re militari florere Epaminondam videbat,
hortari solebat Thebanos ut pacem bello anteferrent,
ne illius imperatoris opera desideraretur.   Huic ille
" Fallis," inquit, " verbo civis tuos, quod eos a bello
avocas[2]; otii enim nomine servitutem concilias;

---

[1] res, *added by Richter.*
[2] avocas, *u, Lambin*; evocas, *MSS.*; revocas, *Klotz.*

but for my own; for I fear that if your money should be taken from you, someone might say that the sum which I had refused when it was offered as a gift had come into my hands through confiscation."

Epaminondas then asked the Persian where he wished to be taken, and when Diomedon named Athens, he gave him an escort, to secure his safe arrival. And he was not even satisfied with that, but through Chabrias, the Athenian, of whom I have already spoken, he saved Diomedon from being molested before he embarked. Of Epaminondas' integrity this will be sufficient proof. As a matter of fact, I might cite a great many instances, but I must use restraint, since I have planned in this one volume to include the lives of several distinguished men, to whose individual deeds various writers before me have devoted many thousand lines.

5. Epaminondas was also so good a speaker that no Theban equalled him in eloquence, and he was not less clever in brief answers than brilliant in a set speech. He had a detractor in the person of one Meneclides, also a native of Thebes and his rival in the administration of the state, who too was a practised speaker, at least for a Theban; for that people possesses more bodily strength than mental ability.[1] This man, observing that warfare brought glory to Epaminondas, used to urge the Thebans to seek peace rather than war, in order that they might not need the aid of that great man as their commander. To him Epaminondas said: "You are deceiving your fellow-citizens by using the wrong word, when you dissuade them from war; for under the name of peace it is slavery that you are recom-

[1] Cf. vii. 11. 3.

4 nam paritur pax bello. Itaque qui ea diutina volunt
frui, bello exercitati esse debent. Qua re si principes Graeciae vultis esse, castris est vobis utendum,
non palaestra."

5 Idem ille Meneclides cum huic obiceret quod
liberos non haberet neque uxorem duxisset, maximeque insolentiam, quod sibi Agamemnonis belli
gloriam videretur consecutus: at ille "Desine,"
inquit, "Meneclida, de uxore mihi exprobrare; nam
nullius in ista re minus uti consilio volo." Habebat
6 enim Meneclides suspicionem adulteri. "Quod
autem me Agamemnonem aemulari putas, falleris.
Namque ille cum universa Graecia vix decem annis
unam cepit urbem, ego contra ea una urbe nostra
dieque uno totam Graeciam, Lacedaemoniis fugatis,
liberavi."

6. Idem cum in conventum venisset Arcadum, petens ut societatem cum Thebanis et Argivis facerent,
contraque Callistratus, Atheniensium legatus, qui
eloquentia omnes eo praestabat tempore, postularet
ut potius amicitiam sequerentur Atticorum, et in
oratione sua multa invectus esset in Thebanos et
2 Argivos in iisque hoc posuisset, animum advertere
debere Arcades quales utraque civitas cives procreasset, ex quibus de ceteris possent iudicare:
Argivos enim fuisse Orestem et Alcmaeonem matri-
cidas; Thebis Oedipum natum, qui, cum patrem
3 suum interfecisset, ex matre liberos procreasset:
huic in respondendo Epaminondas, cum de ceteris

---

mending. As a matter of fact, peace is won by war; hence those who wish to enjoy it for a long time ought to be trained for war. Therefore if you wish to be the leading city of Greece, you must frequent the camp and not the gymnasium."

When this same Meneclides taunted him with not having children or marrying, and especially with arrogance in thinking that he had equalled Agamemnon's renown in war, Epaminondas answered: "Cease, Meneclides, to taunt me about marriage; there is no one whose example in that regard I should be less willing to follow"; and, in fact, Meneclides was suspected of adultery. "Further, in supposing that I regard Agamemnon as a rival, you are mistaken; for he, with all Greece at his back, needed fully ten years to take one city, while I, on the contrary, with this city of ours alone, and in a single day, routed the Lacedaemonians and freed all Greece."[1]

6. Again, when he had entered the assembly of the Arcadians, urging them to conclude an alliance with the Thebans and Argives, Callistratus, the envoy of the Athenians and the most eloquent orator of that time[2] advised them rather to ally themselves with the people of Attica, and in his speech made many attacks upon the Thebans and Argives. For example, he declared that the Arcadians ought to bear in mind the character of some of the citizens that those two cities had produced, since from them they could form an estimate of the rest. Thus from Argos came Orestes and Alcmaeon, the matricides; from Thebes, Oedipus, who, after killing his father, begot children from his mother. In replying to him Epaminondas, after having first discussed the other

perorasset, postquam ad illa duo opprobria pervenit,
admirari se dixit stultitiam rhetoris Attici, qui non
animadverterit, innocentes illos natos domi, scelere
admisso cum patria essent expulsi, receptos esse ab
Atheniensibus.

4   Sed maxime eius eloquentia eluxit Spartae legati
ante pugnam Leuctricam. Quo cum omnium
sociorum convenissent legati, coram frequentissimo
conventu sic Lacedaemoniorum tyrannidem coarguit,
ut non minus illa oratione opes eorum concusserit
quam Leuctrica pugna. Tum enim perfecit, quod
post apparuit, ut auxilio Lacedaemonii sociorum
privarentur.

    7. Fuisse patientem suorumque iniurias ferentem
civium, quod se patriae irasci nefas esse duceret, haec
sunt testimonia. Cum eum propter invidiam cives
sui praeficere exercitui noluissent duxque esset
delectus belli imperitus, cuius errore eo esset deducta
illa multitudo militum ut omnes de salute perti-
mescerent, quod locorum angustiis clausi ab hostibus
obsidebantur, desiderari coepta est Epaminondae
diligentia; erat enim ibi privatus numero militis.
2 A quo cum peterent opem, nullam adhibuit memoriam contumeliae et exercitum obsidione liberatum
3 domum reduxit incolumem. Nec vero hoc semel
fecit, sed saepius. Maxime autem fuit inlustre,

questions, finally came to these two taunts. He was amazed, he said, at the folly of the Attic orator, who did not understand that those men were all blameless at the time of their birth in their native land, but after they had committed their crimes and had been exiled from their country, they had found asylum with the Athenians.

But his most brilliant display of eloquence was at Sparta, as envoy before the battle of Leuctra. For when the representatives of all the allies had assembled there, in the presence of that great throng he denounced the despotism of the Lacedaemonians in such terms that he did not shake the Spartan power more by the battle of Leuctra than by that famous address. For it was then—as afterwards became clear—that he succeeded in depriving the Lacedaemonians of the support of their allies. 371 B.C.

7. That he was patient and submitted to the injustice of his fellow-citizens because he thought it impious to show anger towards his country, appears from the following evidence. The Thebans because of jealousy had refused to make him commander of their army and had chosen a leader without experience in warfare. When the man's blunder had resulted in making that large force of soldiers fearful of their safety, since they were shut up in a narrow defile and blockaded by the enemy, they came to feel the need of Epaminondas' carefulness; and he was present, as it happened, serving as a soldier without a commission. When they appealed to him for help, he entirely overlooked the slight that he had suffered, freed the army from siege, and led it home in safety. And this he did not once, but very often. Conspicuous among these was the time when he led 368 B.C.

cum in Peloponnesum exercitum duxisset adversus Lacedaemonios haberetque collegas duos, quorum alter erat Pelopidas, vir fortis ac strenuus.

Hi cum criminibus adversariorum omnes in invidiam venissent ob eamque rem imperium iis esset abrogatum atque in eorum locum alii praetores 4 successissent, Epaminondas populi scito non paruit idemque ut facerent persuasit collegis, et bellum quod susceperat gessit. Namque animadvertebat, nisi id fecisset, totum exercitum propter praetorum 5 imprudentiam inscitiamque belli periturum. Lex erat Thebis, quae morte multabat, si quis imperium diutius retinuisset quam lege praefinitum foret. Hanc Epaminondas cum rei publicae conservandae causa latam videret, ad perniciem civitatis conferri[1] noluit et quattuor mensibus diutius quam populus iusserat gessit imperium.

8. Postquam domum reditum est, collegae eius hoc crimine accusabantur. Quibus ille permisit ut omnem causam in se transferrent suaque opera factum contenderent, ut legi non oboedirent. Qua defensione illis periculo liberatis, nemo Epaminondam responsurum putabat, quod quid diceret non haberet. 2 At ille in iudicium venit, nihil eorum negavit quae adversarii crimini dabant, omniaque quae collegae dixerant confessus est neque recusavit quominus legis poenam subiret; sed unum ab iis petivit, ut in periculo[2] suo inscriberent:

[1] conferri, *Fleck*; conferre, *MSS.*
[2] periculo, *MSS.*; sepulcro, *Aldus et exc. Pat.*; breviculo, *Heerwagen.*

[1] For this meaning of *periculum* see Cic. *Verr.* iii. 183, eorum hominum fidei tabulae publicae periculaque magistratuum committuntur.

the army to the Peloponnesus against the Lace- 370 B.C.
daemonians and had two colleagues, one of whom was
Pelopidas, a man of courage and energy.

All these generals had become, through the charges
of their opponents, objects of suspicion, and for
that reason their command had been taken from
them and other leaders had been appointed in their
place. Epaminondas refused to obey the people's
decree, persuaded his colleagues to follow his example,
and continued the war which he had begun; for he
knew that unless he did so, the entire army would be
lost, owing to the incapacity of the generals and their
ignorance of warfare. There was a law at Thebes
which punished with death anyone who had retained
a command beyond the time provided by that law.
Since Epaminondas realized that the law in question
had been passed for the safety of his country, he did
not wish it to contribute to the ruin of the state;
consequently, he retained his command for four
months longer than the time fixed by the people.

8. After they returned home, his colleagues were
brought to trial for their disobedience. Epaminondas allowed them to throw the entire responsibility upon him and to urge in their defence that it
was due to him that they had disobeyed the law.
That plea freed them from danger, and no one thought
that Epaminondas would put in an appearance, since
he had nothing to say in his defence. But he came
into court, denied none of the charges of his
opponents, admitted everything that his colleagues
had said, and did not refuse to submit to the penalty
named in the law. He made only one request of the
judges, namely, that they should enter the following
record of his sentence.[1]

3 "Epaminondas a Thebanis morte multatus est,
quod eos coegit apud Leuctra superare Lacedaemonios, quos ante se imperatorem nemo Boeotorum
4 ausus fuit [1] aspicere in acie, quodque uno proelio
non solum Thebas ab interitu retraxit, sed etiam
universam Graeciam in libertatem vindicavit eoque
res utrorumque perduxit, ut Thebani Spartam
5 oppugnarent, Lacedaemonii satis haberent, si salvi
esse possent, neque prius bellare destitit quam,
Messene restituta, urbem eorum obsidione clausit."

Haec cum dixisset, risus omnium cum hilaritate
coortus est, neque quisquam iudex ausus est de eo
ferre suffragium. Sic a iudicio capitis maxima
discessit gloria.

9. Hic extremo tempore imperator apud Manti-
neam cum acie instructa audacius instaret hostes,
cognitus a Lacedaemoniis, quod in unius pernicie eius
patriae sitam putabant salutem, universi in unum
impetum fecerunt neque prius abscesserunt quam
magna caede multisque occisis fortissime ipsum Epaminondam pugnantem, sparo eminus percussum, con-
2 cidere viderunt. Huius casu aliquantum retardati
sunt Boeotii, neque tamen prius pugna excesserunt
3 quam repugnantes profligarunt. At Epaminondas
cum animadverteret mortiferum se vulnus accepisse
simulque, si ferrum, quod ex hastili in corpore
remanserat, extraxisset, animam statim emissurum,
usque eo retinuit, quoad renuntiatum est vicisse
Boeotios. Id postquam audivit, "Satis," inquit,

---

[1] sit, *Halm*; est, *cod. Marcianus.*

"Epaminondas was condemned to death by the Thebans because at Leuctra he compelled them to vanquish the Lacedaemonians, whom before he took command no Boeotian had dared to face in battle, and because in a single contest he not only saved Thebes from destruction, but also secured freedom for all Greece and so changed the situation of the contending parties that the Thebans attacked the Lacedaemonians, while the Lacedaemonians were satisfied with being able to save themselves; and he did not bring the war to an end until by the restoration of Messene he placed Sparta in a state of siege."

When he had said this, there was laughter and merriment throughout the assembly and no juror ventured to vote for his condemnation. Thus from a capital charge he gained the greatest glory.

9. Finally, when commander at Mantinea, in the heat of battle he charged the enemy too boldly. He was recognized by the Lacedaemonians, and since they believed that the death of that one man would ensure the safety of their country, they all directed their attack at him alone and kept on until, after great bloodshed and the loss of many men, they saw Epaminondas himself fall valiantly fighting, struck down by a lance hurled from afar. By his death the 362 B.C. Boeotians were checked for a time, but they did not leave the field until they had completely defeated the enemy. But Epaminondas, realizing that he had received a mortal wound, and at the same time that if he drew out the head of the lance, which was separated from the shaft and fixed in his body, he would at once die, retained it until news came that the Boeotians were victorious. As soon as he heard that,

" vixi; invictus enim morior." Tum, ferro extracto, confestim exanimatus est.

10. Hic uxorem numquam duxit. In quo cum reprehenderetur a Pelopida, qui filium habebat infamem, maleque eum in eo patriae consulere diceret, quod liberos non relinqueret,[1] " Vide," inquit, " ne tu peius consulas, qui talem ex te natum relicturus 2 sis. Neque vero stirps potest mihi deesse; namque ex me natam relinquo pugnam Leuctricam, quae non modo mihi superstes, sed- etiam immortalis sit 3 necesse est." Quo tempore duce Pelopida exsules Thebas occuparunt et praesidium Lacedaemoniorum ex arce expulerunt, Epaminondas, quam diu facta est caedes civium, domo se tenuit, quod neque malos defendere volebat neque impugnare, ne manus suorum sanguine cruentaret; namque omnem civilem victoriam funestam putabat. Idem, postquam apud Cadmeam[2] cum Lacedaemoniis pugnari coeptum est, in primis stetit.

4 Huius de virtutibus vitaque satis erit dictum, si hoc unum adiunxero, quod nemo ibit[3] infitias : Thebas et ante Epaminondam natum et post eiusdem interitum perpetuo alieno paruisse imperio, contra ea, quam diu ille praefuerit rei publicae, caput fuisse totius Graeciae. Ex quo intellegi potest unum hominem pluris quam civitatem fuisse.

[1] quod liberos non relinqueret *after* diceret, *Puteanus*; *after* reprehenderetur, *MSS.*
[2] Cadmeam, *Aldus*; Achademiam (Academiam), *MSS.*
[3] ibit, *Can., Halm*; it, ut, id, eat, *MSS.*

he cried: "I have lived long enough, since I die unconquered." Then he drew out the iron and at once breathed his last.

10. Epaminondas never took a wife. Because of this he was criticized by Pelopidas,[1] who had a son of evil reputation; for his friend said that the great Theban did a wrong to his country in not leaving children. Epaminondas replied; "Take heed that you do not do her a greater wrong in leaving such a son as yours. And besides, I cannot lack offspring; for I leave as my daughter the battle of Leuctra, which is certain, not merely to survive me, but even to be immortal." When the exiles, led by Pelopidas, took Thebes and drove the Lacedaemonian garrison from the citadel, so long as the citizens were being slain Epaminondas remained in his house,[2] since he was unwilling either to aid the traitors or to fight against them, from reluctance to stain his hands with the blood of his countrymen; for he thought that every victory won in a civil war was pernicious. But as soon as the combat began with the Lacedaemonians at the Cadmea, he stood in the forefront.

Enough will have been said of this great man's virtues and of his life, if I add this one thing, which nobody will deny. Before the birth of Epaminondas, and after his death, Thebes was subject constantly to the hegemony [3] of others; but, on the contrary, so long as he was at the head of the state, she was the leading city of all Greece. This fact shows that one man was worth more than the entire body of citizens.

---

[1] Cf. 5. 5.   [2] Cf. xvi. 4. 1.
[3] See note 1, p. 30.

XVI. PELOPIDAS

1. Pelopidas Thebanus, magis historicis quam vulgo notus. Cuius de virtutibus dubito quem ad modum exponam, quod vereor, si res explicare incipiam, ne non vitam eius enarrare, sed historiam videar scribere; sin tantum modo summas attigero, ne rudibus Graecarum litterarum minus dilucide appareat quantus fuerit ille vir. Itaque utrique rei occurram, quantum potuero, et medebor cum satietati tum ignorantiae lectorum.

2 Phoebidas Lacedaemonius cum exercitum Olynthum duceret iterque per Thebas faceret, arcem oppidi, quae Cadmea nominatur, occupavit impulsu paucorum Thebanorum, qui adversariae factioni quo facilius resisterent, Laconum rebus studebant, idque 3 suo privato, non publico fecit consilio. Quo facto eum Lacedaemonii ab exercitu removerunt pecuniaque multarunt, neque eo magis arcem Thebanis reddiderunt, quod susceptis inimicitiis satius ducebant eos obsideri quam liberari; nam post Peloponnesium bellum Athenasque devictas cum Thebanis sibi rem esse existimabant et eos esse solos qui 4 adversus resistere[1] auderent. Hac mente amicis suis summas potestates dederant alteriusque factionis principes partim interfecerant, alios in exsilium eiecerant; in quibus Pelopidas hic, de quo scribere exorsi sumus, pulsus patria carebat.

[1] se sistere, *Andresen.*

---

[1] Nepos makes it clear here that he is not an historian, but a biographer, and that he dwells upon the virtues of his subjects as models for conduct; also that he is addressing the general, unlearned, public.

XVI. PELOPIDAS

1. Pelopidas, the Theban, is better known to historians than to the general public. I am in doubt how to give an account of his merits; for I fear that if I undertake to tell of his deeds, I shall seem to be writing a history rather than a biography; but if I merely touch upon the high points, I am afraid that to those unfamiliar with Grecian literature it will not be perfectly clear how great a man he was. Therefore I shall meet both difficulties as well as I can, having regard both for the weariness and the lack of information of my readers.[1]

When Phoebidas, the Lacedaemonian, was leading his army to Olynthus and went by way of Thebes, he 382 B.C took possession of the citadel of the town, called the Cadmea, at the instigation of a few Thebans, who, in order the more easily to resist the party of their opponents, espoused the cause of the Lacedaemonians; but he did this on his own initiative and not at the direction of his state. Because of this act the Lacedaemonians deprived him of his command and condemned him to pay a fine, but for all that they did not return the citadel to the Thebans, thinking that, having incurred their enmity, it was better to keep them in a state of siege than to free them. Indeed, after the Peloponnesian war and the defeat of Athens they looked upon the Thebans as rivals and as the only people that would dare to resist them. Owing to this feeling, they had given the highest offices at Thebes to their sympathizers, and had either put to death or exiled the leading men of the opposite faction. Among these this Pelopidas, about whom I have begun to write, had been driven from his native land into exile.

2. Hi omnes fere Athenas se contulerant, non quo sequerentur otium, sed ut, quem [1] ex proximo locum fors obtulisset, eo patriam recuperare niterentur.
2 Itaque, cum tempus est visum rei gerendae, communiter cum iis qui Thebis idem sentiebant diem delegerunt ad inimicos opprimendos civitatemque liberandam eum quo maximi magistratus simul
3 consuerant epulari. Magnae saepe res non ita magnis copiis sunt gestae, sed profecto numquam tam ab tenui initio tantae opes sunt profligatae; nam duodecim adulescentuli coierunt ex iis qui exsilio erant multati, cum omnino non essent amplius centum, qui tanto se offerrent periculo. Qua paucitate percussa est Lacedaemoniorum potentia.
4 Hi enim non magis adversariorum factioni quam Spartanis eo tempore bellum intulerunt, qui principes erant totius Graeciae; quorum imperii maiestas, neque ita multo post, Leuctrica pugna ab hoc initio perculsa concidit.
5 Illi igitur duodecim, quorum dux erat Pelopidas, cum Athenis interdiu exissent, ut vesperascente caelo Thebas possent pervenire, cum canibus venaticis exierunt,[2] retia ferentes, vestitu agresti, quo minore suspicione facerent iter. Qui cum tempore ipso quo studerant pervenissent, domum Charonis deverterunt,[3] a quo et tempus et dies erat datus.

3. Hoc loco libet interponere, etsi seiunctum ab re

---

[1] quem, *Madvig*; quemque, *MSS.*
[2] exierunt, *omitted by Richter, Guill.*
[3] deverterunt, *Lambin*; devenerunt, *MSS.*

---

[1] The festival of the Aphrodisia, at the end of the term of office of the three annually elected polemarchs.

2. Nearly all those who had been banished took refuge in Athens, not in order to live in idleness, but to make an effort to recover their native land at the very first opportunity that fortune offered. Accordingly, as soon as they thought that the time for action had come, with those of their fellow-citizens in Thebes who had the same sentiments they agreed upon a time when they were to surprise their enemies 379 B.C. and free the city, choosing the day on which the chief magistrates were in the habit of meeting at a banquet.[1] Great things have often been accomplished with not so very great forces, but surely never did so humble a beginning result in the overthrow of so mighty a power. For only a dozen young men came together of those who had been punished with exile, and there were not more than a hundred in all to confront so great a peril. Yet it was by that small number that the power of Lacedaemon was shattered. For they made war, not more upon the party of their opponents than on the Spartans, and that too when the Spartans were the masters of all Greece. But Sparta's imposing power, after being shaken by this enterprise, soon afterward fell in ruins at the battle of Leuctra.

Those twelve heroes, then, led by Pelopidas, left Athens by day, in order to be able to reach Thebes at nightfall. They took with them hunting dogs and nets, and wore the garb of peasants, that their expedition might attract less attention. At the very time that they had planned they arrived at Thebes, and went to lodge at the house of Charon, the man who had named the day and hour.

3. Here I should like to digress, although it has no direct connection with my narrative, to point out how

proposita est, nimia fiducia quantae calamitati soleat
esse. Nam magistratuum Thebanorum statim ad
aures pervenit exsules in urbem venisse. Id illi
vino epulisque dediti usque eo despexerunt, ut ne
2 quaerere quidem de tanta re laborarint. Accessit
etiam quod magis aperiret eorum dementiam.
Adlata est enim epistula Athenis ab Archino uni [1] ex
his, Archiae, qui tum maximum magistratum Thebis
obtinebat, in qua omnia de profectione eorum perscripta erant. Quae cum iam accubanti in convivio
esset data, sicut erat signata, sub pulvinum subiciens,
3 " In crastinum," inquit, " differo res severas." At
illi omnes, cum iam nox processisset, vinolenti ab
exsulibus duce Pelopida sunt interfecti. Quibus
rebus confectis, vulgo ad arma libertatemque vocato,
non solum qui in urbe erant, sed etiam undique
ex agris concurrerunt, praesidium Lacedaemoniorum
ex arce pepulerunt, patriam obsidione liberarunt,
auctores Cadmeae occupandae partim occiderunt,
partim in exsilium eiecerunt.

4. Hoc tam turbido tempore, sicut supra docuimus,
Epaminondas, quoad cum civibus dimicatum est,
domi quietus fuit. Itaque haec liberandarum
Thebarum propria laus est Pelopidae, ceterae fere
2 communes cum Epaminonda. Namque in [2] Leuctrica
pugna, imperatore Epaminonda, hic fuit dux delectae

[1] uni, *Bosius*; uno, *MSS.* (viro, *Can.*).
[2] in, *Can., Lambin*; *the other MSS. omit.*

[1] He was one of the Boeotarchs, or representatives of the
cities of the Boeotian league, of which Thebes had two.

great danger there usually is in excessive confidence. For it came at once to the ears of the Theban magistrates that the exiles had arrived in the city; but busy as they were in drinking and feasting, they considered the news so unimportant that they did not even take the trouble to inquire into a matter of such moment. Another thing made their folly still more apparent; for a letter was brought from Athens, written by Archinus to one of their number, Archias, who at the time was the chief magistrate in Thebes,[1] in which full details of the expedition were given. The letter was handed to Archias when he had already taken his place at the banquet, but without breaking the seal he put it under his pillow, with the remark: "Serious matters may wait until to-morrow." Now all those magistrates, in the course of that night, were slain in their cups by the exiles, headed by Pelopidas. That done, the people were called to arms and to liberty; they hastened to the spot, not only from the city, but from all the country-side, drove the Lacedaemonian garrison from the citadel, and freed their country from oppression. Of those who had caused the occupation of the Cadmea some were slain, others driven into exile.

4. During this time, so full of trouble, Epaminondas, as I have already said,[2] remained quietly at home, so long as the contest was with fellow-citizens. Hence this glorious deed of freeing Thebes belongs wholly to Pelopidas, but almost all the rest of his renown was shared with Epaminondas. For example, in the battle of Leuctra, although Epaminondas was commander-in-chief, Pelopidas was the

---

[2] Cf. xv. 10. 3.

manus quae prima phalangem prostravit Laconum.
3 Omnibus praeterea periculis eius[1] adfuit—sicut,
Spartam cum oppugnavit, alterum tenuit cornu—
quoque Messena celerius restitueretur, legatus in
Persas est profectus. Denique haec fuit altera
persona Thebis, sed tamen secunda ita ut proxima
esset Epaminondae.

5. Conflictatus autem est etiam adversa fortuna.
Nam et initio, sicut ostendimus, exsul patria caruit et,
cum Thessaliam in potestatem Thebanorum cuperet
redigere legationisque iure satis tectum se arbitraretur, quod apud omnes gentes sanctum esse
consuesset, a tyranno Alexandro Pheraeo simul cum
2 Ismenia comprehensus in vincla coniectus est. Hunc
Epaminondas recuperavit, bello persequens Alexandrum. Post id factum numquam animo placari
pótuit in eum a quo erat violatus. Itaque persuasit
Thebanis ut subsidio Thessaliae proficiscerentur
3 tyrannosque eius expellerent. Cuius belli cum ei
summa esset data eoque cum exercitu profectus
esset, non dubitavit, simul ac conspexit hostem,
4 confligere. In quo proelio Alexandrum ut animadvertit, incensus ira equum in eum concitavit proculque
digressus a suis, coniectu telorum confossus concidit.
Atque hoc secunda victoria accidit; nam iam inclina-
5 tae erant tyrannorum copiae. Quo facto omnes
Thessaliae civitates interfectum Pelopidam coronis
aureis et statuis aeneis liberosque eius multo agro
donarunt.

---

[1] eius, *added by Halm.*

---

[1] The so-called Sacred Band of 300 heavy-armed soldiers,
in which pairs of intimate friends fought side by side.
[2] Pelopidas went to Persia in 367 B.C.; Messene had been
restored (that is, made an independent state) in 370 B.C.

leader of the select corps [1] that was first to break the
Lacedaemonian phalanx. Moreover, he shared in all
his other dangers (thus in the attack on Sparta he
commanded one wing), and in order to hasten the
restoration of Messene, he went as an envoy to the
Persians.[2] In short, he was one of the two great
citizens of Thebes, and although he was second, yet
he was next to Epaminondas.

5. But Pelopidas contended also with ill fortune;
for in the beginning, as I have stated, he was driven
from his country into exile, and when he wished to
bring Thessaly under the sway of Thebes and thought 368 B.C.
that he was amply protected by the inviolability of
ambassadors, since that was observed sacredly by all
nations, he was arrested with Ismenias by Alexander,
tyrant of Pherae, and thrown into prison. He
was rescued by Epaminondas, who made war upon
Alexander. After that experience Pelopidas could
never be reconciled with the man who had outraged
him, and it was for that reason that he persuaded the
Thebans to go to the aid of Thessaly and free it of its
tyrants. When he had been given the chief command
in that war and had set out with his army, he did not
hesitate to join battle immediately on catching sight
of the enemy. In the action that followed, inflamed
with wrath at the very first sight of Alexander, he
spurred his horse against the tyrant, and being thus
separated some distance from his men, he fell,
struck down by a shower of weapons. This happened in the full tide of victory, for the tyrants' forces
had already given way. Because of that exploit all
the states of Thessaly presented the dead Pelopidas
with crowns of gold and statues of bronze, and his
children with a great amount of land.

XVII. AGESILAUS

1. Agesilaus Lacedaemonius cum a ceteris scriptoribus tum eximie a Xenophonte Socratico conlaudatus est; eo enim usus est familiarissime.

2 Hic primum de regno cum Leotychide, fratris filio, habuit contentionem. Mos erat[1] enim a maioribus Lacedaemoniis traditus, ut duos haberent semper reges, nomine magis quam imperio, ex duabus familiis Procli et Eurysthenis, qui principes 3 ex progenie Herculis Spartae reges fuerunt. Horum ex altera in alterius familiae locum regem[2] fieri non licebat; ita suum utraque retinebat ordinem. Primum ratio habebatur, qui maximus natu esset ex liberis eius qui regnans decessisset; sin is virile secus non reliquisset, tum deligebatur qui proximus esset pro- 4 pinquitate. Mortuus erat Agis rex, frater Agesilai; filium reliquerat Leotychidem. Quem ille natum non agnorat, eundem moriens suum esse dixerat. Is de honore regni cum Agesilao, patruo suo, con- 5 tendit neque id quod petivit consecutus est; nam Lysandro suffragante, homine, ut ostendimus supra, factioso et iis temporibus potente, Agesilaus antelatus est.

2. Hic simul atque imperii potitus est, persuasit Lacedaemoniis ut exercitus emitterent[3] in Asiam bellumque regi facerent, docens satius esse in Asia quam in Europa dimicari. Namque fama exierat Artaxerxen comparare classes pedestresque exerci- 2 tus, quos in Graeciam mitteret. Data potestate tanta

---

[1] erat, *Fleck.*; est, *MSS.*   [2] regem, *added by Fleck.*
[3] exercitum et se mitterent, *Guill.*

---

[1] Artaxerxes Mnemon is meant.

XVII. AGESILAUS

1. Agesilaus the Lacedaemonian was praised, not only by all other historians, but in particular by Xenophon, the disciple of Socrates, whose intimate friend he was.

He began by having a dispute about the throne with Leotychides, his brother's son; for it was the custom of the Lacedaemonians, handed down from their forefathers, always to have two kings (whose power, however, was rather nominal than real) from the families of Procles and Eurysthenes, who were descendants of Hercules and the first kings at Sparta. It was not lawful for one of these to be made king from one family in place of the other; so each family kept its order of succession. Consideration was first given to the eldest of the children of the one who had died upon the throne; but if he had left no male offspring, then his nearest relative was chosen. Now King Agis, the brother of Agesilaus, had died, leaving a son Leoty- 399 B.C. chides; he had not acknowledged the boy at his birth, but on his death-bed he declared that he was his son. He it was that disputed the title of king with his uncle Agesilaus, but he was unsuccessful; for thanks to the support of Lysander, a man, as we have already shown, who at that time was ambitious and powerful, Agesilaus was preferred.

2. As soon as Agesilaus was in possession of the throne, he persuaded the Lacedaemonians to send out armies to Asia and make war upon the king, 396 B.C. pointing out that it would be better to fight in Asia than in Europe; for the rumour had gone forth that Artaxerxes [1] was equipping a fleet and land forces to send to Greece. As soon as permission was given

193

celeritate usus est, ut prius in Asiam cum copiis per-
venerit quam regii satrapae eum scirent profectum.
Quo factum est ut omnes imparatos imprudentesque
3 offenderet. Id ut cognovit Tissaphernes, qui summum imperium tum inter praefectos habebat regios,
indutias a Lacone petivit, simulans se dare operam
ut Lacedaemoniis cum rege conveniret, re autem
vera ad copias comparandas, easque impetravit
4 trimenstres. Iuravit autem uterque se sine dolo
indutias conservaturum.

In qua pactione summa fide mansit Agesilaus;
contra ea Tissaphernes nihil aliud quam bellum
5 comparavit. Id etsi sentiebat Laco, tamen iusiurandum servabat multumque in eo se consequi dicebat,
quod Tissaphernes periurio suo et homines suis
rebus abalienaret et deos sibi iratos redderet, se
autem, conservata religione, confirmare exercitum,
cum animadverteret deum numen facere secum
hominesque sibi conciliari amiciores, quod iis
studere consuessent quos conservare fidem viderent.

3. Postquam indutiarum praeteriit dies, barbarus
non dubitans, quod ipsius erant plurima domicilia in
Caria et ea regio iis temporibus ,multo putabatur
locupletissima, eo potissimum hostes impetum
2 facturos, omnes suas copias eo contraxerat. At
Agesilaus in Phrygiam se convertit eamque prius
depopulatus est quam Tissaphernes usquam se
moveret. Magna praeda militibus locupletatis,

---

[1] The statement is true of Lydia rather than of Caria.

him, Agesilaus acted with such rapidity that he arrived in Asia with his forces before the king's satraps knew that he was on his way. The result was that he surprised them all and caught them all unprepared. As soon as his arrival became known to Tissaphernes, who then held the chief authority among the king's governors, he asked the Laconian for a truce, under pretext of trying to reconcile the Lacedaemonians and the king, but actually for the purpose of mustering his forces; and he obtained a truce of three months. The two parties took oath that they would loyally observe the armistice.

That promise Agesilaus kept with the utmost scrupulousness; Tissaphernes, on the contrary, devoted all his time to preparing for war. Although the Laconian knew this, he nevertheless kept his oath and said that in so doing he gained a great advantage, since Tissaphernes by his perjury not only turned men against him but also incurred the wrath of the gods; while he, on the contrary, by keeping his pledge, inspired confidence in his army, because they saw that they had the favour of the gods, while men were more sympathetic towards them, since they commonly side with those whom they see keeping their faith.

3. As soon as the period of the truce came to an end, since the barbarian had many palaces in Caria and that region in those times was regarded as by far the richest part of the kingdom,[1] he felt sure that it was against this that the enemy would be most likely to direct their attack. Accordingly he massed all his troops there. But Agesilaus turned towards Phrygia and laid that country waste before Tissaphernes could make any move. The great booty enriched his

Ephesum hiematum exercitum reduxit atque ibi officinis armorum institutis, magna industria bellum apparavit. Et quo studiosius armarentur insigniusque ornarentur, praemia proposuit quibus donarentur

3 quorum egregia in ea re fuisset industria. Fecit idem in exercitationum generibus, ut, qui ceteris praestitissent, eos magnis adficeret muneribus. His igitur rebus effecit ut et ornatissimum et exercitatissimum haberet exercitum.

4 Huic cum tempus esset visum copias extrahere ex hibernaculis, vidit, si quo esset iter facturus palam pronuntiasset, hostis non credituros aliasque regiones praesidiis occupaturos neque dubitaturos aliud eum [1]

5 facturum ac pronuntiasset. Itaque cum ille Sardis iturum se dixisset, Tissaphernes eandem Cariam defendendam putavit. In quo cum eum opinio fefellisset victumque se vidisset consilio, sero suis praesidio profectus est; nam cum illo venisset, iam Agesilaus, multis locis expugnatis, magna erat

6 praeda potitus. Laco autem cum videret hostis equitatu superare, numquam in campo sui fecit potestatem et iis locis manum conseruit quibus plus pedestres copiae valerent. Pepulit ergo, quotienscumque congressus est, multo maiores adversariorum copias et sic in Asia versatus est, ut omnium opinione victor duceretur.

4. Hic cum iam animo meditaretur proficisci in

---

[1] eum, *P u*; esse, *the other MSS.*

soldiers, and Agesilaus led his army back to Ephesus for the winter; there he established manufactories of arms and prepared for war with great energy. And in order that the arms might be made with greater care and adorned more artistically, he offered rewards to those who showed the greatest energy in their manufacture. He followed the same plan with regard to various forms of exercise, giving handsome prizes to those who excelled their fellows; and in that way he succeeded in having an army both finely equipped and excellently trained.

When it appeared to him to be time to lead his troops from their winter quarters, he saw that if he openly announced in advance where he was going to march, the enemy would not believe him and would post their garrisons in other regions, feeling sure that he would do something different from what he had said. And in fact, when he announced that he would march upon Sardis, Tissaphernes, as before, thought that it was Caria that he ought to defend. And when he was mistaken in that, and saw that he had been outwitted, he was too late in going to the defence of his countrymen; for when he arrived at the spot, Agesilaus had already stormed many places and got possession of a great amount of booty. Moreover, since the Laconian perceived that the enemy were superior in cavalry, he always avoided meeting them on level ground, but joined battle in places where infantry was more effective; and so, whenever he engaged, he routed far superior forces of his opponents, and conducted his campaigns in Asia in such a manner that in the judgment of all men he was regarded as the victor. 395 B.C.

4. Agesilaus was already planning to march against

Persas et ipsum regem adoriri, nuntius ei domo venit
ephororum missu,[1] bellum Athenienses et Boeotos
indixisse Lacedaemoniis : qua re venire ne dubitaret.
2 In hoc non minus eius pietas suspicienda est quam
virtus bellica; qui cum victori praeesset exercitui
maximamque haberet fiduciam regni Persarum
potiundi, tanta modestia dicto audiens fuit iussis
absentium magistratuum, ut si privatus in comitio
esset Spartae. Cuius exemplum utinam imperatores
3 nostri sequi voluissent! Sed illuc redeamus. Agesilaus opulentissimo regno praeposuit bonam existimationem multoque gloriosius duxit si institutis
patriae paruisset, quam si bello superasset Asiam.
4 Hac igitur mente Hellespontum copias traiecit
tantaque usus est celeritate ut, quod iter Xerxes
anno vertente confecerat, hic transierit XXX diebus.
5 Cum iam haud ita longe abesset a Peloponneso,
obsistere ei conati sunt Athenienses et Boeotii
ceterique eorum socii apud Coroneam; quos omnes
gravi proelio vicit.
6 Huius victoriae vel maxima fuit laus, quod, cum
plerique ex fuga se in templum Minervae coniecissent
quaerereturque ab eo quid iis vellet fieri, etsi aliquot
vulnera acceperat eo proelio et iratus videbatur
omnibus qui adversus arma tulerant, tamen antetulit

---

[1] missu, *A Dan. (written above)* and u in margin; iussus, *A*
(*written above*) *and the other MSS.*

---

[1] See ix. 2. 4.
[2] As Roman writers frequently do, Nepos uses the Roman
term *comitium* for the corresponding place in Sparta, either
the Ephoreium, the place of meeting of the ephors, or perhaps
the agora.

the Persians and attack the king himself, when a message from home arrived, sent by the ephors, that the Athenians and Boeotians had declared war upon the Lacedaemonians;[1] that he must therefore return at once. At this juncture his patriotism is no less to be admired than his valour in war; for although he was at the head of a victorious army and had the fullest confidence in his ability to conquer the kingdom of Persia, he showed as much deference in obeying the orders of the magistrates, far away as they were, as if he had been a private citizen in the Ephoreium[2] at Sparta. An example that I only wish our generals had been willing to follow![3] But let us return to our subject. Agesilaus preferred good repute to the richest of kingdoms, and thought it far more glorious to conform to the customs of his native land than to vanquish Asia by his arms. Because of that feeling, then, he led his forces across the Hellespont, and showed such speed that in thirty days he completed the march which had occupied Xerxes for an entire year.[4] He was already nearing the Peloponnesus, when the Athenians, the Boeotians 394 B.C. and their allies attempted to stop him at Coronea; but he defeated them all in a sanguinary battle.

Of that victory the most glorious feature was this: many of the fugitives had rushed into the temple of Minerva,[5] and when Agesilaus was asked what he wished to be done with them, although he had received several wounds in the battle and was obviously incensed with all those who had borne arms against Sparta, yet he subordinated his anger to

[3] Referring to Julius Caesar, Antony and Octavian, all of whom had refused to obey the senate.
[4] See note on ii. 5. 2.   [5] See n. 3, p. 54).

7 irae religionem et eos vetuit violari. Neque vero
hoc solum in Graecia fecit, ut templa deorum sancta
haberet, sed etiam apud barbaros summa religione
8 omnia simulacra arasque conservavit. Itaque praedi-
cabat mirari se non sacrilegorum numero haberi
qui supplicibus eorum[1] nocuissent, aut non graviori-
bus poenis adfici qui religionem minuerent, quam
qui fana spoliarent.

5. Post hoc proelium conlatum omne bellum est circa
Corinthum ideoque Corinthium[2] est appellatum.
2 Hic cum una pugna decem milia hostium Agesilao
duce cecidissent eoque facto opes adversariorum
debilitatae viderentur, tantum afuit ab insolentia
gloriae, ut commiseratus sit fortunam Graeciae, quod
tam multi a se victi vitio adversariorum concidissent:
namque illa multitudine, si sana mens esset, Graeciae
3 supplicium Persas dare potuisse. Idem cum adversarios intra moenia compulisset et ut Corinthum
oppugnaret multi hortarentur, negavit id suae
virtuti convenire: se enim eum esse dixit qui ad
officium peccantes redire cogeret, non qui urbes
nobilissimas expugnaret Graeciae. " Nam si," inquit
" eos exstinguere voluerimus qui nobiscum adversus
barbaros steterunt, nosmet ipsi nos expugnaverimus,
illis quiescentibus. Quo facto sine negotio, cum
voluerint, nos oppriment."

6. Interim accidit illa calamitas apud Leuctra[3] Lacedaemoniis. Quo ne proficisceretur, cum a plerisque

---

[1] deorum, *Magius and B as a correction.*
[2] Corinthium, *Ascensius and u*; Corinthum, *MSS.*
[3] Leuctra, *u*; Leuctram, *MSS.* (Leuctrum, *B*).

---

[1] Until 387 B.C.

respect for religion and forbade their being injured. And it was not in Greece alone that he held the temples of the gods sacred, but among the barbarians also he was most scrupulous in sparing all their statues and altars. Indeed, he openly declared that he was surprised that those who had injured their suppliants who had taken refuge in such places were not regarded as guilty of sacrilege, or that those were not more severely punished who made light of sacred obligations than those who robbed temples.

5. After this battle[1] the entire war centred about Corinth and hence was known as the Corinthian war. There in a single battle under the lead of Agesilaus ten thousand of the enemy were slain, and in consequence of that disaster the power of his adversaries seemed to be shattered. Yet he was so far from feeling boastful arrogance, that he lamented the fortune of Greece, because through the fault of his opponents his victory had cost the lives of so many of her citizens : for with that great number, if the Greeks had been sensible, they might have been able to take vengeance on the Persians. Again, when he had driven his foes within the walls and many were urging him to attack Corinth, he said that such an act was unworthy of his valour; for it was his part to recall to their duty those who had gone astray, not to storm the most famous cities of Greece. " For," said he, " if we set about destroying those who have stood side by side with us against the barbarians, we ourselves shall triumph over one another, while they quietly look on. That done, they will crush us without difficulty, whenever they wish."

6. In the meantime that famous disaster at Leuctra 371 B.C. befell the Lacedaemonians. Not wishing to embark

ad exeundum premeretur, ut si de exitu divinaret, exire noluit.[1] Idem, cum Epaminondas Spartam oppugnaret essetque sine muris oppidum, talem se imperatorem praebuit, ut eo tempore omnibus apparuerit, nisi ille fuisset, Spartam futuram non 2 fuisse. In quo quidem discrimine celeritas eius consilii saluti fuit universis. Nam cum quidam adulescentuli, hostium adventu perterriti, ad Thebanos transfugere vellent et locum extra urbem editum cepissent, Agesilaus, qui perniciosissimum fore videret si animadversum esset quemquam ad hostis transfugere conari, cum suis eo venit atque, ut si bono animo fecissent, laudavit consilium eorum, quod eum locum occupassent; se quoque id[2] fieri 3 debere animadvertisse. Sic adulescentis simulata laudatione recuperavit et, adiunctis de suis comitibus, locum tutum reliquit. Namque illi, aucto[3] numero eorum qui expertes erant consilii, commovere se non sunt ausi eoque libentius, quod latere arbitrabantur quae cogitaverant.

7. Sine dubio post Leuctricam pugnam Lacedaemonii se numquam refecerunt neque pristinum imperium recuperarunt, cum interim numquam Agesilaus destitit quibuscumque rebus posset patriam 2 iuvare. Nam cum praecipue Lacedaemonii indigerent pecunia, ille omnibus qui a rege defecerant

---

[1] exire noluit, *MSS.*; valetudinem excusavit, *Halm*; ex. senectutem, *Fleck*; aegrotare se finxit et *before* cum a plerisque, *suggested by Radermacher*; exire noluit idem, cum . . . tamen talem (*adding* recusavit *after* premeretur), *Wagner.*

[2] et se id quoque, *MSS.*; et, *omitted by Andresen*; quoque *put after* id *in ed. Vulpiana.*

[3] aucti, *Bosius.*

on that campaign, although he was urged by many
to go, as if he divined the outcome he refused to do
so.[1] Again, when Epaminondas was attacking
Sparta and the city was without walls, he showed
himself so able a commander, that it was evident to
all that if it had not been for him Sparta would at
that time have ceased to exist.[2] In fact, in that
critical situation it was his quickness of wit that saved
all the citizens. For some young men, panic-stricken
by the arrival of the enemy, wished to desert to
the Thebans and had taken possession of an elevated
place outside the city; then Agesilaus, realizing that
the knowledge that anyone was trying to go over to
the enemy would be most dangerous, joined them with
his troops and commended their good judgment in
occupying such a position, pretending to believe that
they had done so with good intent, and saying that he
too had seen the advisability of such a step. Thus
by his pretended praise he won back the young men,
and by joining with them some of his own companions he left the position safe. For they, when
the number of those who were not implicated in the
plot was increased, did not dare to make any move,
and remained quiet the more willingly because they
thought that their real designs were not known.

7. It is beyond question that after the battle of
Leuctra the Lacedaemonians never recovered their
strength or regained their former hegemony, although
in the meantime Agesilaus never ceased to aid his
country in whatever way he could. For example,
when the Lacedaemonians were above all in need of
funds, he went to the help of all those who had

---

[1] The sentence is an awkward one; see the crit. note.
[2] See note 3, p. 129.

praesidio fuit; a quibus magna donatus pecunia
3 patriam sublevavit. Atque in hoc illud imprimis
fuit admirabile, cum maxima munera ei ab regibus
ac dynastis civitatibusque conferrentur, quod nihil
umquam domum suam contulit, nihil de victu,
4 nihil de vestitu Laconum mutavit. Domo eadem
fuit contentus qua Eurysthenes, progenitor maiorum
suorum, fuerat usus; quam qui intrarat nullum
signum libidinis, nullum luxuriae videre poterat,
contra ea plurima patientiae atque abstinentiae.
Sic enim erat instructa, ut in nulla re differret a [1]
cuiusvis inopis atque privati.

8. Atque hic tantus vir ut naturam fautricem ha-
buerat in tribuendis animi virtutibus, sic maleficam
nactus est in corpore fingendo; nam et statura
fuit humili et corpore exiguo et claudus altero pede.
Quae res etiam nonnullam adferebat deformitatem,
atque ignoti, faciem eius cum intuerentur, contemne-
bant; qui autem virtutes noverant non poterant
2 admirari satis. Quod ei usu venit, cum annorum
LXXX subsidio Tacho in Aegyptum iisset et in acta
cum suis accubuisset sine ullo tecto stratumque
haberet tale, ut terra tecta esset stramentis neque
huc amplius quam pellis esset iniecta, eodemque
comites omnes accubuissent vestitu humili atque
obsoleto, ut eorum ornatus non modo in iis regem
neminem significaret, sed homines non beatissimos
esse suspicionem praeberet.
3 Huius de adventu fama cum ad regios esset perlata,
celeriter munera eo cuiusque generis sunt adlata.

---

[1] a, *added by Cobet.*

---

[1] Cf. xii. 2. 3.
[2] Agesilaus was of the line of Procles, not Eurysthenes.

revolted against the great king, and when they gave him large sums of money he devoted it to the service of his country. And a trait of his that was especially worthy of admiration was this: although lavish gifts were bestowed upon him by kings, princes and nations, he never took anything home with him,[1] and made no change in the manner of life and dress usual with the Laconians. He was content with the same house that had been used by Eurysthenes, the first of his line[2]; on entering it, no sign of licence, no sign of luxury was visible, but on the contrary many indications of austerity and frugality; in fact, in its equipment the house did not differ from that of any private citizen of humble means.

8. But although Nature had favoured this great man in bestowing qualities of mind, in fashioning his body he found her unkindly; for he was short of stature, of slender frame, and lame in one foot. These defects made him somewhat ill-favoured, and strangers, who judged him from his appearance, were apt to look upon him with contempt; but those who knew his good qualities could not sufficiently admire him. That was his experience when, at the age of eighty, he had gone to the help of Tachos in Egypt. 361 B.C. He had taken his place at meat with his men on the shore, without any shelter and having for a couch straw spread on the ground and covered with nothing but a skin; and there too all his companions reclined beside him in plain and well-worn clothing. Their appearance, far from suggesting that there was a king among them, would indicate that they were men of no great wealth.

When the report of the Spartan's arrival had reached the king's officers, they hastened to bring to his camp

His quaerentibus Agesilaum vix fides facta est,
4 unum esse ex iis qui tum accubabant. Qui cum
regis verbis quae attulerant dedissent, ille praeter
vitulinam et eius modi genera obsonii quae praesens
tempus desiderabat, nihil accepit; unguenta, coronas
secundamque mensam servis dispertiit, cetera referri
5 iussit. Quo facto, eum barbari magis etiam con-
tempserunt,´ quod eum ignorantia bonarum rerum
vilia potissimum sumpsisse arbitrabantur.
6 Hic cum ex Aegypto reverteretur, donatus ab
rege Nectanabide ducentis viginti talentis, quae ille
muneri populo suo daret, venissetque in portum qui
Menelai vocatur, iacens inter Cyrenas et Aegyptum,
7 in morbum implicitus decessit. Ibi eum amici, quo
Spartam facilius perferre possent, quod mel non
habebant, cera circumfuderunt atque ita domum
rettulerunt.

XVIII. EUMENES

1. Eumenes Cardianus. Huius si virtuti par data
esset fortuna, non ille quidem maior exstitisset[1]—
quod magnos homines virtute metimur, non fortuna[2]
2 —sed multo illustrior atque etiam honoratior. Nam
cum aetas eius incidisset in ea tempora quibus
Macedones florerent, multum ei detraxit inter eos

[1] exstitisset, *added by Halm*; fuisset, *Lambin.*
[2] quod . . . fortuna *after* honoratior, *MSS.*; *transposed by Pluygers.*

---

[1] The bodies of Spartan kings who died abroad were usually embalmed in honey. The friends of Agesilaus substituted melted wax.

gifts of every kind. When they inquired for Agesilaus, they could hardly believe that he was one of those who were then at meat. When they offered him in the name of the king what they had brought, he refused everything except some veal and similar kinds of food which his circumstances made necessary; perfumes, garlands and desserts he distributed among his servants, the rest he ordered to be taken back. Such conduct led the barbarians to hold him in still greater contempt, since they supposed that he had made his choice through lack of acquaintance with fine things.

When Agesilaus was on his way back from Egypt after having received from King Nectenebis two hundred and twenty talents to give as a gift to his country, on arriving at the place called the Port of Menelaus, situated between Cyrene and Egypt, he fell ill and died. Thereupon his friends, in order that his body might the more readily be taken to Sparta, having no honey,[1] covered it with wax and thus bore it to his native land.

XVIII. EUMENES

1. Eumenes of Cardia.[2] If this man's merit had been attended by equal good fortune, he would not, it is true, have turned out greater (for we measure a man's greatness by his merit and not by his fortune), but he would have been much more famous and even more honoured. For his lifetime fell in the period when the Macedonians were at the height of their power, and living as he did in their country, it was

[2] A different person, of course, from Eumenes of Pergamum, mentioned in xxiii. 11.

viventi, quod alienae erat civitatis, neque aliud huic
3 defuit quam generosa stirps. Etsi ille domestico
summo genere erat, tamen Macedones eum sibi
aliquando anteponi indigne ferebant, neque tamen
non patiebantur; vincebat enim omnes cura, vigi-
lantia, patientia, calliditate et celeritate ingenii.
4 Hic peradulescentulus ad amicitiam accessit
Philippi, Amyntae filii, brevique tempore in intimam
pervenit familiaritatem; fulgebat enim iam in
5 adulescentulo indoles virtutis. Itaque eum habuit
ad manum scribae loco, quod multo apud Graios
honorificentius est quam apud Romanos. Namque
apud nos, re vera sicut sunt, mercennarii scribae
existimantur; at apud illos e contrario [1] nemo ad id
officium admittitur nisi honesto loco, et fide et
industria cognita, quod necesse est omnium consilio-
6 rum eum esse participem. Hunc locum tenuit
amicitiae apud Philippum annos septem. Illo
interfecto, eodem gradu fuit apud Alexandrum
annos tredecim. Novissimo tempore praefuit etiam
alterae equitum alae, quae Hetaerice appellabatur.
Utrique autem in consilio semper adfuit et omnium
rerum habitus est particeps.

2. Alexandro Babylone mortuo, cum regna singulis
familiaribus dispertirentur et summa tradita esset
tuenda eidem cui Alexander moriens anulum suum
2 dederat, Perdiccae—ex quo omnes coniecerant eum

---

[1] e contrario, *R, Lambin*; contrario, *the other MSS.*

---

[1] That is, from a noble Macedonian family.
[2] This applies only to such exceptional positions as that of
Eumenes. There were similar positions in Rome; thus
Horace was offered the post of secretary to the Emperor
Augustus (Suet. *Vit. Hor.*).

greatly to his disadvantage that he was a native of a
foreign state; for he lacked nothing except noble
descent.[1] Although he was of the highest rank in
his own country, yet the Macedonians were indignant
that he was sometimes preferred to them; but they
were obliged to put up with it, since he excelled them
all in diligence, in watchfulness and in endurance, as
well as in skill and mental alertness.

Eumenes, when very young, became the friend of 342 B.7
Philip, son of Amyntas, and soon grew very intimate
with the king, being conspicuous even in his youth for
his high character. Therefore Philip kept him near
his person, in the capacity of secretary, a position
much more highly honoured among the Greeks than
with the Romans. With us, indeed, scribes are
considered hirelings, as in fact they are; in Greece,
on the contrary, no one is accepted for such a position
unless he is of respectable family and of proven
fidelity and ability, since he is necessarily acquainted
with all his superior's plans.[2] This position of
friendship with Philip Eumenes held for seven years.
When Philip was assassinated, he held the same rank
with Alexander for thirteen years. During the latter 336–323
part of that time [3] he commanded one of the two B.C.
corps of cavalry known as "The Band of Comrades."
Moreover, he was always asked for his advice by
both kings and given a share in all their affairs.

2. When Alexander died at Babylon, his provinces 323 B.C.
were divided among his friends and the supreme
power was committed to the care of Perdiccas, to
whom Alexander on his death-bed had given his ring.
From this act of Alexander's all had inferred that he

---

[3] That is, after 325 B.C.

regnum ei commisisse,[1] quoad liberi eius in suam
tutelam pervenissent; aberat enim Crateros et
Antipater, qui antecedere hunc videbantur; mortuus
erat Hephaestio, quem unum Alexander, quod
facile intellegi posset, plurimi fecerat. Hoc tempore
data est Eumeni Cappadocia, sive potius dicta; nam
3 tum in hostium erat potestate. Hunc sibi Perdiccas
adiunxerat magno studio, quod in homine fidem et
industriam magnam videbat, non dubitans, si eum
pellexisset, magno usui fore sibi in iis rebus quas
apparabat. Cogitabat enim, quod fere omnes in
magnis imperiis concupiscunt, omnium partis corri-
4 pere atque complecti. Neque vero hoc ille solus
fecit, sed ceteri quoque omnes qui Alexandri fuerant
amici. Primus Leonnatus Macedoniam praeoccu-
pare destinavit.[2] Hic multis magnisque pollicita-
tionibus persuadere Eumeni studuit, ut Perdiccam
5 desereret ac secum faceret societatem. Cum per-
ducere eum non posset, interficere conatus est; et
fecisset, nisi ille clam noctu ex praesidiis eius effu-
gisset.

3. Interim conflata sunt illa bella quae ad inter-
necionem post Alexandri mortem gesta sunt, omnesque concurrerunt ad Perdiccam opprimendum.
Quem etsi infirmum videbat, quod unus omnibus
resistere cogebatur, tamen amicum non deseruit
2 neque salutis quam fidei fuit cupidior. Praefecerat
hunc Perdiccas ei parti Asiae quae inter Taurum
montem iacet atque Hellespontum, et illum unum
opposuerat Europaeis adversariis; ipse Aegyptum

---

[1] commisisse, *Benecke;* commisisse vel commendasse,
Leid. A P B R F λ μ; commendasse, π *M u* (*u in margin has*
" *al.* commisisse ").
[2] destinavit, *u;* praedestinavit (—averat, *M*), *MSS.*

had entrusted the rule to Perdiccas until his own
children should come of age; for Craterus and
Antipater were not present, who obviously had
better claims than Perdiccas; Hephaestion was dead,
whom Alexander esteemed most of all, as could
readily be seen. At that time Cappadocia was
given to Eumenes, or rather, promised to him, since
it was then in possession of the enemy. Perdiccas
had made every effort to win his friendship, realizing
the man's great loyalty and ability, and had no doubt
that, if he should gain his regard, Eumenes would be
very useful to him in carrying out his plans; for it was
his design to do what almost all who hold great power
aspire to, namely, seize the shares of all the others
and unite them. But he was not the only one who
had this design, for it was entertained by all the rest
who had been friends of Alexander. First, Leonnatus proposed to usurp Macedonia, and tried by
many lavish promises to induce Eumenes to desert
Perdiccas and form an alliance with him. Failing in
that, Leonnatus tried to kill Eumenes, and would
have succeeded if his intended victim had not eluded
his guards by night and made his escape.

3. Meanwhile those notorious wars of extermina- 321 B.C.
tion broke out which followed the death of Alexander,
and all united in an attack upon Perdiccas, to rid
themselves of him. Although Eumenes saw the
weakness of his friend's position, in being obliged to
resist all the others single-handed, yet he did not
desert him nor desire safety at the expense of
loyalty. Perdiccas had made him governor of the
part of Asia lying between the Taurus mountains
and the Hellespont and had left him to face his
European opponents alone; he himself had gone to

oppugnatum adversus Ptolemaeum erat profectus.
3 Eumenes cum neque magnas copias neque firmas
haberet, quod et inexercitatae et non multo ante
erant contractae, adventare autem dicerentur Helles-
pontumque transisse Antipater et Crateros magno
cum exercitu Macedonum, viri cum claritate tum
usu belli praestantes—Macedones vero milites ea
4 tum erant fama, qua nunc Romani feruntur; etenim
semper habiti sunt fortissimi, qui summi[1] imperii
potirentur—Eumenes intellegebat, si copiae suae
cognossent adversus quos ducerentur, non modo non
ituras, sed simul cum nuntio dilapsuras.
5 Itaque hoc ei visum est[2] prudentissimum, ut deviis
itineribus milites duceret, in quibus vera audire non
possent, et iis persuaderet se contra quosdam bar-
6 baros proficisci. Itaque tenuit hoc propositum et
prius in aciem exercitum eduxit proeliumque commisit, quam milites sui scirent cum quibus arma
conferrent. Effecit etiam illud locorum praeoccu-
patione, ut equitatu potius dimicaret, quo plus
valebat, quam peditatu, quo erat deterior.

4. Quorum acerrimo concursu cum magnam partem
diei esset oppugnatum,[3] cadit Crateros dux et
Neoptolemus, qui secundum locum imperii tenebat.
2 Cum hoc concurrit ipse Eumenes. Qui cum inter
se complexi in terram ex equis decidissent, ut facile
intellegi possent inimica mente contendisse animoque
magis etiam pugnasse quam corpore, non prius

---

[1] summi, *Madvig*; summam. *Dan. A M P R*; summa, *B u.*
[2] ei visum est, *Nipp.*; eius fuit, *MSS.*
[3] pugnatum, *u.*

Egypt, to war against Ptolemy. The troops of
Eumenes were neither numerous nor strong, since
they had been enrolled not long before and lacked
training; moreover, it was said that Antipater and
Craterus, two men eminent both for their renown and
their military experience, had crossed the Hellespont
with a great army of Macedonians. In those days
the Macedonian soldiers had the reputation that the
Romans now enjoy, since those have always been
regarded as of the greatest valour who rule the whole
world, and Eumenes understood that if his troops
knew against whom they were being led, they would
not only refuse to go, but immediately on hearing
the news would melt away.

It therefore seemed wisest to lead the soldiers
over by-ways, where they could not learn the truth,
and make them believe that they were marching
against some barbarian tribe or other. And so well
did Eumenes carry out this plan, that his army was
already drawn up and had begun the battle before
the soldiers knew with whom they were to fight.
He also, by choosing his ground in advance of the
enemy, made the brunt of the battle fall on his
cavalry, in which he was the stronger, rather than
on the infantry, in which he was inferior.

4. They engaged for a greater part of a day in a
fierce struggle, in which Craterus fell, the leader
of the enemy, as well as Neoptolemus, who was
second in command. With the latter Eumenes fought
hand to hand. When the two had grappled and had
fallen from their horses to the ground, it could
easily be seen that they were personal enemies, and
that their contest was one of the spirit even more
than of body; for they could not be separated until

distracti sunt quam alterum anima relinqueret.
Ab hoc aliquot plagis Eumenes vulneratur neque
eo magis ex proelio excessit, sed acrius hostis institit.
3 Hic equitibus profligatis, interfecto duce Cratero,
multis praeterea et maxime nobilibus captis, pedester
exercitus, quod in ea loca erat deductus ut invito
Eumene elabi non posset, pacem ab eo petit.   Quam
cum impetrasset, in fide non mansit et se, simul ac
potuit, ad Antipatrum recepit.
4   Eumenes Craterum ex acie semivivum elatum
recreare studuit; cum id non posset, pro hominis
dignitate proque pristina amicitia—namque illo
usus erat Alexandro vivo familiariter—amplo funere [1]
extulit ossaque in Macedoniam uxori eius ac liberis
remisit.

   5. Haec dum apud Hellespontum geruntur, Perdiccas apud Nilum flumen interficitur ab Seleuco et
Antigene,[2] rerumque summa ad Antipatrum defertur.
Hic qui deseruerant, exercitu suffragium ferente,
capitis absentes damnantur, in iis Eumenes.   Hac
ille perculsus plaga, non succubuit neque eo setius
bellum administravit.   Sed exiles res animi magnitudinem, etsi non frangebant, tamen minuebant.
2 Hunc persequens Antigonus, cum omni genere
copiarum abundaret, saepe in itineribus vexabatur,
neque umquam ad manum accedere licebat nisi iis
3 locis quibus pauci multis possent resistere.   Sed
extremo tempore, cum consilio capi non posset,

[1] funere, *M R A* (*written above*); munere, *the other MSS.*
[2] Antigene, *Van Staveren*; Antigono, *MSS.*

one of the two had been killed. From his opponent Eumenes suffered several wounds, but he did not on that account leave the field, but attacked the enemy with renewed vigour. Then, after the cavalry had been routed, their leader Craterus killed, and many prisoners taken besides, including men of very high rank, the enemy's infantry was decoyed into a position from which it could not escape without the consent of Eumenes, and sued for a truce. Having obtained it, they did not keep faith, but returned as soon as possible to Antipater.

Eumenes tried to cure Craterus, who had been carried off the field still living; when that proved impossible, bearing in mind the high position of the deceased and their former friendship (for the two had been intimate during the lifetime of Alexander) he gave him a funeral with great ceremony and sent his ashes to his wife and children in Macedonia.

5. While these events were taking place at the Hellespont, Perdiccas was slain near the river Nile by Seleucus and Antigenes, and the supreme power passed to Antipater. Then those who had not sided with the new ruler were condemned to death in their absence by vote of his army, including Eumenes. He, although the blow was a heavy one, did not succumb to it, but continued none the less to carry on the war; but his slender resources, although they did not break his high spirit, nevertheless impaired it. Antigonus pursued him, but although he had 320 B.C. an abundance of troops of every kind and often harassed Eumenes on the march, he never succeeded in engaging him in battle except in places where a few could resist great numbers. At last, however, though he could not be taken off his guard by

multitudine circumitus est. Hinc tamen, multis suis
amissis, se expedivit et in castellum Phrygiae, quod
Nora appellatur, confugit.

4 In quo cum circumsederetur et vereretur ne, uno
loco manens, equos militares perderet, quod spatium
non esset agitandi, callidum fuit eius inventum quem
ad modum stans iumentum concalfieri exercerique
posset, quo libentius et cibo uteretur et a corporis
5 motu non removeretur. Substringebat caput loro
altius quam ut prioribus pedibus plene terram posset
attingere, deinde post [1] verberibus cogebat exsultare
et calces remittere; qui motus non minus sudorem
6 excutiebat, quam si in spatio decurreret. Quo
factum est, quod omnibus mirabile est visum, ut
aeque nitida iumenta ex castello educeret, cum
complures menses in obsidione fuisset, ac si in
7 campestribus ea locis habuisset. In hac conclusione,
quotienscumque voluit, apparatum et munitiones
Antigoni alias incendit, alias disiecit. Tenuit autem
se uno loco quam diu hiems fuit, quod castra sub
divo habere non poterat. Ver appropinquabat;
simulata deditione, dum de condicionibus tractat,
praefectis Antigoni imposuit seque ac suos omnis
extraxit incolumis.

6. Ad hunc Olympias, mater quae fuerat Alexandri,
cum litteras et nuntios misisset in Asiam, consultum
utrum regnum [2] repetitum in Macedoniam veniret—
2 nam tum in Epiro habitabat—et eas res occuparet,
huic ille primum suasit ne se moveret et exspectaret
quoad Alexandri filius regnum adipisceretur; sin

---

[1] pastum, *Wagner.*   [2] regnum, *added by Nipp.*

---

[1] That is, the front part of its body.
[2] Namely, Alexander, son of Roxane.

strategy, Eumenes was surrounded by superior numbers. Yet he made his escape with the loss of many of his men, and took refuge in a fortified place in Phrygia, called Nora.

Being besieged there and fearing that by remaining in one place he might ruin the horses of his army, because there was no room for exercising them, Eumenes hit upon a clever device by which an animal standing in one place might be warmed and exercised, so that it would have a better appetite and not lose its bodily activity. He drew up its head[1] with a thong so high that it could not quite touch the ground with its forefeet, and then forced it by blows of a whip to bound and kick out behind, an exercise which produced no less sweat than running on a race-course. The result was that, to the surprise of all, the animals were led out of the fortress after a siege of several months in as good condition as if he had kept them in pasture. During this blockade, as often as he wished, he set fire to some part of the works and fortifications of Antigonus and threw down others. Furthermore, he remained in the same place as long as the winter lasted, because he could not camp in the open. When spring drew near, pretending a surrender, he outwitted Antigonus' officers while the terms were under discussion, and made his escape without the loss of a man.

6. To Eumenes, when he was in Asia, Olympias, 319 b.c. the mother of Alexander, had sent a letter and messengers, to ask his advice as to coming to Macedonia to claim the throne (for she was then living in Epirus) and to make herself ruler there. He advised her above all things to make no move, but to wait until Alexander's son[2] gained the throne; but if she was

aliqua cupiditate raperetur in Macedoniam, oblivisceretur omnium iniuriarum et in neminem acerbiore
3 uteretur imperio. Horum illa nihil fecit nam et in Macedoniam profecta est et ibi crudelissime se gessit. Petit autem ab Eumene absente ne pateretur Philippi domus ac familiae inimicissimos stirpem quoque interimere, ferretque opem liberis Alexandri.
4 Quam veniam si daret, quam primum exercitus pararet quos sibi subsidio adduceret. Id quo facilius faceret, se omnibus praefectis qui in officio manebant misisse litteras, ut ei parerent eiusque consiliis
5 uterentur. His rebus Eumenes permotus, satius duxit, si ita tulisset fortuna, perire bene meritis referentem gratiam quam ingratum vivere.

7. Itaque copias contraxit, bellum adversus Antigonum comparavit. Quod una erant Macedones complures nobiles, in iis Peucestes, qui corporis custos fuerat Alexandri, tum autem obtinebat Persidem, et Antigenes, cuius sub imperio phalanx erat Macedonum, invidiam verens—quam tamen effugere non potuit—si potius ipse alienigena summi
2 imperii potiretur quam alii Macedonum, quorum ibi erat multitudo, in principiis Alexandri nomine tabernaculum statuit in eoque sellam auream cum sceptro ac diademate iussit poni eoque omnes cottidie convenire, ut ibi de summis rebus consilia caperentur; credens minore se invidia fore, si

---

1 The body-guard of Alexander was an official of high rank.
1 "The others, of the (that is, 'who were,') Macedonians"; Eumenes was not a Macedonian.

strongly drawn towards Macedonia, to forget all her
wrongs and not exercise her power with too great
severity against anyone. She adopted neither of
these recommendations; for she proceeded to
Macedonia and conducted herself there most cruelly.
Then she besought Eumenes, who was far away, not
to allow the bitter enemies of Philip's house and
family to destroy his stock as well, but to bear aid to
the children of Alexander. If he would grant her
prayer, she said, he must equip armies and lead them
to her assistance as soon as possible. In order to
make that easier, she had sent letters to all the
governors who had remained loyal, instructing them
to obey him and follow his directions. Deeply
moved by these communications, Eumenes thought
it better, if such were Fortune's will, to lose his
life in requiting kindnesses than save it by ingratitude.

7. Accordingly, he mustered his forces and prepared to make war upon Antigonus. Since he had
with him a number of Macedonian nobles, including
Peucestes, formerly Alexander's body-guard[1] and
then governor of Persia, and Antigenes, commander
of the Macedonian phalanx, he feared ill-feeling
(which after all he could not escape) if he, a foreigner,
should hold the chief command rather than one of the
Macedonians,[2] of whom there were very many
there. He therefore set up a tent at the army
headquarters in the name of Alexander, and gave
orders that there should be placed in it the
golden throne with the sceptre and diadem, and
that all should meet there daily, in order to
make it the place where matters of highest moment
were discussed. For he believed that he would

specie imperii nominisque simulatione Alexandri
3 bellum videretur administrare. Quod effecit; [1] nam
cum non ad Eumenis principia, sed ad regia conveniretur atque ibi de rebus deliberaretur, quodam
modo latebat, cum tamen per eum unum gererentur
omnia.

8. Hic in Paraetacis cum Antigono conflixit, non
acie instructa, sed in itinere, eumque male acceptum
in Mediam hiematum coegit redire. Ipse in finitima
regione Persidis hiematum copias divisit, non ut
2 voluit, sed ut militum cogebat voluntas. Namque
illa phalanx Alexandri Magni, quae Asiam pera-
grarat deviceratque Persas, inveterata cum gloria
tum etiam licentia, non parere se ducibus, sed
imperare postulabat, ut nunc veterani faciunt nostri.
Itaque periculum est ne faciant quod illi fecerunt,
sua intemperantia nimiaque licentia ut omnia
perdant neque minus eos cum quibus fecerint, quam
3 adversus quos steterint. Quod si quis illorum veteranorum legat facta, paria horum cognoscat neque
rem ullam nisi tempus interesse iudicet. Sed ad
illos revertar. Hiberna sumpserant non ad usum
belli, sed ad ipsorum luxuriam, longeque inter se
4 discesserant. Hoc Antigonus cum comperisset intel-
legeretque se parem non esse paratis adversariis,
statuit aliquid sibi consilii novi esse capiendum.

Duae erant viae qua ex Medis, ubi ille hiemabat,
ad adversariorum hibernacula posset perveniri.

---

[1] effecit, *Heusinger*; et fecit, *MSS.*

arouse less jealousy if he seemed to carry on the war with the mere appearance of leadership, and pretended to act in the name of Alexander. And so it turned out; for since they met and held council, not at the headquarters of Eumenes, but at those of Alexander, Eumenes remained to a certain extent in the background, while in fact everything was done by his direction alone.

8. He fought with Antigonus at Paraetacae, not 317 B.C. in order of battle, but while on the march, and having worsted him, compelled him to return to Media to pass the winter. He for his part in the neighbouring region of Persia distributed the winter quarters of his soldiers, not according to his own wishes, but as their desires dictated. For that famous phalanx of Alexander the Great, which had overrun Asia and conquered the Persians, after a long career of glory as well as of licence claimed the right to command its leaders instead of obeying them, even as our veterans do to-day. And so there is danger that our soldiers may do what the Macedonians did, and ruin everything by their licence and lawlessness, their friends as well as their enemies. For if anyone should read the history of those veterans of old, he would recognize a parallel in our own, and decide that the only difference is one of time. But let me return to those of former days. They had chosen their winter quarters with an eye rather to their own pleasure than to the requirements of war, and were widely separated. When Antiochus learned of this, knowing that he was no match for his opponents when they were on their guard, he decided to resort to some new plan.

There were two roads leading from Media, where he was wintering, to the winter quarters of the

5 Quarum brevior per loca deserta, quae nemo incolebat
propter aquae inopiam, ceterum dierum erat fere
decem; illa autem qua omnes commeabant altero
tanto longiorem habebat anfractum, sed erat copiosa
6 omniumque rerum abundans. Hac si proficisceretur,
intellegebat prius adversarios rescituros de suo
adventu quam ipse tertiam partem confecisset
itineris; sin per loca sola contenderet, sperabat se
7 imprudentem hostem oppressurum. Ad hanc rem
conficiendam imperavit quam plurimos utris atque
etiam culleos comparari; post haec pabulum;
praeterea cibaria cocta dierum decem, ut quam
minime fieret ignis in castris. Iter quo habeat[1] omnis
celat. Sic paratus, qua constituerat proficiscitur.

9. Dimidium fere spatium confecerat, cum ex fumo
castrorum eius suspicio adlata est ad Eumenem
hostem appropinquare. Conveniunt duces; quaeri-
tur quid opus sit facto. Intellegebant omnes tam
celeriter copias ipsorum contrahi non posse, quam
2 Antigonus adfuturus videbatur. Hic, omnibus titu-
bantibus et de rebus summis desperantibus, Eumenes ait, si celeritatem velint adhibere et imperata
facere, quod ante non fecerint, se rem expediturum.
Nam quod diebus quinque hostis transisse posset, se
effecturum ut non minus totidem dierum spatio
retardaretur; qua re circumirent, suas quisque
contraheret copias.
3 Ad Antigoni autem refrenandum impetum tale
capit consilium. Certos mittit homines ad infimos

---

[1] quo habeat, *Nipp.*; quod (quot, *B¹ R*) habebat, *MSS.*

---

[1] The soldiers, because of the cold, disobeyed Antiochus
and built fires at night; it was the light from these, rather
than the smoke, that betrayed him.

enemy. The shorter of these was through desert
regions, which because of lack of water were unin-
habited, but it was a journey of only about ten days;
the other, however, which everyone used, was a
circuitous route of twice that length, but rich in
supplies and abounding in all kinds of commodities.
If he marched by the latter road, he knew that his
opponents would be informed of his coming before
he had gone a third part of the way; but if he made a
quick march through the desert, he hoped to surprise the enemy and rout him. With that end in
view, he ordered the greatest possible number of
bladders as well as leathern bags to be procured, then
forage, and finally cooked food for ten days, wishing
to make the fewest possible camp-fires. He concealed
his proposed route from everyone. Thus prepared,
he set out by the road which he had selected.

9. He had covered nearly half the distance, when
the smoke from his camp [1] led Eumenes to suspect
that the enemy were approaching. He held a
meeting with his generals; they deliberated as to
what should be done. It was evident to all that
their own troops could not be assembled quickly
enough to meet the arrival of Antigonus. At this
juncture, when all were in a panic and believed that
they were lost, Eumenes said that if they would act
quickly and obey his orders, which they had not
done before, he would save the day. For whereas
the enemy had but five days' journey left, he would
contrive to delay them at least as many days longer;
therefore his officers must go about and each collect
his own troops.

Now, to check the speed of Antiochus he devised
the following plan. He sent trustworthy men to the

montes, qui obvii erant itineri adversariorum, iisque
praecipit [1] ut prima nocte quam latissime possint
ignes faciant quam maximos atque hos secunda
4 vigilia minuant, tertia perexiguos reddant et, assimu-
lata castrorum consuetudine, suspicionem iniciant
hostibus iis locis esse castra ac de eorum adventu
esse praenuntiatum; idemque postera nocte faciant.
5 Quibus imperatum erat diligenter praeceptum
curant. Antigonus tenebris obortis ignes conspica-
tur; credit de suo adventu esse auditum et adver-
6 sarios illuc suas contraxisse copias. Mutat consilium et, quoniam imprudentes [2] adoriri non posset,
flectit iter suum et illum anfractum longiorem
copiosae viae capit ibique diem unum opperitur ad
lassitudinem sedandam militum ac reficienda iumenta,
quo integriore exercitu decerneret.

10. Sic [3] Eumenes callidum imperatorem vicit
consilio celeritatemque impedivit eius, neque tamen
2 multum profecit; nam invidia ducum, cum quibus
erat, perfidiaque Macedonum veteranorum, cum
superior proelio discessisset, Antigono est deditus,
cum exercitus ei ter ante separatis temporibus iuras-
set se eum defensurum neque umquam deserturum.
Sed tanta fuit nonnullorum virtutis obtrectatio, ut
fidem amittere mallent quam eum non perdere.
3 Atque hunc Antigonus, cum ei fuisset infestissi-
mus, conservasset, si per suos esset licitum, quod
ab nullo se plus adiuvari posse intellegebat in iis

---

[1] praecipit, *Lambin*; praecepit, *MSS.*
[2] imprudentes, *Lambin*; imprudentem, *MSS.*
[3] sic, *Heusinger*; hic, *MSS.*

---

[1] For *iumenta* in this sense cf. 5. 4.

foot of the mountains which crossed the enemy's line of march, with orders to light great fires in the early part of the night over the widest possible space and let them die down in the second watch. In the third watch they must let them nearly go out, and thus, by imitating what was usual in a camp, lead the enemy to suspect that Eumenes was encamped there, and that their coming had been reported; and they must do the same on the following night. Those to whom these orders had been given executed them to the letter. Antigonus saw the fires at nightfall; he believed that his coming was known and that his foes had massed their forces there to meet him. He altered his plan, and since he thought that he could not attack them unawares, he changed his course and chose the longer detour where supplies were plentiful, halting where he was for one day to rest his men and refresh his horses,[1] in order to fight with his army in better condition.

10. Thus it was that Eumenes outwitted a crafty general and checked his rapid advance, but it did not profit him greatly; for through the jealousy of his fellow-generals and the treachery of the Macedonian veterans, although he was victorious in the battle, he was betrayed into the hands of Antigonus. 316 B.C. And yet the army had on three separate occasions before that sworn to defend him and never desert him. But some of them were so ill-disposed towards true worth, that they preferred to break their oath rather than not to ruin him.

Yet after all, Antigonus would have saved him, although Eumenes had been his bitter enemy, if his associates would have consented, knowing as he did that no one could render him greater assistance in

rebus quas impendere iam apparebat omnibus.
Imminebant enim Seleucus, Lysimachus, Ptolemaeus,
opibus iam valentes, cum quibus ei de summis rebus
4 erat dimicandum. Sed non passi sunt ii qui circa
erant, quod videbant Eumene recepto omnes prae
illo parvi futuros. Ipse autem Antigonus adeo erat
incensus, ut nisi magna spe maximarum rerum leniri
non posset.

11. Itaque cum eum in custodiam dedisset et praefectus custodum quaesisset, quem ad modum servari
vellet, " Ut acerrimum," inquit, " leonem aut fero-
cissimum elephantum"; nondum enim statuerat,
2 conservaret eum necne. Veniebat autem ad Eumenem utrumque genus hominum, et qui propter odium
fructum oculis ex eius casu capere vellent, et qui
propter veterem amicitiam colloqui consolarique
cuperent, multi etiam, qui eius formam cognoscere
studebant, qualis esset quem tam diu tamque valde
timuissent, cuius in pernicie positam spem habuissent
victoriae.

3 At Eumenes, cum diutius in vinclis esset, ait Onomarcho, penes quem summa imperii erat custodiae,
se mirari qua re iam tertium diem sic teneretur;
non enim hoc convenire Antigoni prudentiae, ut
sic deuteretur victo[1]: quin aut interfici aut missum
4 fieri iuberet. Hic cum ferocius Onomarcho loqui
videretur, " Quid? Tu," inquit, " animo si isto
eras, cur non in proelio cecidisti potius quam in

---

[1] uteretur devicto, *Nipp.*

the crisis that all now perceived to be imminent. For Antigonus was menaced by Seleucus, Lysimachus and Ptolemy, men already possessed of formidable power, with whom he must fight for the supremacy. But his associates would not consent, because they saw that if he should be reconciled with Eumenes, they would all be of small account in comparison with that great man. And besides, Antigonus himself was so incensed that he could not be appeased except by great hope of the greatest advantages.

11. Therefore, when he had put Eumenes in prison, and the commander of the guards had asked how he wished him to be guarded, Antigonus replied: "Like the fiercest of lions or the most savage of elephants." For he had not yet made up his mind whether to spare his life or not. Now, Eumenes was visited by two classes of men, those who because of hatred wished to feast their eyes on his misfortune, and those who because of long-standing friendship desired to talk with him and console him; there were also many who were eager to see how he looked, what manner of man it was that they had feared so long and so mightily, that on his downfall had depended their hope of victory.

But Eumenes, after having been in prison for some time, said to Onomarchus, who held the chief command of the guards, that he was surprised that he had been thus confined for three full days; that it was not in accordance with Antiochus' usual wisdom thus to mistreat a defeated enemy; why did he not bid him be executed or set free? Since it seemed to Onomachus that this remark was over-arrogant, he retorted: "Well, if that was your feeling, why did you not die in battle rather than

5 potestatem inimici venires?" Huic Eumenes:
"Utinam quidem istud evenisset! Sed eo non
accidit, quod numquam cum fortiore sum congressus;
non enim cum quoquam arma contuli, quin is mihi
succubuerit." Neque id erat falsum; non enim virtute
hostium, sed amicorum perfidia decidit[1] . . .[2] nam et
dignitate fuit honesta et viribus ad laborem ferendum
firmis neque tam magno corpore quam figura venusta.

12. De hoc Antigonus cum solus constituere non
auderet, ad consilium rettulit. Hic cum omnes primo
perturbati admirarentur non iam de eo sumptum
esse supplicium, a quo tot annos adeo essent male
habiti, ut saepe ad desperationem forent adducti,
2 quique maximos duces interfecisset, denique in quo
uno tantum esset, ut, quoad ille viveret, ipsi securi
esse non possent, interfecto nihil habituri negotii
essent; postremo, si illi redderet salutem, quaerebant
quibus amicis esset usurus: sese enim cum Eumene
3 apud eum non futuros. Hic cognita consīlii voluntate
tamen usque ad septimum diem deliberandi sibi
spatium reliquit. Tum autem, cum iam vereretur
ne qua seditio exercitus oriretur, vetuit quemquam
ad eum admitti et cottidianum victum removeri
iussit; nam negabat se ei vim adlaturum qui ali-
4 quando fuisset amicus. Hic tamen non amplius
quam triduum fame fatigatus, cum castra moverentur,
insciente Antigono iugulatus est a custodibus.

---

[1] non enim . . . decidit *after* falsum, *Fleck.*; non enim . . .
decidi *after* succubuerit, *MSS.*
[2] *A lacuna after* falsum *was inferred by Buchner*; *Heusinger
and Bremi deleted* nam . . . venusta; *Vonck put* et viribus
. . . firmis *after* nam.

---

fall into the hands of your enemy?" To which Eumenes answered: "Would that what you say had happened; but the reason that it did not is because I have never encountered a foeman stronger than myself; for I have never joined battle with anyone that he did not yield to me." And that was true, since it was not the enemy's valour, but a friend's treachery, that undid him [1] . . . for he had an imposing appearance, powers of endurance that enabled him to bear hardship, and a graceful figure rather than great size of body.

12. Since Antigonus did not dare to decide the fate of his enemy on his own responsibility, he referred the matter to a council. In that assembly all were at first disturbed, wondering at the delay in executing a man from whom they had suffered so much during so many years, that they had often been reduced to despair, and who had slain their greatest generals; in short, the only man who, so long as he lived, could threaten their peace of mind, and whose death would relieve them from all trouble. Finally, they asked, if Antigonus spared him, on what friends could he rely? For, they said, they would not remain in his service in company with Eumenes. Antigonus, after learning the decision of the council, nevertheless allowed himself a period of six days for reflection. But then, beginning to fear the outbreak of a revolt in the army, he forbade anyone to have access to the prisoner, and gave orders that he should be deprived of his daily food; for he declared that he would not do violence to a man who had once been his friend. However, Eumenes had not suffered hunger for more than two days when, as they were moving camp, he was strangled by his guards without the knowledge of Antigonus.

13. Sic Eumenes annorum V et XL, cum ab anno
vicesimo, uti supra ostendimus, septem annos
Philippo apparuisset, tredecim apud Alexandrum
eundem locum obtinuisset, in his unum equitum
alae praefuisset, post autem Alexandri Magni
mortem imperator exercitus duxisset summosque
duces partim reppulisset, partim interfecisset, captus
non Antigoni virtute, sed Macedonum periurio
talem habuit exitum vitae. In quo quanta omnium
2 fuerit opinio eorum qui post Alexandrum Magnum
reges sunt appellati ex hoc facillime potest iudicari,
3 quod, nemo Eumene vivo rex appellatus est, sed
praefectus, eidem post huius occasum statim regium
ornatum nomenque sumpserunt, neque, quod initio
praedicarant, se Alexandri liberis regnum servare,
praestare voluerunt, et, uno propugnatore sublato,
quid sentirent aperuerunt. Huius sceleris principes
fuerunt Antigonus, Ptolemaeus, Seleucus, Lysimachus, Cassandrus.
4 Antigonus autem Eumenem mortuum propinquis
eius sepeliendum tradidit. Hi militari honestoque
funere, comitante toto exercitu, humaverunt ossaque
eius in Cappadociam ad matrem atque uxorem
liberosque eius deportanda curarunt.

XIX. PHOCION

1. Phocion Atheniensis etsi saepe exercitibus
praefuit summosque magistratus cepit, tamen multo
eius notior est integritas[1] vitae quam rei militaris

[1] est integritas, *u, Fleck.*; integ. est, *M.*; *the other MSS.
omit* est.

13. Thus it was that Eumenes at the age of forty-
five, having from his twentieth year served Philip,
as I said above, having held the same position with
Alexander for thirteen years, and having during
that time commanded a corps of cavalry for a year;
having been, after the death of Alexander the Great,
at the head of an army and either defeated or slain
the greatest generals, fell victim, not to the valour
of Antigonus, but to the false witness of the Macedonians, and ended his life as I have described. How
high he stood in the estimation of all those who after
the death of Alexander the Great assumed the title
of king may most easily be judged from the fact
that while Eumenes lived no one was called king,
but only prefect. But after his death those same
men at once assumed the state and name of king,
and no one, as all had professed in the beginning,
attempted to maintain that he was keeping the
throne for the children of Alexander, but after
getting rid of their only champion, the rivals disclosed their real designs. The leaders in that crime
were Antigonus, Ptolemy, Seleucus, Lysimachus
and Cassander.

Antiochus, however, sent the body of Eumenes
to his relatives for burial. They gave him a funeral
worthy of a soldier and an eminent man, which was
attended by all the army; and they had his ashes
taken to his mother, wife and children in Cappadocia.

XIX. PHOCION

1. Phocion, the Athenian, although he often
commanded armies and held the highest offices,
yet was much better known for the integrity of his

labor. Itaque huius memoria est nulla, illius autem magna fama, ex quo cognomine Bonus est appellatus.
2 Fuit enim perpetuo pauper, cum divitissimus esse posset propter frequentis delatos honores potesta-
3 tesque summas, quae ei a populo dabantur. Hic cum a rege Philippo munera magnae pecuniae repudiaret legatique hortarentur accipere simulque admonerent, si ipse iis facile careret, liberis tamen suis prospiceret, quibus difficile esset in summa paupertate tantam
4 paternam tueri gloriam, his ille "Si mei similes erunt, idem hic," inquit, "agellus illos alet qui me ad hanc dignitatem perduxit; sin dissimiles sunt futuri, nolo meis impensis illorum ali augerique luxuriam."

2. Idem[1] cum prope ad annum octogesimum prospera pervenisset fortuna, extremis temporibus
2 magnum in odium pervenit suorum civium, primo quod cum Demade de urbe tradenda Antipatro consenserat eiusque consilio Demosthenes cum ceteris qui bene de re publica meriti existimabantur populi scito in exsilium erant expulsi. Neque in eo solum offenderat, quod patriae male consuluerat, sed
3 etiam quod amicitiae fidem non praestiterat. Namque auctus adiutusque a Demosthene eum quem tenebat ascenderat gradum, cum adversus Charetem eum subornaret; ab eodem in iudiciis, cum capitis causam

---

[1] idem, *Schoppius*; eidem, *MSS.*

---

[1] *Honores* are magistracies; *potestates* is a more general term. Both are Roman terms; cf. n. 2, p. 198.
[2] That is, at the expense of his good name.
[3] The second reason follows in § 4.
[4] See xii. 3, 1, and note 4.

life than for his work as a soldier. And so no one remembers the latter, while the former is widely known and led to his surname of "The Good." In fact, he was always in moderate circumstances, although he might have acquired great wealth because of the frequent offices and commissions which the people conferred upon him.[1] When he had refused the gift of a large sum of money from King Philip, the king's envoys urged him to take it, at the same time reminding him that even if he himself could readily do without such things, yet he ought to consider his children, who would find it difficult with narrow means to live up to the great glory inherited from their father. But he replied to them: "If they are like me, they will live on this same little farm which has brought me to my present rank; but if they are going to be different, I do not wish their luxury to be nourished and grow at my expense."[2]

2. After good fortune had attended him almost to his eightieth year, at the end of his life he incurred 322 B.C. the bitter hatred of his fellow-citizens; at first,[3] because he had made an agreement with Demades to turn the city over to Antipater, and because it was by his advice that Demosthenes and the rest who were thought to have served their country well had been exiled by decree of the people. And in the latter instance he was censured, not merely for having acted contrary to the interests of his country, but also for disloyalty to a friend. For it was through the aid and support of Demosthenes that Phocion had reached the rank that he enjoyed, having gained the orator's secret support against Chares;[4] he had also on several occasions been defended by Demos-

diceret, defensus aliquotiens, liberatus discesserat.
Hunc non solum in periculis non defendit, sed etiam
prodidit.

4 Concidit autem maxime uno crimine, quod, cum
apud eum summum esset imperium populi iussu[1] et
Nicanorem, Cassandri praefectum, insidiari Piraeo
Atheniensium a Dercylo moneretur idemque[2] postularet ut provideret ne commeatibus civitas privaretur,
huic audiente populo Phocion negavit esse periculum
5 seque eius rei obsidem fore pollicitus est. Neque
ita multo post Nicanor Piraeo est potitus, sine quo
Athenae omnino esse non possunt.[3] Ad quem recupe-
randum cum populus armatus concurrisset, ille non
modo neminem ad arma vocavit, sed ne armatis
quidem praeesse voluit.

3. Erant eo tempore Athenis duae factiones,
quarum una populi causam agebat, altera optimatium.
In hac erat Phocion et Demetrius Phalereus. Harum
utraque Macedonum patrociniis utebatur; nam
populares Polyperchonti favebant, optimates cum
2 Cassandro sentiebant. Interim a Polyperchonte
Cassandrus Macedonia pulsus est. Quo facto populus
superior factus, statim duces adversariae factionis
capitis damnatos patria propulit, in iis Phocionem et
Demetrium Phalereum, deque ea re legatos ad

---

[1] iussu, *added by Andresen.*
[2] idemque, *u*; eidemque, *MSS.*
[3] *Transposed by Kraffert; after* voluit *in MSS.; put after*
insidiari Piraeo *by Guill. (Döderlein), who puts* Atheniensium
after populi.

---

[1] That of στρατηγός, or general.
[2] Although the Piraeus had been destroyed in the first
Mithridatic war, the harbour was still important in the time
of Nepos. For the position of this phrase see the crit. note.

thenes, when charged with capital offences, and had been acquitted. This benefactor Phocion not only did not defend in time of danger, but he even betrayed him.

But his downfall was due particularly to one 317 B.C offence, committed when he held the highest office in the gift of the people.[1] On that occasion, being warned by Dercylus that Nicanor, one of Cassander's prefects, was plotting an attack on the Piraeus of the Athenians, and being urged to take heed that the state should not be deprived of supplies, Phocion replied in the hearing of the people that there was no danger and promised to assume all responsibility. Not long afterwards Nicanor got possession of the Piraeus, without which Athens cannot[2] exist at all; and when the people united to recover it by force, Phocion not only issued no call to arms, but refused to take command of the people when they had armed themselves.

3. There were at Athens at that time two parties, one of which favoured the populace, the other the aristocrats. To the latter belonged Phocion and Demetrius of Phalerum. Both these parties depended upon the patronage of the Macedonians; for the popular party sided with Polyperchon, the aristocrats with Cassander. While these events were going on, Cassander was driven from Macedonia by Polyperchon. When that happened, the people, having gained the upper hand, at once outlawed the leaders of the opposing party and drove them from Athens,[3] including Phocion and Demetrius of Phalerum; then with reference to that action they

[3] Some were banished; others were condemned to death and fled from the city.

Polyperchontem misit, qui ab eo peterent ut sua
3 decreta confirmaret. Huc[1] eodem profectus est
Phocion. Quo ut venit, causam apud Philippum
regem verbo, re ipsa quidem apud Polyperchontem
iussus est dicere ; namque is tum regis rebus praeerat.
4 Hic ab Agnone accusatus, quod Piraeum Nicanori
prodidisset, ex consilii sententia in custodiam coniectus, Athenas deductus est, ut ibi de eo legibus
fieret iudicium.

4. Huc ut perventum est, cum propter aetatem
pedibus iam non valeret vehiculoque portaretur,
magni concursus sunt facti, cum alii, reminiscentes
veteris famae, aetatis misererentur, plurimi vero ira
exacuerentur propter proditionis suspicionem Piraei
maximeque quod adversus populi commoda in senec-
2 tute steterat. Quare ne[2] perorandi quidem ei data
est facultas et dicendi causam. Inde iudicio legi-
timis quibusdam confectis damnatus, traditus est
undecimviris, quibus ad supplicium more Athenien-
3 sium publice damnati tradi solent. Hic cum ad
mortem duceretur, obvius ei fuit Euphiletus, quo
familiariter fuerat usus. Is cum lacrimans dixisset
" O quam indigna perpeteris, Phocion ! " huic ille
" At non inopinata," inquit; " hunc enim exitum
4 plerique clari viri habuerunt Athenienses." In hoc

---

[1] huc, *Lambin*; hoc, *MSS.*
[2] quare ne, *Nipp.*; quo harene, *A P*; qua de re ne, *the other
MSS.*

---

[1] This was Philippus Arrhidaeus, half-brother and nominal
successor of Alexander the Great.

sent envoys to Polyperchon, to beg him to confirm their decrees. Phocion also went to Polyperchon. On his arrival he was ordered to plead his cause, ostensibly before King Philip,[1] but actually before Polyperchon; for he then had the management of the king's affairs. Phocion was accused by Hagnon of having betrayed the Piraeus to Nicanor, was imprisoned by the decision of the council, and was then taken to Athens, in order that he might there be judged according to the laws of the Athenians.

4. When he arrived in the city, he was now unable to proceed on foot because of his age, and was taken to the court in a carriage. A great crowd collected, some of whom remembered his past glory and pitied his years, although the greater number were filled with bitter anger because of their suspicion that he had betrayed the Piraeus, and especially because in his old age he had opposed the interests of the people. In consequence, he was not even given the opportunity of making a speech and of pleading his cause. Then he was condemned by the court, after certain legal forms had been observed, and was turned over to the Eleven, who, according to the custom of the Athenians, regularly have official charge of the punishment of the condemned.[2] As he was being led to execution, he was met by Euphiletus, who had been his intimate friend. When the latter said with tears in his eyes: " Oh, how unmerited is the treatment you are suffering, Phocion! " the prisoner replied: " But it is not unexpected; for nearly all the distinguished men of Athens have met this end." Such was the hatred

---

[2] They had charge of executions, which were actually performed by an executioner.

tantum fuit odium multitudinis, ut nemo ausus sit
eum liber sepelire. Itaque a servis sepultus est.

XX. TIMOLEON

1. Timoleon Corinthius. Sine dubio magnus
omnium iudicio hic vir exstitit. Namque huic uni
contigit, quod nescio an nulli,[1] ut et patriam in qua
erat natus, oppressam a tyranno liberaret, et a
Syracusanis, quibus auxilio erat missus, iam invetera-
tam servitutem depelleret totamque Siciliam, multos
annos bello vexatam a barbarisque oppressam, suo
adventu in pristinum restitueret.

2 Sed in his rebus non simplici fortuna conflictatus
est et, id quod difficilius putatur, multo sapientius
3 tulit secundam quam adversam fortunam. Nam cum
frater eius Timophanes, dux a Corinthiis delectus,
tyrannidem per milites mercennarios occupasset
particepsque regni ipse posset esse, tantum afuit a
societate sceleris, ut antetulerit civium suorum
libertatem fratris saluti et parere legibus quam im-
4 perare patriae satius duxerit. Hac mente per haru-
spicem communemque adfinem, cui soror ex iisdem
parentibus nata nupta erat, fratrem tyrannum interficiundum curavit. Ipse non modo manus non attulit,
sed ne aspicere quidem fraternum sanguinem voluit.
Nam dum res conficeretur, procul in praesidio fuit,
ne quis satelles posset succurrere.

---

[1] nulli, π[1] (n *deleted by second hand*), *Lambin*; ulli, *MSS.*

---

[1] Since he had been executed for high treason, he could not
be buried within the limits of Attica; see Val. Max. v. 3. ext.
3; Plut. *Phoc.* 37.
[2] 365 or 364 B.C.

of the people for him, that no freeborn man ventured
to bury him; and so he was buried by slaves.[1]

XX. TIMOLEON

1. Timoleon, the Corinthian. Without doubt this
man has shown himself great in the estimation of all.
For he alone had the good fortune, which I am
inclined to think fell to the lot of no one else, to
free the land of his birth from a tyrant's oppression,
to rescue the Syracusans, whom he had been sent to
help, from long-continued slavery, and by his mere
arrival to restore all Sicily to its former condition,
after it had for many years been harassed by wars
and subject to barbarians.

But in the course of these events he had to struggle
with varied fortune, and he did what is regarded
as especially difficult, that is, showed himself far
wiser in prosperity than in adversity. For when
his brother Timophanes, who had been chosen general
by the Corinthians, made himself tyrant with the
aid of mercenary troops,[2] although Timoleon might
have shared in his power, so far was he from partici-
pating in the crime, that he valued the liberty of his
fellow-citizens above his brother's life and considered obedience to its laws preferable to ruling
over his country. Owing to that feeling, through
the aid of a soothsayer and of a relative by marriage,
the husband of their own sister, he caused the death
of the tyrant, his own brother. He himself not only
did not lay hands upon him, but he did not wish
even to look upon his brother's blood; for while
the deed was being done he was some distance
away, keeping guard to prevent any palace guard
from coming to the tyrant's aid.

5 Hoc praeclarissimum eius factum non pari modo probatum est ab omnibus ; nonnulli enim laesam ab eo pietatem putabant et invidia laudem virtutis obterebant. Mater vero post id factum neque domum ad se filium admisit neque aspexit quin eum fratricidam
6 impiumque detestans compellaret. Quibus rebus ille adeo est commotus, ut nonnumquam vitae finem facere voluerit atque ex ingratorum hominum conspectu morte decedere.

2. Interim Dione Syracusis interfecto, Dionysius rursus Syracusarum potitus est. Cuius adversarii opem a Corinthiis petierunt ducemque quo in bello uterentur postularunt. Huc Timoleon missus, incredibili felicitate Dionysium tota Sicilia depulit.
2 Cum interficere posset, noluit tutoque ut Corinthum perveniret effecit, quod utrorumque Dionysiorum opibus Corinthii saepe adiuti fuerant, cuius benignitatis memoriam volebat exstare, eamque praeclaram victoriam ducebat in qua plus esset clementiae quam crudelitatis ; postremo ut non solum auribus acciperetur, sed etiam oculis cerneretur quem et ex quanto
3 regno ad quam fortunam detulisset. Post Dionysii decessum cum Hiceta bellavit, qui adversatus erat Dionysio ; quem non odio tyrannidis dissensisse, sed cupiditate indicio fuit quod ipse, expulso Dionysio, imperium dimittere noluit.
4 Hoc superato, Timoleon maximas copias Kartha-

---

[1] 346 B.C. Dionysius the Younger is meant.
[2] 344 B.C.

This glorious deed of his did not meet with equal approval from all; for some thought that he had been false to fraternal loyalty and through jealousy disparaged the glory of his exploit. As for his mother, after that act she would not admit her son to her presence, and she never saw him without calling him an impious fratricide and cursing him. This treatment so affected Timoleon that he sometimes thought of ending his life, and, since men were ungrateful, of leaving their presence by death.

2. In the meantime Dion had been killed at Syracuse and Dionysius had again gained possession of the city.[1] His opponents sought aid from Corinth and asked for a leader to conduct the war. Timoleon was sent to them and with incredible good fortune drove Dionysius from all Sicily.[2] Although he might have put the tyrant to death, he did not choose to do so, but enabled him to reach Corinth in safety; for the Corinthians had often been aided by the power of the two Dionysii, and he wished the memory of that kindness to endure; moreover, he considered that the most glorious victory was one which was marked by greater mercy than cruelty. Finally, he wished men, not only to hear, but to see with their own eyes, what a tyrant he had overcome and from what great power to how humble a fortune he had reduced him. After the departure of Dionysius, Timoleon made war upon Hicetas, who had been the tyrant's opponent; but that his hostility to Dionysius was due rather to ambition than to hatred of tyranny was shown by the fact that after the tyrant was driven from his throne, Hicetas refused to renounce the supreme power.

After overcoming Hicetas, Timoleon routed a huge

giniensium apud Crinissum flumen fugavit ac satis habere coegit si liceret Africam obtinere, qui iam complures annos possessionem Siciliae tenebant. Cepit etiam Mamercum, Italicum ducem, hominem bellicosum et potentem, qui tyrannos adiutum in Siciliam venerat.

3. Quibus rebus confectis, cum propter diuturnitatem belli non solum regiones, sed etiam urbes desertas videret, conquisivit quos potuit primum Siculos, dein Corintho arcessivit colonos, quod ab iis 2 initio Syracusae erant conditae. Civibus veteribus sua restituit, novis bello vacuefactas possessiones divisit, urbium moenia disiecta fanaque deserta refecit, civitatibus leges libertatemque reddidit; ex maximo bello tantum otium totae insulae conciliavit, ut hic conditor urbium earum, non illi qui initio 3 deduxerant, videretur. Arcem Syracusis, quam munierat Dionysius ad urbem obsidendam, a fundamentis disiecit, cetera tyrannidis propugnacula demolitus est deditque operam, ut quam minime multa vestigia servitutis manerent.

4 Cum tantis esset opibus, ut etiam invitis imperare posset, tantum autem amorem haberet omnium Siculorum, ut nullo recusante regnum obtinere,[1] maluit se diligi quam metui. Itaque, cum primum potuit, imperium deposuit ac privatus Syracusis, quod

---

[1] obtinere, *Freinshem*; obtineret, *MSS.*; obtinere liceret, *Heerwagen*.

force of Carthaginians at the river Crinissus and compelled them to be satisfied with being allowed to possess Africa, after they had for many years been masters of Sicily. He also made a prisoner of an Italian general called Mamercus, a warlike and powerful man, who had come to Sicily to aid the tyrants.

3. After these exploits, seeing that because of the long duration of the war not only the country districts but also the cities were deserted, he first hunted up what Sicilians he could and then summoned settlers from Corinth, because in the beginning Corinthians had founded Syracuse. To the former citizens he restored their property, to the new ones he distributed the estates that had become vacant as the result of war; he repaired the shattered walls of the cities and the deserted temples, and restored to the states their laws and liberty; after a terrible war he won such complete peace for the whole island, that he was regarded as the founder of those cities rather than the men who had first established the colonies. The citadel of Syracuse, which Dionysius had fortified as a menace to the city, he destroyed from its foundations; the other strongholds of the tyranny he demolished, taking care that the fewest possible traces of slavery should survive.

Although Timoleon's power was so great that he might have ruled his fellow-citizens even against their will, and although he possessed the affection of all the Sicilians to such a degree that he might have mounted the throne without opposition, he preferred to be loved rather than feared. Therefore, as soon as he could, he laid down his office and

5 reliquum vitae fuit, vixit. Neque vero id imperite
fecit; nam quod ceteri reges imperio potuerunt, hic
benevolentia tenuit. Nullus honos huic defuit, neque
postea res ulla Syracusis gesta est publice, de qua
prius sit decretum quam Timoleontis sententia cog-
6 nita. Nullius umquam consilium non modo ante-
latum, sed ne comparatum quidem est. Neque id
magis benevolentia factum est quam prudentia.

4. Hic cum aetate iam provectus esset, sine ullo
morbo lumina oculorum amisit. Quam calamitatem
ita moderate tulit, ut neque eum querentem quisquam audierit neque eo minus privatis publicisque
2 rebus interfuerit. Veniebat autem in theatrum,
cum ibi concilium populi haberetur, propter valetudinem vectus iumentis iunctis, atque ita de vehiculo
quae videbantur dicebat. Neque hoc illi quisquam
tribuebat superbiae; nihil enim umquam neque
3 insolens neque gloriosum ex ore eius exiit. Qui
quidem, cum suas laudes audiret praedicari, numquam aliud dixit quam se in ea re maxime dis agere
gratias atque habere, quod, cum Siciliam recreare
constituissent, tum se potissimum ducem esse voluis-
4 sent. Nihil enim rerum humanarum sine deorum
numine geri putabat; itaque suae domi sacellum
Automatias constituerat idque sanctissime colebat.

5. Ad hanc hominis excellentem bonitatem mira-
biles accesserant casus; nam proelia maxima natali
244

lived the rest of his life as a private citizen of Syracuse. And, indeed, he acted wisely in so doing; for the authority which others enjoyed by becoming kings he gained through good-will. There was no office that was not conferred upon him, and after that time no public action was taken at Syracuse without first learning what Timoleon thought about it. Not only was no one's advice never preferred to his, but no one else's was ever even considered. And that was due less to good-will than to discretion.

4. When he was already advanced in years, without suffering any disease he lost the sight of his eyes. This affliction he endured with such patience that no one ever heard him complain, nor did he because of it cease to busy himself with private and public affairs. Moreover, he came to the theatre, when the assembly of the people was held there, riding behind a pair of mules because of his infirmity, and gave his opinion without leaving his carriage. And no one regarded this as arrogance on his part; for nothing either arrogant or boastful ever passed his lips. In fact, when he heard his praises sounded, he never said but one thing, namely, that the main reason why he was particularly thankful to the gods and felt most grateful to them was this, that when they had resolved to restore Sicily, they had chosen him in preference to all others to be their instrument. For he believed that nothing in human affairs happened without the design of the gods; and for that reason he had established in his house a shrine of Fortune, which he venerated most religiously.

5. To this surpassing goodness of the man were

suo die fecit omnia, quo factum est ut eius diem
2 natalem festum haberet universa Sicilia. Huic quidam Laphystius,[1] homo petulans et ingratus, vadimonium cum vellet imponere, quod cum illo se lege
agere diceret, et complures concurrissent, qui pro-
cacitatem hominis manibus coercere conarentur,
Timoleon oravit omnes ne id facerent. Namque id
ut Laphystio et cuivis liceret, se maximos labores
summaque adiisse pericula. Hanc enim speciem
libertatis esse, si omnibus, quod quisque vellet, legibus
3 experiri liceret. Idem, cum quidam Laphystii
similis, nomine Demaenetus, in contione populi de
rebus gestis eius detrahere coepisset ac nonnulla
inveheretur in Timoleonta, dixit nunc demum se voti
esse damnatum; namque hoc a dis immortalibus
semper precatum, ut talem libertatem restitueret
Syracusanis in qua cuivis liceret de quo vellet quod
vellet impune dicere.

4   Hic cum diem supremum obisset, publice a Syracusanis in gymnasio quod Timoleonteum appellatur,
tota celebrante Sicilia, sepultus est.

XXI. DE REGIBUS [2]

1. Hi fere fuerunt Graecae [3] gentis duces qui
memoria digni videantur, praeter reges; namque

---

[1] Laphystius, *Longueil*; Lamistius, *etc.*, *MSS.*
[2] *Joined in the MSS. to the Life of Timoleon, first separated
from it by Caelius Curio, with the title "De Regibus brevis
notatio."*
[3] Graecae, *u*; Graeciae, *MSS.*

added remarkable instances of good luck. Thus he fought his most important battles without exception on his birthday, and in consequence all Sicily celebrated that day as a public festival. Once when a certain Laphystius, a quarrelsome and ungrateful fellow, wished to issue a summons against him, saying that he desired to go to law with him, many citizens had come together and were attempting to check the man's effrontery by force; but Timoleon begged them all to desist, saying that this was just the reason why he had undergone great toil and extreme danger, in order that Laphystius, or anyone else, might be allowed to do just that thing. For that was the ideal of liberty, when all were allowed to resort to law for any purpose that anyone wished. Again, when a man like Laphystius, Demaenetus by name, in an assembly of the people had begun to disparage Timoleon's acts and made some attacks upon him, he declared that at last his vow was fulfilled; for he had always prayed the immortal gods to restore such liberty to the Syracusans that anyone might be allowed with impunity to say what he wished on any subject he wished.

When he ended his life, he was buried at public expense by the Syracusans in the gymnasium called Timoleonteum,[1] and all Sicily attended his funeral.

XXI. ON KINGS

1. These have been about all the generals of the Greek nation who seem worthy of mention, with the exception of kings; for upon kings I have been

---

[1] He was buried in the agora, and the gymnasium was built afterwards at the place where he was interred; see Plut. *Tim.* 39.

eos attingere noluimus, quod omnium res gestae
2 separatim sunt relatae. Neque tamen ii admodum
sunt multi. Lacedaemonius autem Agesilaus nomine, non potestate fuit rex, sicut ceteri Spartani.
Ex iis vero qui dominatum imperio tenuerunt excel-
lentissimi fuerunt, ut nos iudicamus, Persarum Cyrus
et Darius, Hystaspi filius, quorum uterque privatus
virtute regnum est adeptus. Prior horum apud
Massagetas in proelio cecidit, Darius senectute diem
3 obiit supremum. Tres sunt praeterea eiusdem
generis: Xerxes et duo Artaxerxae,[1] Macrochir
cognomine[2] et Mnemon. Xerxi maxime est illustre,
quod maximis post hominum memoriam exercitibus
4 terra marique bellum intulit Graeciae. At Macrochir praecipuam habet laudem amplissimae pulcher-
rimaeque corporis formae, quam incredibili ornavit
virtute belli; namque illo Perses nemo manu fuit
fortior. Mnemon autem iustitiae fama floruit; nam
cum matris suae scelere amisisset uxorem, tantum
5 indulsit dolori, ut eum pietas vinceret. Ex his duo
eodem nomine morbo naturae debitum reddiderunt,
tertius ab Artabano praefecto ferro interemptus est.

2. Ex Macedonum autem gente duo multo ceteros
antecesserunt rerum gestarum gloria: Philippus,
Amyntae filius, et Alexander Magnus. Horum alter

---

[1] Artaxerxae, *Heusinger*; Artaxerxe, *P A*; Artaxerxes, *B R M.*

[2] cognomine, *Nipp.*; quoque, *A B M P V*; que, *R*; *omitted in u.*

---

[1] In the book entitled *De Regibus Exterarum Gentium;* see
Introd., p. xi. In his second edition (see Introd., p. xiii)
Nepos here added an account of some kings who were also
great generals.

[2] That is, kings who were also generals.

unwilling to touch, because the history of all of them has been related in another place.[1] But, after all, these[2] are not very numerous. Now Agesilaus, the Lacedaemonian, had the title, but not the power, of a king, as was true of the other Spartans of that rank. But of those who joined to their title absolute dominion, the most eminent in my estimation were the Persians Cyrus and Darius, son of Hystaspes, both of whom were private citizens who attained royal power through merit. Of these the former fell in battle in the land of the Massagetae; Darius died of old age. There are besides three other eminent kings of the same nation: Xerxes and the two Artaxerxes, surnamed Macrochir, or " Long-hand," and Mnemon, or " of Good Memory."[3] Xerxes owes his fame in particular to having made war on Greece by land and sea with the greatest armies within the memory of man; but Macrochir is principally known for his imposing and handsome figure, which he enhanced by incredible valour in war; for no one of the Persians excelled him in deeds of arms. Mnemon, on the contrary, was celebrated for his justice; for when he had lost his wife through the crime of his mother, he confined the indulgence of his resentment within the bounds of filial piety.[4] Of these kings the two that bore the same name paid their debt to nature as the result of disease; the third was murdered by his prefect Artabanus.

2. Now, among the people of Macedonia two kings far surpassed the rest in the glory of their deeds: Philip, son of Amyntas, and Alexander the

559–529 and 521–543 B.C.

485–464 B.C.

[3] Macrochir reigned from 464 to 425; Mnemon, from 405 to 359 B.C.

[4] He banished her to Babylon.

Babylone morbo consumptus est, Philippus Aegiis a
Pausania, cum spectatum ludos iret, iuxta theatrum
occisus est.   Unus Epirotes, Pyrrhus, qui cum populo
2 Romano bellavit.   Is cum Argos oppidum oppugnaret in Peloponneso, lapide ictus interiit.   Unus
item Siculus, Dionysius prior.   Nam et manu fortis
et belli peritus fuit et, id quod in tyranno non facile
reperitur, minime libidinosus, non luxuriosus, non
avarus, nullius denique rei cupidus nisi singularis per-
petuique imperii ob eamque rem crudelis ; nam dum
id studuit munire, nullius pepercit vitae, quem eius
3 insidiatorem putaret.   Hic cum virtute tyrannidem
sibi peperisset, magna retinuit felicitate ; maior enim
annos sexaginta natus decessit, florente regno.
Neque in tam multis annis cuiusquam ex sua stirpe
funus vidit, cum ex tribus uxoribus liberos procreasset
multique ei nati essent nepótes.

   3. Fuerunt praeterea magni reges ex amicis Alexandri Magni, qui post obitum eius imperia ceperunt, in
iis Antigonus et huius filius Demetrius, Lysimachus,
2 Seleucus, Ptolemaeus.   Ex his Antigonus in proelio,
cum adversus Seleucum et Lysimachum dimicaret,
occisus est.   Pari leto adfectus est Lysimachus ab
Seleuco ; namque, societate dissoluta, bellum inter se
3 gesserunt.   At Demetrius, cum filiam suam Seleuco
in matrimonium dedisset neque eo magis fida inter
eos amicitia manere potuisset, captus bello in custodia

---

[1] It was a tile, hurled from a housetop by a woman.
[2] See x, *passim.*

Great. Of these the latter died a natural death at Babylon; Philip was murdered by Pausanias at Aegiae near the theatre, when he was on his way to see the plays. There was one celebrated Epirote king, Pyrrhus, who made war upon the Romans. When he was attacking Argos, a town in the Peloponnesus, he was killed by a blow from a stone.[1] There was also one great Sicilian king, the elder Dionysius; for he was personally valiant and skilled in warfare, and besides—a quality rarely found in a tyrant—he was free from licentiousness, extravagance and avarice, in a word, from all passions except that for absolute and permanent dominion. That, however, led to cruelty; for in his desire to make his power secure he spared no one whom he suspected of threatening it. Having made himself tyrant by valour, he retained his power with great good-fortune.[2] He was more than sixty years old when he died, leaving his realm in a prosperous condition. And in all those years he did not witness the death of any one of his descendants, although he had begotten children from three wives and had a great number of grandchildren.

3. There were besides many kings among the friends of Alexander the Great, who assumed their power after his death, including Antigonus and his son Demetrius, Lysimachus, Seleucus and Ptolemy. Of these Antigonus was slain in battle, fighting against Seleucus and Lysimachus. A like death overtook Lysimachus at the hands of Seleucus; for they broke off their alliance and warred with each other. But Demetrius, after giving his daughter in marriage to Seleucus, without thereby ensuring the permanence of their friendship, was taken captive and

4 socer generi periit a morbo. Neque ita multo post
Seleucus a Ptolemaeo Cerauno dolo interfectus est,
quem ille a patre expulsum Alexandrea alienarum
opum indigentem receperat. Ipse autem Ptolemaeus, cum vivus filio regnum tradidisset, ab illo
eodem vita privatus dicitur.

5   De quibus quoniam satis dictum putamus, non
incommodum videtur non praeterire Hamilcarem et
Hannibalem, quos et animi magnitudine et calliditate
omnes in Africa natos praestitisse constat.

XXII. HAMILCAR

1. Hamilcar, Hannibalis filius, cognomine Barca,
Karthaginiensis, primo Poenico bello, sed temporibus
extremis, admodum adulescentulus in Sicilia praeesse
2 coepit exercitui. Cum ante eius adventum et mari
et terra male res gererentur Karthaginiensium, ipse
ubi adfuit, numquam hosti cessit neque locum nocendi
dedit, saepeque e contrario, occasione data, lacessivit
semperque superior discessit. Quo facto, cum paene
omnia in Sicilia Poeni amisissent, ille Erycem sic
defendit, ut bellum eo loco gestum non videretur.
3 Interim Karthaginienses, classe apud insulas Aegatis
a C. Lutatio, consule Romanorum, superati, statue-
runt belli facere finem eamque rem arbitrio permi-
serunt Hamilcaris.

---

1 In the book *De Regibus Exterarum Gentium.*
2 C. Lutatius Catulus, called Catulus in § 5.

died a natural death in the custody of his son-in-law. 283 B.C.
And not very long after that Seleucus was treacher-
ously killed by Ptolemaeus, surnamed Ceraunus or 280 B.C.
"the Thunderbolt," to whom, when he was exiled by
his father from Alexandria and was in need of help
from others, Seleucus had given asylum. But
Ptolemaeus himself, having made over his kingdom
to his son while still living, by him, they say, was 283 B.C.
put to death.

Since I think that I have said enough about these
kings,[1] it seems fitting not to pass over Hamilcar
and Hannibal, who are generally admitted to have
surpassed all men of African birth in greatness of
soul and in sagacity.

XXII. HAMILCAR

1. Hamilcar the Carthaginian, son of Hannibal and
surnamed Barca, in the first Punic war, but when it
was nearly ended, was first put in command of an
army in Sicily, when he was a very young man.
Although before his arrival the Carthaginians
were faring badly by land and sea, wherever he was
present in person he never yielded to the enemy
or gave them a chance to do harm; on the contrary,
he often attacked them, when opportunity offered,
and invariably came off victor. Besides that, when
the Carthaginians had lost almost everything in Sicily,
he defended Eryx with such success that one might
have thought that there had been no war in that
quarter. In the meantime the Carthaginians, after
being defeated in a naval battle off the Aegates 241 B.C.
islands by Gaius Lutatius,[2] the Roman consul, determined to put an end to the war and gave Hamilcar
full powers to conduct the negotiations.

253

Ille etsi flagrabat bellandi cupiditate, tamen paci
4 serviundum putavit, quod patriam exhaustam sumpti-
bus diutius calamitates belli ferre non posse intellegebat, sed ita ut statim mente agitaret, si paulum
modo res essent refectae, bellum renovare Romanos-
que armis persequi, donicum aut virtute vicissent aut
5 victi manus dedissent. Hoc consilio pacem conciliavit, in quo[1] tanta fuit ferocia, cum Catulus negaret
bellum compositurum, nisi ille cum suis, qui Erycem
tenuerunt, armis relictis, Sicilia decederent, ut, suc-
cumbente patria, ipse periturum se potius dixerit,
quam cum tanto flagitio domum rediret; non enim
suae esse virtutis arma a patria accepta adversus
hostes adversariis tradere. Huius pertinaciae cessit
Catulus.

2. At ille ut Karthaginem venit, multo aliter ac
sperarat rem publicam se habentem cognovit.
Namque diuturnitate externi mali tantum exarsit
intestinum bellum, ut numquam in pari periculo
2 fuerit Karthago nisi cum deleta est. Primo mercennarii milites, qui adversus Romanos fuerant, descive-
runt, quorum numerus erat $\overline{\text{XX}}$. Hi totam abaliena-
runt Africam, ipsam Karthaginem oppugnarunt.
3 Quibus malis adeo sunt Poeni perterriti, ut etiam
auxilia ab Romanis petierint, eaque impetrarint.
Sed extremo, cum prope iam ad desperationem pervenissent, Hamilcarem imperatorem fecerunt.

---

[1] in quo, *u*; in qua, *MSS.*

Though he burned with desire for war, yet Hamilcar thought that he ought to strive for peace; for he knew that his country was in financial straits and could no longer support the disasters of war. But in so doing he at once began to plan to renew the war, if only Carthage should recover a little strength, and to bear arms against the Romans until his countrymen won the victory by their valour or were defeated and gave up the contest. It was with that end in view that he conducted the negotiations, in the course of which he was so self-confident that, when Catulus declared that he would not cease from war unless his opponent and all those who defended Eryx would lay down their arms and leave Sicily, he declared that his country should fall and he himself perish before he would return home in such disgrace; for it was unworthy of his courage to surrender to her foes the arms which he had received from his country to use against her enemies. And such was his obstinacy that Catulus yielded.

2. But when he came to Carthage, he learned that the state was in a far different condition than he had hoped; for by the long-continued ill-fortune abroad so serious a civil war had been kindled that 240–238 Carthage was never in so great danger except when B.C. the city was destroyed. To begin with, the mercenary soldiers whom they had used against the Romans had revolted, to the number of twenty thousand men. They roused all Africa to rebellion and even attacked Carthage. By these troubles the Carthaginians were so greatly alarmed that they even asked help of the Romans, and obtained it. But finally, being almost reduced to despair, they made Hamilcar commander-in-chief.　232 B.C.

4 Is non solum hostis a muris Karthaginis removit,
cum amplius centum milia facta essent armatorum,
sed etiam eo compulit ut, locorum angustiis clausi,
plures fame quam ferro interirent. Omnia oppida
abalienata, in iis Uticam atque Hipponem, valentis-
5 sima totius Africae, restituit patriae. Neque eo fuit
contentus, sed etiam fines imperii propagavit, tota
Africa tantum otium reddidit, ut nullum in ea bellum
videretur multis annis fuisse.

3. Rebus his ex sententia peractis, fidenti animo
atque infesto Romanis, quo facilius causam bellandi
reperiret, effecit ut imperator cum exercitu in Hispaniam mitteretur, eoque secum duxit filium Hanni-
2 balem annorum novem. Erat praeterea cum eo
adulescens illustris, formosus, Hasdrubal, quem
nonnulli diligi turpius quam par erat ab Hamilcare
loquebantur; non enim maledici tanto viro deesse
poterant. Quo factum est ut a praefecto morum
Hasdrubal cum eo vetaretur esse. Huic ille filiam
suam in matrimonium dedit, quod moribus eorum non
3 poterat interdici socero genero. De hoc ideo mentionem fecimus, quod, Hamilcare occiso, ille exercitui
praefuit resque magnas gessit et princeps largitione
vetustos pervertit mores Karthaginiensium eiusdemque post mortem Hannibal ab exercitu accedit imperium.

---

[1] This official is mentioned nowhere else.
[2] This law also is mentioned by Nepos alone.
[3] From 229 to 221 B.C.

That general not only drove the enemy from the walls of Carthage, although they now numbered more than a hundred thousand armed men, but even succeeded in shutting them up in a narrow defile, where more of them died of hunger than by the sword. All the disaffected towns, among which were Utica and Hippo, the strongest places in all Africa, he restored to his country. And not content with that, he even extended the Carthaginian frontiers, and brought about such a state of peace all over Africa as to make it seem that there had been no war there for many years.

3. After finishing these tasks to his satisfaction, confident in spirit and hating the Romans, with the view of more readily finding a pretext for war, he contrived to be sent to Spain in command of an 237 B.C. army, and with him he took his son Hannibal, then nine years old. He was accompanied also by a distinguished and handsome young man, Hasdrubal by name, whom some said that Hamilcar loved less honourably than was proper; for so great a man could not escape being slandered. Because of that charge the censor of morals[1] forbade Hasdrubal to be with Hamilcar; but the general gave the young man his daughter in marriage, since according to the code of the Carthaginians a father-in-law could not be denied the society of his son-in-law.[2] I have spoken of Hasdrubal because, when Hamilcar was killed, he commanded the army[3] and accomplished great things, but he was the first by gifts of money to undermine the old-time morals of the Carthaginians; it was after his death too that Hannibal succeeded to the chief command by choice of the army.

4. At Hamilcar, posteaquam mare transiit in Hispaniamque venit, magnas res secunda gessit fortuna; maximas bellicosissimasque gentes subegit, equis, 2 armis, viris, pecunia totam locupletavit Africam. Hic cum in Italiam bellum inferre meditaretur, nono anno postquam in Hispaniam venerat, in proelio pugnans 3 adversus Vettones occisus est. Huius perpetuum odium erga Romanos maxime concitasse videtur secundum bellum Poenicum; namque Hannibal, filius eius, assiduis patris obtestationibus eo est perductus, ut interire quam Romanos non experiri mallet.

XXIII. HANNIBAL

1. Hannibal, Hamilcaris filius, Karthaginiensis. Si verum est, quod nemo dubitat, ut populus Romanus omnes gentes virtute superarit, non est infitiandum Hannibalem tanto praestitisse ceteros imperatores prudentia quanto populus Romanus antecedat forti- 2 tudine cunctas nationes. Nam quotienscumque cum eo congressus est in Italia, semper discessit superior. Quod nisi domi civium suorum invidia debilitatus esset, Romanos videtur superare potuisse. Sed multorum obtrectatio devicit unius virtutem.

3 Hic autem, velut hereditate relictum, odium paternum erga Romanos sic conservavit, ut prius animam quam id deposuerit, qui quidem, cum patria pulsus esset et alienarum opum indigeret, numquam

4. But Hamilcar, after crossing the sea and coming into Spain, did great deeds through the favour of fortune. He subdued mighty and warlike nations and enriched all Africa with horses, arms, men and money. As he was planning to carry the war into Italy, in the ninth year after his arrival in Spain, he fell in battle, fighting against the Vettones. It was this man's inveterate hatred of Rome that seems to have been the special cause of the second Punic war. For his son Hannibal was so affected by his father's constant entreaties that he preferred to die rather than fail to measure his strength against the Romans.

XXIII. HANNIBAL

1. Hannibal the Carthaginian, son of Hamilcar. If it be true, as no one doubts, that the Roman people have surpassed all other nations in valour, it must be admitted that Hannibal excelled all other commanders in skill as much as the Roman people are superior to all nations in bravery. For as often as he engaged with that people in Italy, he invariably came off victor; and if his strength had not been impaired by the jealousy of his fellow-citizens at home, he would have been able, to all appearance, to conquer the Romans. But the disparagement of the multitude overcame the courage of one man.

Yet after all, he so cherished the hatred of the Romans which had, as it were, been left him as an inheritance by his father, that he would have given up his life rather than renounce it. Indeed, even after he had been driven from his native land and was dependent on the aid of foreigners, he never

destiterit animo bellare cum Romanis. **2.** Nam ut omittam Philippum, quem absens hostem reddidit Romanis, omnium iis temporibus potentissimus rex Antiochus fuit. Hunc tanta cupiditate incendit bellandi, ut usque a rubro mari arma conatus sit inferre Italiae.

2 Ad quem cum legati venissent Romani, qui de eius voluntate explorarent darentque operam consiliis clandestinis ut Hannibalem in suspicionem regi adducerent, tamquam ab ipsis corruptus alia atque antea sentiret,[1] neque id frustra fecissent idque Hannibal comperisset seque ab interioribus consiliis segregari

3 vidisset, tempore dato adiit ad regem, eique cum multa de fide sua et odio in Romanos commemorasset, hoc adiunxit: "Pater meus," inquit, "Hamilcar puerulo me, utpote non amplius novem annos nato, in Hispaniam imperator proficiscens, Karthagine Iovi

4 optimo maximo hostias immolavit. Quae divina res dum conficiebatur, quaesivit a me vellemne secum in castra proficisci. Id cum libenter accepissem atque ab eo petere coepissem ne dubitaret ducere, tum ille, ' Faciam,' inquit, ' si mihi fidem quam postulo dederis.' Simul me ad aram adduxit apud quam sacrificare instituerat eamque ceteris remotis tenentem iurare iussit numquam me in amicitia cum Romanis fore.

5 Id ego iusiurandum patri datum usque ad hanc aetatem ita conservavi, ut nemini dubium esse debeat quin reliquo tempore eadem mente sim futurus.

---

[1] corruptus . . . sentiret, *Bosius*; corruptum . . . sentire, *MSS.*

---

[1] Philip V, of Macedon (220–179 B.C.).
[2] From 215 to 205 B.C.
[3] The Persian Gulf.   [4] 192 B.C.

ceased to war with the Romans in spirit. 2. For
not to mention Philip,[1] whom from afar he made an
enemy of the Romans,[2] he fired Antiochus, the most
powerful of all kings in those times, with such a
desire for war, that from far away on the Red Sea[3]
he made preparations to invade Italy.[4]

To his court came envoys from Rome to sound his
intentions and try by secret intrigues to arouse his
suspicions of Hannibal, alleging that they had
bribed him and that he had changed his sentiments.
These attempts were not made in vain, and when
Hannibal learned it and noticed that he was excluded
from the king's more intimate councils, he went to
Antiochus, as soon as the opportunity offered, and
after calling to mind many proofs of his loyalty and
his hatred of the Romans, he added: " My father
Hamilcar, when I was a small boy not more than
nine years old, just as he was setting out from
Carthage to Spain as commander-in-chief, offered up
victims to Jupiter, Greatest and Best of gods.[5]
While this ceremony was being performed, he asked
me if I would like to go with him on the campaign.
I eagerly accepted and began to beg him not to
hesitate to take me with him. Thereupon he said:
' I will do it, provided you will give me the pledge
that I ask.' With that he led me to the altar on
which he had begun his sacrifice, and having dis-
missed all the others, he bade me lay hold of the
altar and swear that I would never be a friend to the
Romans. For my part, up to my present time of
life, I have kept the oath which I swore to my father
so faithfully, that no one ought to doubt that in the
future I shall be of the same mind. Therefore, if

---

[5] Really to Baal, the great god of the Carthaginians.

6 Quare si quid amice de Romanis cogitabis, non imprudenter feceris, si me celaris; cum quidem bellum parabis, te ipsum frustraberis, si non me in eo principem posueris."

3. Hac igitur qua diximus aetate cum patre in Hispaniam profectus est, cuius post obitum, Hasdrubale imperatore suffecto, equitatui omni praefuit. Hoc quoque interfecto, exercitus summam imperii ad eum detulit. Id Karthaginem delatum publice comprobatum est. 2 Sic Hannibal minor V et XX annis natus imperator factus, proximo triennio omnes gentes Hispaniae bello subegit, Saguntum, foederatam civitatem, vi expugnavit, tres exercitus maximos 3 comparavit. Ex his unum in Africam misit, alterum cum Hasdrubale fratre in Hispania reliquit, tertium in Italiam secum duxit. Saltum Pyrenaeum transiit; quacumque iter fecit, cum omnibus incolis conflixit, neminem nisi victum dimisit.

4 Ad Alpes posteaquam venit, quae Italiam ab Gallia seiungunt, quas nemo umquam cum exercitu ante eum praeter Herculem Graium transierat—quo facto is hodie saltus Graius appellatur—Alpicos conantes prohibere transitu concidit, loca patefecit, itinera muniit, effecit ut ea elephantus ornatus ire posset qua antea unus homo inermis vix poterat repere. Hac copias traduxit in Italiamque pervenit.

---

[1] In reality, he was twenty-six.
[2] The origin of the name is uncertain; it may come from some unknown tribe.

you have any kindly intentions with regard to the Roman people, you will be wise to hide them from me; but when you prepare war, you will go counter to your own interests if you do not make me the leader in that enterprise."

3. Accordingly, at the age which I have named, Hannibal went with his father to Spain, and after Hamilcar died and Hasdrubal succeeded to the chief command, he was given charge of all the cavalry. When Hasdrubal died in his turn, the army chose Hannibal as its commander, and on their action being reported at Carthage, it was officially 221 B.C. confirmed. So it was that when he was less than twenty-five years old,[1] Hannibal became commander-in-chief; and within the next three years he subdued all the peoples of Spain by force of arms, stormed Saguntum, a town allied with Rome, and mustered 219 B.C three great armies. Of these armies he sent one to Africa, left the second with his brother Hasdrubal in Spain, and led the third with him into Italy. He crossed the range of the Pyrenees. Wherever he marched, he warred with all the natives, and he was everywhere victorious.

When he came to the Alps separating Italy from Gaul, which no one before him had ever crossed with an army except the Grecian Hercules—because of which that place is called the Grecian Pass [2]—he cut to pieces the Alpine tribes that tried to keep him from crossing, opened up the region, built roads, and made it possible for an elephant with its equipment to go over places along which before that a single unarmed man could barely creep. By this route he led his forces across the Alps and came into Italy.

4. Conflixerat apud Rhodanum cum P. Cornelio
Scipione consule eumque pepulerat. Cum hoc eodem
Clastidi apud Padum decernit sauciumque inde ac
2 fugatum dimittit. Tertio idem Scipio cum collega
Ti. Longo apud Trebiam adversus eum venit. Cum
his manum conseruit utrosque profligavit. Inde per
3 Ligures Appenninum transiit, petens Etruriam. Hoc
itinere adeo gravi morbo adficitur oculorum, ut postea
numquam dextro aeque bene usus sit. Qua valetudine cum etiam tum [1] premeretur lecticaque ferretur,
C. Flaminium consulem apud Trasumenum cum
exercitu insidiis circumventum occidit, neque multo
post C. Centenium praetorem cum delecta manu
saltus occupantem.

4 Hinc in Apuliam pervenit. Ibi obviam ei venerunt
duo consules, C. Terentius et L. Aemilius. Utriusque
exercitus uno proelio fugavit, Paulum consulem
occidit et aliquot praeterea consulares, in his Cn.[2]
Servilium Geminum, qui superiore anno fuerat consul.

5. Hac pugna pugnata, Romam profectus nullo re-
sistente, in propinquis urbi [3] montibus moratus est.
Cum aliquot ibi dies castra habuisset et Capuam
reverteretur, Q. Fabius Maximus, dictator Romanus,
2 in agro Falerno ei se obiecit. Hic, clausus locorum
angustiis, noctu sine ullo detrimento exercitus se
expedivit Fabioque, callidissimo imperatori, dedit
verba; namque obducta nocte sarmenta in cornibus

---

[1] etiam tum, *R M*; etiamnum, *A u*; etiam nunc, *B*; nimium,
P.

[2] Cn. *Lambin*; P., *MSS.*

[3] urbi, *Fleck.*; urbis, *MSS.*

4. He had already fought at the Rhone with Publius Cornelius Scipio, the consul, and routed him; with the same man he engaged at Clastidium on the Po, wounded him, and drove him from the field. A third time that same Scipio, with his colleague Tiberius Longus, opposed him at the Trebia. With those two he joined battle and routed 216 B.C. them both. Then he passed through the country of the Ligurians over the Apennines, on his way to Etruria. In the course of that march he contracted such a severe eye trouble that he never afterwards had equally good use of his right eye. While he was still suffering from that complaint and was carried in a litter, he ambushed the consul Gaius Flaminius with his army at Trasumenus and slew him; and 217 B.C. not long afterwards Gaius Centenius, the praetor, who was holding a pass with a body of picked men, met the same fate.

Next, he arrived in Apulia. There he was opposed by two consuls, Gaius Terentius and Lucius Aemilius, 216 B.C. both of whose armies he put to flight in a single battle; the consul Paulus was slain, besides several ex-consuls, including Gnaeus Servilius Geminus, who had been consul the year before.

5. After having fought that battle, Hannibal advanced upon Rome without resistance. He halted in the hills near the city. After he had remained in camp there for several days and was returning to Capua, the Roman dictator Quintus Fabius Maximus 211 B.C. opposed himself to him in the Falernian region. But Hannibal, although caught in a defile, extricated himself by night without the loss of any of his men, and thus tricked Fabius, that most skilful of generals. For under cover of night the Carthaginian bound

iuvencorum deligata incendit eiusque generis multitudinem magnam dispalatam immisit. Quo repentino obiecto visu[1] tantum terrorem iniecit exercitui Romanorum, ut egredi extra vallum nemo sit ausus.

3 Hanc post rem gestam non ita multis diebus M. Minucium Rufum, magistrum equitum pari ac dictatorem imperio, dolo productum in proelium, fugavit. Ti. Sempronium Gracchum, iterum consulem, in Lucanis absens in insidias inductum sustulit. M. Claudium Marcellum, quinquiens consulem, apud Venusiam pari modo interfecit.

4 Longum est omnia enumerare proelia. Qua re hoc unum satis erit dictum, ex quo intellegi possit quantus ille fuerit: quamdiu in Italia fuit, nemo ei in acie restitit, nemo adversus eum post Cannensem pugnam in campo castra posuit.

6. Hinc invictus patriam defensum revocatus, bellum gessit adversus P. Scipionem, filium eius[2] quem ipse primo apud Rhodanum, iterum apud Padum, 2 tertio apud Trebiam fugarat. Cum hoc, exhaustis iam patriae facultatibus, cupivit impraesentiarum bellum componere, quo valentior postea congrederetur. In colloquium convenit, condiciones non con- 3 venerunt. Post id factum paucis diebus apud Zamam cum eodem conflixit; pulsus—incredibile dictu— biduo et duabus noctibus Hadrumetum pervenit, quod

[1] obiecto visu, *C. W. Nauck*; obiectu viso, *MSS.*
[2] S. filium eius (eius *omitted by M*) R M F λ u; filium eius *omitted by P A B π μ*; S. f. eius Scipionis, *Nipp.*

---

[1] Nepos should have written *bis* and *quintum*; see Gellius, x. 1.
[2] The battle actually took place on the day after the conference.

faggots to the horns of cattle and set fire to them, then sent a great number of animals in that condition to wander about in all directions. The sudden appearance of such a sight caused so great a panic in the Roman army that no one ventured to go outside the entrenchments. Not so many days after this exploit, when Marcus Minucius Rufus, master of horse, had been given the same powers as the dictator, he craftily lured him into fighting, and utterly defeated the Roman. Although not present in person, he enticed Tiberius Sempronius Gracchus, who had been twice consul,[1] into an ambuscade in 212 B.C. Lucania and destroyed him. In a similar manner, at Venusia, he slew Marcus Claudius Marcellus, who was 208 B.C. holding his fifth consulship.[1]

It would be a long story to enumerate all his battles. Therefore it will suffice to add this one fact, to show how great a man he was: so long as he was in Italy, no one was a match for him in the field, and after the battle of Cannae no one encamped face to face with him on open ground.

6. Then, undefeated, he was recalled to defend his 202 B.C. native land; there he carried on war against Publius Scipio, the son of that Scipio whom he had put to flight first at the Rhone, then at the Po, and a third time at the Trebia. With him, since the resources of his country were now exhausted, he wished to arrange a truce for a time, in order to carry on the war later with renewed strength. He had an interview with Scipio, but they could not agree upon terms. A few days[2] after the conference he fought with Scipio at Zama. Defeated—incredible to relate 202 B.C. —he succeeded in a day and two nights in reaching Hadrumetum, distant from Zama about three

4 abest ab Zama circiter milia passuum[1] trecenta. In
hac fuga Numidae qui simul cum eo ex acie excesse-
rant insidiati sunt ei, quos non solum effugit, sed
etiam ipsos oppressit. Hadrumeti reliquos e fuga
conlegit, novis dilectibus paucis diebus multos
contraxit.

7. Cum in apparando acerrime esset occupatus,
Karthaginienses bellum cum Romanis composuerunt.
Ille nihilo setius exercitui postea praefuit resque in
Africa gessit[2] usque ad P. Sulpicium C. Aurelium con-
2 sules. His enim magistratibus legati Karthaginienses
Romam venerunt, qui senatui populoque Romano
gratias agerent, quod cum iis pacem fecissent ob
eamque rem corona aurea eos donarent simulque
peterent ut obsides eorum Fregellis essent captivique
3 redderentur. His ex senatus consulto responsum
est : munus eorum gratum acceptumque esse;
obsides quo loco rogarent futuros; captivos non
remissuros, quod Hannibalem, cuius opera susceptum
bellum foret, inimicissimum nomini Romano, etiam-
nunc cum imperio apud exercitum haberent itemque
4 fratrem eius Magonem. Hoc responso Karthaginienses cognito, Hannibalem domum et Magonem revo-
carunt. Huc ut rediit, rex[3] factus est, postquam
praetor[4] fuerat anno secundo et vicesimo—ut enim
Romae consules, sic Karthagine quotannis annui bini
reges creabantur.

[1] passuum, *Ascensius, Can.*; passus, *the other MSS.*
[2] *After* gessit *the MSS.* have itemque Mago frater eius;
deleted by Bosius.
[3] rex, *Heusinger*; praetor, *MSS.*
[4] praetor, *Heusinger* (imperator, *Nipp.*); rex, *MSS.*

hundred miles. In the course of that retreat the Numidians who had left the field with him laid a trap for him, but he not only eluded them, but even crushed the plotters. At Hadrumetum he rallied the survivors of the retreat and by means of new levies mustered a large number of soldiers within a few days.

7. While he was busily engaged in these preparations, the Carthaginians made peace with the Romans. 201 B.C. Hannibal, however, continued after that to command the army and carried on war in Africa until the consulship of Publius Sulpicius and Gaius Aurelius. For 200 B.C. in the time of those magistrates Carthaginian envoys came to Rome, to return thanks to the Roman senate and people for having made peace with them; and as a mark of gratitude they presented them with a golden crown, at the same time asking that their hostages might live at Fregellae and that their prisoners should be returned. To them, in accordance with a decree of the senate, the following answer was made: that their gift was received with thanks; that the hostages should live where they had requested; that they would not return the prisoners, because Hannibal, who had caused the war and was bitterly hostile to the Roman nation, still held command in their army, as well as his brother Mago. Upon receiving that reply the Carthaginians recalled Hannibal and Mago to Carthage. On his return Hannibal was made a king,[1] after he had been general for twenty-one years. For, as is true of the consuls at Rome, so at Carthage two kings were elected annually for a term of one year.

----

[1] Really, one of the highest magistrates at Carthage, called *suffetes*, or judges.

5 In eo magistratu pari diligentia se Hannibal
praebuit ac fuerat in bello. Namque effecit ex novis
vectigalibus non solum ut esset pecunia quae Romanis
ex foedere penderetur, sed etiam superesset quae in
6 aerario reponeretur. Deinde [1] M. Claudio L. Furio
consulibus, Roma legati Karthaginem venerunt.
Hos Hannibal ratus sui exposcendi gratia missos,
priusquam iis senatus daretur, navem ascendit clam
7 atque in Syriam ad Antiochum perfugit. Hac re
palam facta, Poeni naves duas quae eum comprehenderent, si possent consequi, miserunt, bona eius
publicarunt, domum a fundamentis disiecerunt, ipsum
exsulem iudicarunt.

8. At Hannibal anno tertio [2] postquam domo pro-
fugerat, L. Cornelio Q. Minucio consulibus, cum
quinque navibus Africam accessit in finibus Cyrenaeo-
rum, si forte Karthaginienses ad bellum Antiochi spe
fiduciaque inducere posset, cui iam persuaserat ut
cum exercitibus in Italiam proficisceretur. Huc
2 Magonem fratrem excivit. Id ubi Poeni resciverunt,
Magonem eadem qua fratrem absentem adfecerunt
poena. Illi, desperatis rebus, cum solvissent naves ac
vela ventis dedissent, Hannibal ad Antiochum pervenit. De Magonis interitu duplex memoria prodita
est: namque alii naufragio, alii a servolis ipsius inter-

---

[1] *The MSS. have* anno post praeturam *after* deinde; *deleted
by Fleck.*; praeturam *deleted by Heusinger.*
[2] quarto, *Nipp.*

---

[1] The Carthaginian body corresponding to the Roman
senate.

In that office Hannibal gave proof of the same energy that he had shown in war. For by means of new taxes he provided, not only that there should be money to pay to the Romans according to the treaty, but also that there should be a surplus to be deposited in the treasury. Then in the following year, when Marcus Claudius and Lucius Furius were consuls, envoys came to Carthage from Rome. Hannibal thought that they had been sent to demand his surrender; therefore, before they were given audience by the senate,[1] he secretly embarked on a ship and took refuge with King Antiochus in Syria. When this became known, the Carthaginians sent two ships to arrest Hannibal, if they could overtake him; then they confiscated his property, demolished his house from its foundations, and declared him an outlaw.

8. But Hannibal, in the third[2] year after he had fled from his country, in the consulship of Lucius Cornelius and Quintus Minucius, with five ships landed in Africa in the territories of Cyrene, to see whether the Carthaginians could by any chance be induced to make war by the hope of aid from King Antiochus, whom Hannibal had already persuaded to march upon Italy with his armies. To Italy also he dispatched his brother Mago. When the Carthaginians learned this, they inflicted on Mago in his absence the same penalty that Hannibal had suffered. The brothers, regarding the situation as desperate, raised anchor and set sail. Hannibal reached Antiochus; as to the death of Mago there are two accounts; some have written that he was shipwrecked; others,

196 B.C.

193 B.C.

---

[2] According to the usual Roman method of reckoning it would be the fourth year, and Nipperdey emended *tertio* to *quarto*.

3 fectum eum scriptum reliquerunt. Antiochus autem si tam in agendo [1] bello consiliis eius parere voluisset, quam in suscipiendo instituerat, propius Tiberi quam Thermopylis de summa imperii dimicasset. Quem etsi multa stulte conari videbat, tamen nulla deseruit 4 in re. Praefuit paucis navibus, quas ex Syria iussus erat in Asiam ducere, iisque adversus Rhodiorum classem in Pamphylio mari conflixit. Quo cum multitudine adversariorum sui superarentur, ipse quo cornu rem gessit fuit superior.

9. Antiocho fugato, verens ne dederetur, quod sine dubio accidisset, si sui fecisset potestatem, Cretam ad Gortynios venit, ut ibi quo se conferret consideraret. 2 Vidit autem vir omnium callidissimus in [2] magno se fore periculo, nisi quid providisset, propter avaritiam Cretensium; magnam enim secum pecuniam portabat, de qua sciebat exisse famam. Itaque capit tale 3 consilium. Amphoras complures complet plumbo, summas operit auro et argento. Has, praesentibus principibus, deponit in templo Dianae, simulans se suas fortunas illorum fidei credere. His in errorem inductis, statuas aeneas, quas secum portabat, omni [3] sua pecunia complet easque in propatulo domi abicit. 4 Gortynii templum magna cura custodiunt, non tam a

---

[1] agendo, *MSS.*; cf. *Sallust, Or. Cott.* 11 *(p.* 412, *L.C.L.) belli ab aliis acti ratio*; gerendo, *Lambin.*
[2] in, *added by Fleck.*
[3] omni, *Nipp.*; omnes, *MSS.*

---

[1] He was defeated at Thermopylae in 191 B.C.

that he was killed by his own slaves. As for Antiochus, if he had been as willing to follow Hannibal's
advice in the conduct of the war as he had been in
declaring it, he would not have fought for the rule
of the world at Thermopylae,[1] but nearer to the
Tiber. But although Hannibal saw that many of the
king's plans were unwise, yet he never deserted him.
On one occasion he commanded a few ships, which
he had been ordered to take from Syria to Asia, and
with them he fought against a fleet of the Rhodians in
the Pamphylian Sea. Although in that engagement
his forces were defeated by the superior numbers of
their opponents, he was victorious on the wing where
he fought in person.

9. After Antiochus had been defeated, Hannibal, 190 B.C.
fearing that he would be surrendered to the Romans
—as undoubtedly would have happened, if he had
let himself be taken—came to the Gortynians in
Crete, there to deliberate where to seek asylum.
But being the shrewdest of all men, he realized that
he would be in great danger, unless he devised some
means of escaping the avarice of the Cretans; for
he was carrying with him a large sum of money, and
he knew that news of this had leaked out. He
therefore devised the following plan: he filled a
number of large jars with lead and covered their
tops with gold and silver. These, in the presence of
the leading citizens, he deposited in the temple of
Diana, pretending that he was entrusting his property
to their protection. Having thus misled them, he
filled some bronze statues which he was carrying with
him with all his money and threw them carelessly
down in the courtyard of his house. The Gortynians
guarded the temple with great care, not so much

273

ceteris quam ab Hannibale, ne ille inscientibus iis tolleret secumque duceret.

10. Sic conservatis suis rebus, Poenus illusis Cretensibus omnibus, ad Prusiam in Pontum pervenit. Apud quem eodem animo fuit erga Italiam neque aliud quicquam egit quam regem armavit et exercuit [1] 2 adversus Romanos. Quem cum videret domesticis opibus minus esse robustum, conciliabat ceteros reges adiungebat bellicosas nationes. Dissidebat ab eo Pergamenus rex Eumenes, Romanis amicissimus, 3 bellumque inter eos gerebatur et mari et terra. Sed utrobique Eumenes plus valebat propter Romanorum societatem.[2] Quo magis cupiebat eum Hannibal opprimi; quem si removisset, faciliora sibi cetera fore arbitrabatur.

Ad hunc interficiundum talem iniit rationem. 4 Classe paucis diebus erant decreturi. Superabatur navium multitudine; dolo erat pugnandum, cum par non esset armis. Imperavit quam plurimas venenatas serpentes vivas conligi easque in vasa fictilia conici. 5 Harum cum effecisset magnam multitudinem, die ipso quo facturus erat navale proelium classiarios convocat iisque praecipit, omnes ut in unam Eumenis regis concurrant navem, a ceteris tantum satis habeant se defendere. Id illos facile serpentium multitudine 6 consecuturos. Rex autem in qua nave veheretur ut

[1] exacuit, *Heinrich.*
[2] sed . . . societatem, *transposed by Fleck.; after* opprimi *in MSS.*

---

[1] Prusias was king of Bithynia. Why he was in Pontus is not stated.
[2] See note 1, p. 207.

against others as against Hannibal, to prevent him from taking anything without their knowledge and carrying it off with him.

10. Thus he saved his goods, and having tricked all the Cretans, the Carthaginian joined Prusias in Pontus.[1] At his court he was of the same mind towards Italy and gave his entire attention to arming the king and training his forces to meet the Romans. And seeing that Prusias' personal resources did not give him great strength, he won him the friendship of the other kings of that region and allied him with warlike nations. Prusias had quarrelled with Eumenes, 184 B.C. king of Pergamum,[2] a strong friend of the Romans, and they were fighting with each other by land and sea. But Eumenes was everywhere the stronger because of his alliance with the Romans, and for that reason Hannibal was the more eager for his overthrow, thinking that if he got rid of him, all his difficulties would be ended.

To cause his death, he formed the following plan. Within a few days they were intending to fight a decisive naval battle. Hannibal was outnumbered in ships; therefore it was necessary to resort to a ruse, since he was unequal to his opponent in arms. He gave orders to collect the greatest possible number of venomous snakes and put them alive in earthenware jars. When he had got together a great number of these, on the very day when the sea-fight was going to take place he called the marines together and bade them concentrate their attack on the ship of Eumenes and be satisfied with merely defending themselves against the rest; this they could easily do, thanks to the great number of snakes. Furthermore, he promised to let them know in what ship Eumenes was

scirent se facturum; quem si aut cepissent aut interfecissent, magno iis pollicetur praemio fore.

11. Tali cohortatione militum facta, classis ab utrisque in proelium deducitur. Quarum acie constituta,
priusquam signum pugnae daretur, Hannibal, ut palam faceret suis quo loco Eumenes esset, tabellarium
2 in scapha cum caduceo mittit. Qui ubi ad naves
adversariorum pervenit epistulamque ostendens, se
regem professus est quaerere, statim ad Eumenem
deductus est, quod nemo dubitabat quin aliquid de
pace esset scriptum. Tabellarius, ducis nave de-
clarata suis, eodem unde erat egressus se recepit.
3 At Eumenes soluta epistula nihil in ea repperit nisi
quae ad irridendum eum pertinerent. Cuius etsi
causam mirabatur neque reperiebat,[1] tamen proelium
statim committere non dubitavit.
4 Horum in concursu Bithynii Hannibalis praecepto
universi navem Eumenis adoriuntur. Quorum vim
rex cum sustinere non posset, fuga salutem petiit,
quam consecutus non esset, nisi intra sua praesidia
se recepisset, quae in proximo litore erant conlocata.
5 Reliquae Pergamenae naves cum adversarios preme-
rent acrius, repente in eas vasa fictilia de quibus
supra mentionem fecimus conici coepta sunt. Quae
iacta initio risum pugnantibus concitarunt, neque
6 qua re id fieret poterat intellegi. Postquam autem
naves suas oppletas conspexerunt serpentibus, nova
re perterriti, cum quid potissimum vitarent non vide-

---

[1] reperiebat, *Lambin*; reperiebatur, *MSS*.

sailing, and to give them a generous reward if they succeeded in either capturing or killing the king.

11. After he had encouraged the soldiers in this way, the fleets on both sides were brought out for battle. When they were drawn up in line, before the signal for action was given, in order that Hannibal might make it clear to his men where Eumenes was, he sent a messenger in a skiff with a herald's staff. When the emissary came to the ships of the enemy, he exhibited a letter and said that he was looking for the king. He was at once taken to Eumenes, since no one doubted that it was some communication about peace. The letter-carrier, having pointed out the commander's ship to his men, returned to the place from which he came. But Eumenes, on opening the missive, found nothing in it except what was designed to mock at him. Although he wondered at the reason for such conduct and could not find one, he nevertheless did not hesitate to join battle at once.

When the clash came, the Bithynians did as Hannibal had ordered and fell upon the ship of Eumenes in a body. Since the king could not resist their force, he sought safety in flight, which he secured only by retreating within the entrenchments which had been thrown up on the neighbouring shore. When the other Pergamene ships began to press their opponents too hard, on a sudden the earthenware jars of which I have spoken began to be hurled at them. At first these projectiles excited the laughter of the combatants, and they could not understand what it meant. But as soon as they saw their ships filled with snakes, terrified by the strange weapons and not knowing how to avoid them, they turned

rent, puppes verterunt[1] seque ad sua castra nautica

7 rettulerunt. Sic Hannibal consilio arma Pergamenorum superavit, neque tum solum, sed saepe alias pedestribus copiis pari prudentia pepulit adversarios.

12. Quae dum in Asia geruntur, accidit casu ut legati Prusiae Romae apud T.[2] Quinctium Flamininum[3] consularem cenarent, atque ibi de Hannibale mentione facta, ex iis unus diceret eum in Prusiae

2 regno esse. Id postero die Flamininus senatui detulit. Patres conscripti, qui Hannibale vivo numquam se sine insidiis futuros existimarent, legatos in Bithyniam miserunt, in iis Flamininum, qui ab rege peterent ne inimicissimum suum secum haberet

3 sibique dederet. His Prusia negare ausus non est; illud recusavit, ne id a se fieri postularent quod adversus ius hospitii esset: ipsi, si possent, comprehenderent; locum, ubi esset, facile inventuros. Hannibal enim uno loco se tenebat, in castello quod ei a rege datum erat muneri idque sic aedificarat, ut in omnibus partibus aedificii exitus haberet, scilicet verens ne usu veniret quod accidit.

4 Huc cum legati Romanorum venissent ac multitudine domum eius circumdedissent, puer, ab ianua prospiciens, Hannibali dixit plures praeter consuetudinem armatos apparere. Qui imperavit ei ut omnes fores aedificii circumiret ac propere sibi nuntiaret num eodem modo undique obsideretur.

---

[1] verterunt, *Nipp.*; averterunt, *MSS.*; converterunt, *Buchner.*

[2] T., *Magius*; L., *MSS.*

[3] Flamininum, *Lambin*; Flamminium, etc., *MSS.*

---

[1] The *praesidia* of § 4.

their ships about and retreated to their naval camp.[1]
Thus Hannibal overcame the arms of Pergamum by
strategy; and that was not the only instance of the
kind, but on many other occasions in land battles
he defeated his antagonists by a similar bit of
cleverness.

12. While this was taking place in Asia, it chanced
that in Rome envoys of Prusias were dining with
Titus Quinctius Flamininus, the ex-consul, and that 183 B.C.
mention being made of Hannibal, one of the envoys
said that he was in the kingdom of Prusias. On the
following day Flamininus informed the senate. The
Fathers, believing that while Hannibal lived they
would never be free from plots, sent envoys to
Bithynia, among them Flamininus, to request the
king not to keep their bitterest foe at his court, but
to surrender him to the Romans. Prusias did not
dare to refuse; he did, however, stipulate that they
would not ask him to do anything which was in
violation of the laws of hospitality. They themselves, if they could, might take him; they would
easily find his place of abode. As a matter of fact,
Hannibal kept himself in one place, in a stronghold
which the king had given him, and he had so arranged
it that he had exits in every part of the building,
evidently being in fear of experiencing what actually
happened.

When the envoys of the Romans had come to the
place and surrounded his house with a great body of
troops, a slave looking out from one of the doors
reported that an unusual number of armed men were
in sight. Hannibal ordered him to go about to all
the doors of the building and hasten to inform him
whether he was beset in the same way on every side.

5 Puer cum celeriter quid esset renuntiasset omnisque exitus occupatos ostendisset, sensit id non fortuito factum, sed se peti neque sibi diutius vitam esse retinendam. Quam ne alieno arbitrio dimitteret, memor pristinarum virtutum, venenum quod semper secum habere consuerat sumpsit.

13. Sic vir fortissimus, multis variisque perfunctus laboribus, anno adquievit septuagesimo. Quibus consulibus interierit non convenit. Namque Atticus M. Claudió Marcello Q. Fabio Labeone consulibus mortuum in Annali suo scriptum reliquit, at Polybius L. Aemilio Paulo Cn. Baebio Tamphilo, Sulpicius autem Blitho P. Cornelio Cethego M. Baebio Tam-
2 philo. Atque hic tantus vir tantisque bellis districtus non nihil temporis tribuit litteris. Namque aliquot eius libri sunt, Graeco sermone confecti, in iis ad Rhodios de Cn. Manlii Volsonis in Asia rebus gestis.
3 Huius belli gesta multi memoriae prodiderunt, sed ex iis duo, qui cum eo in castris fuerunt simulque vixerunt, quam diu fortuna passa est, Silenus et Sosylus Lacedaemonius. Atque hoc Sosylo Hannibal litterarum Graecarum usus est doctore.
4 Sed nos tempus est huius libri facere finem et Romanorum explicare imperatores, quo facilius, collatis utrorumque factis, qui viri praeferendi sint possit iudicari.[1]

---

[1] For the verses added in A P and a few other MSS. see Introd., pp. xi f.

---

[1] In a ring; cf. Juvenal x. 164, sed ille Cannarum vindex ac tanti sanguinis ultor, anulus.

[2] In 183 B.C. Hannibal was sixty-three years old.

[3] See xxv. 18. 1.

[4] Cn. Manlius Volso defeated the Gauls in Asia Minor in 189 B.C., and in the following year brought about peace with

The slave having quickly reported the facts and told him that all the exits were guarded, Hannibal knew that it was no accident; that it was he whom they were after and he must no longer think of preserving his life. But not wishing to lose it at another's will, and remembering his past deeds of valour, he took the poison which he always carried about his person.[1]

13. Thus that bravest of men, after having performed many and varied labours, entered into rest in his seventieth[2] year. Under what consuls he died is disputed. For Atticus has recorded in his *Annals*[3] that he died in the consulate of Marcus Claudius Marcellus and Quintus Fabius Labeo; Polybius, under Lucius Aemilius Paulus and Gnaeus Baebius Tamphilus; and Sulpicius Blitho, in the time of Publius Cornelius Cethegus and Marcus Baebius Tamphilus. And that great man, although busied with such great wars, devoted some time to letters; for there are several books of his, written in Greek, among them one, addressed to the Rhodians, on the deeds of Gnaeus Manlius Volso in Asia.[4] Hannibal's deeds of arms have been recorded by many writers, among them two men who were with him in camp and lived with him so long as fortune allowed, Silenus and Sosylus of Lacedaemon. And it was this Sosylus whom Hannibal employed as his teacher of Greek.

But it is time for us to put an end to this book and give an account of the Roman generals, to make it possible by comparing their deeds with those of the foreigners to judge which heroes ought to be given the higher rank.

183 B.C.
182 B.C.
181 B.C.

Antiochus. The Rhodians had joined with the Romans in the campaigns.

CORNELIUS NEPOS

XXIV. CATO

EXCERPTUM E LIBRO CORNELII NEPOTIS DE LATINIS
HISTORICIS

1. M.[1] Cato, ortus municipio Tusculo, adulescentulus, priusquam honoribus operam daret, versatus est in Sabinis, quod ibi heredium a patre
relictum habebat. Inde hortatu L. Valerii Flacci,
quem in consulatu censuraque habuit collegam, ut
M. Perpenna censorius [2] narrare solitus est, Romam
2 demigravit in foroque esse coepit. Primum stipen-
dium meruit annorum decem septemque. Q. Fabio
M. Claudio consulibus tribunus militum in Sicilia
fuit. Inde ut rediit, castra secutus est C.[3] Claudii
Neronis, magnique opera eius existimata est in
proelio apud Senam, quo cecidit Hasdrubal, frater
3 Hannibalis. Quaestor obtigit P. Africano consuli,
cum quo non pro sortis necessitudine vixit; namque
ab eo perpetua dissensit vita. Aedilis plebi factus
4 est cum C. Helvio. Praetor provinciam obtinuit
Sardiniam, ex qua quaestor superiore tempore ex
Africa decedens, Q. Ennium poetam deduxerat,
quod non minoris aestimamus quam quemlibet
amplissimum Sardiniensem triumphum.

2. Consulatum gessit cum L. Valerio Flacco.

---

[1] M., *A*; *the other MSS. omit.*
[2] censorius, *Magius*; censorinus, *A B P R.*
[3] C. *Lambin*; P., *MSS.*

---

[1] More commonly known as the battle of the Metaurus
river, 207 B.C.
[2] P. Scipio Africanus, the conqueror of Hannibal.
[3] The relations of a quaestor to the consul or praetor under
whom he served were like those of a son to his father; cf.
Cic. *Div. in Caec.* 61.

XXIV. CATO

AN EXTRACT FROM THE BOOK OF CORNELIUS NEPOS ON
LATIN HISTORIANS

1. Marcus Cato, born in the town of Tusculum, in
his early youth, before entering on an official career,
lived in the land of the Sabines, since he had there
an hereditary property, left him by his father. Then,
with the encouragement of Lucius Valerius Flaccus,
later his colleague in the consulship and the censor-
ship—as Marcus Perpenna, the ex-censor, was fond of
mentioning—he moved to Rome and entered public
life. He served his first campaign at the age of 215 B.C.
seventeen. In the consulate of Quintus Fabius and 125 B.C.
Marcus Claudius he was tribune of the soldiers in
Sicily. On his return from there he joined the
army of Gaius Claudius Nero and won high praise in
the battle at Sena,[1] in which Hasdrubal, the brother of
Hannibal, fell. As quaestor the chance of the lot
assigned him to the consul Publius Africanus,[2] with
whom he did not live as the intimacy of their associa-
tion demanded;[3] for he disagreed with him throughout his whole life. He was chosen plebeian aedile 199 B.C.
with Gaius Helvius. As praetor he was allotted the
province of Sardinia, from which at an earlier time, 198 B.C.
when leaving Africa after his quaestorship, he had
brought the poet Ennius to Rome—an act which, in
my opinion, was no less glorious than the greatest
possible victory in Sardinia.[4]

2. He was consul with Lucius Valerius Flaccus, 195 B.C.

[4] That Ennius came back with Cato was mere chance.
Cato was bitterly opposed to the tendencies which Ennius
represented.

283

Sorte provinciam nactus Hispaniam citeriorem, exque
2 ea triumphum deportavit. Ibi cum diutius mora-
retur, P. Scipio Africanus consul iterum, cuius in
priore consulatu quaestor fuerat, voluit eum de
provincia depellere et ipse ei succedere; neque hoc
per senatum efficere potuit, cum quidem Scipio
principatum in civitate obtineret, quod tum non
potentia, sed iure res publica administrabatur. Qua
ex re iratus senatui, consulatu [1] peracto, privatus in
3 urbe mansit. At Cato, censor cum eodem Flacco
factus, severe praefuit ei potestati; nam et in complures nobiles animadvertit et multas res novas in
edictum addidit qua re luxuria reprimeretur, quae
4 iam tum incipiebat pullulare. Circiter annos octo-
ginta, usque ad extremam aetatem ab adulescentia,
rei publicae causa suscipere inimicitias non destitit.
A multis temptatus, non modo nullum detrimentum
existimationis fecit, sed quoad vixit virtutum laude
crevit.

3. In omnibus rebus singulari fuit industria; nam
et agricola sollers et peritus [2] iuris consultus et
magnus imperator et probabilis orator et cupidis-
2 simus litterarum fuit. Quarum studium etsi senior
adripuerat, tamen tantum progressum fecit, ut non
facile reperiri possit neque de Graecis neque de
3 Italicis rebus quod ei fuerit incognitum. Ab adulescentia confecit orationes. Senex historias scribere
instituit. Earum sunt libri septem. Primus con-

---

[1] consulatu, *added by Bosius.*
[2] peritus, *Klotz;* rei publicae peritus, *MSS.*

---

[1] The censor's edict contained numerous standing provisions
(*edictum tralaticium*) handed down from his predecessors, to
which new ones were added from time to time.

and being allotted the province of Hither Spain, from 194 B.C. it won a triumph. When he lingered there somewhat too long, Publius Scipio Africanus, then consul for the second time—in his former consulship Cato had been his quaestor—wished to force him to leave the province, in order himself to succeed him. But the senate would not support Scipio in the attempt, although he was the leading man in the state, because in those days the government was administered, not by influence, but by justice. Therefore Scipio was at odds with the senate and, after his consulship was ended, he lived the life of a private citizen in Rome. But Cato was chosen censor, once more with Flaccus 184 B.C. as his colleague, and administered the office with severity; for he inflicted punishment upon several nobles, and added to his edict[1] many new provisions for checking luxury, which even then was beginning to grow rank. For about eighty years, from youth to the end of his life, he never ceased to incur enmity through his devotion to his country. But although often attacked, he not only suffered no loss of reputation, but as long as he lived the fame of his virtues increased.

3. In all lines he was a man of extraordinary activity; for he was an expert husbandman, an able jurist, a great general, a praiseworthy[2] orator and greatly devoted to letters. Although he took up literary work late in life, yet he made such progress that it is not easy to find anything either in the history of Greece or of Italy which was unknown to him. From early youth he composed speeches. He was already an old man when he began to write history, of which he left seven books. The first contains

---

[1] Cato was the greatest orator of his time.

tinet res gestas regum populi Romani, secundus et
tertius unde quaeque civitas orta sit Italica; ob
quam rem omnes Origines videtur appellasse. In
quarto: autem bellum Poenicum est primum, in
4 quinto secundum. Atque haec omnia capitulatim
sunt dicta; reliquaque bella pari modo persecutus
est usque ad praeturam Ser. Galbae, qui diripuit
Lusitanos. Atque horum bellorum duces non nomi-
navit, sed sine nominibus res notavit. In iisdem
exposuit quae in Italia Hispaniisque aut fierent aut
viderentur admiranda; in quibus multa industria et
diligentia comparet, nulla doctrina.

5 Huius de vita et moribus plura in eo libro perse-
cuti sumus quem separatim de eo fecimus · rogatu
T. Pomponii Attici. Qua re studiosos Catonis ad
illud volumen delegamus.

XXV. ATTICUS

1. T. Pomponius Atticus, ab origine ultima stirpis
Romanae generatus, perpetuo a maioribus acceptam
2 equestrem obtinuit dignitatem. Patre usus est
diligente et, ut tum erant tempora, diti imprimisque
studioso litterarum. Hic, prout ipse amabat litteras,
omnibus doctrinis quibus puerilis aetas impertiri
3 debet filium erudivit. Erat autem in puero praeter
docilitatem ingenii summa suavitas oris atque vocis,

---

[1] This extract is therefore only a brief summary of his larger
work, put in to make his list of *Roman Historians* complete,
just as the brief extract *XXI, De Regibus,* is added to make
his list of *Generals of Foreign Nations* complete; see note 1,
p. 248.

an account of the kings of the Roman people; the second and third, the origin of all the states of Italy —and it seems to be for that reason that he called the entire work *The Origins*. Then in the fourth book we have the first Punic war, and in the fifth, the second. All this is told in summary fashion, and he treated the other wars in the same manner down to the praetorship of Servius Galba, who plundered the 150 B.C. Lusitanians. In his account of all these wars he did not name the leaders, but related the events without mentioning names. In the same work he gave an account of noteworthy occurrences and sights in Italy and the Spains; and in it he showed great industry and carefulness, but no learning.

Concerning this man's life and character I have given fuller details in the separate book which I devoted to his biography at the urgent request of Titus Pomponius Atticus. Therefore I may refer those who are interested in Cato to that volume.[1]

XXV. ATTICUS

1. Titus Pomponius Atticus, descended from the most ancient Roman stock,[2] never abandoned the equestrian rank which he had inherited from his ancestors. His father was attentive to business and rich for those days. He was besides particularly interested in literature, and because of his own love of letters, trained his son in all the studies essential for the education of the young. Moreover, the boy had, in addition to a capacity for learning, a most

---

[2] The Pomponii claimed descent from Pompo, a son of King Numa. Such fanciful family trees were not uncommon; cf. *e.g.* Suet. *Galba*, 2; *Vesp.* 12.

ut non solum celeriter acciperet quae tradebantur,
sed etiam excellenter pronuntiaret. Qua ex re in
pueritia nobilis inter aequales ferebatur clariusque
exsplendescebat quam generosi condiscipuli animo
4 aequo ferre possent. Itaque incitabat omnes studio
suo, quo in numero fuerunt L. Torquatus, C. Marius
filius, M. Cicero; quos consuetudine sua sic devinxit,
ut nemo iis perpetuo [1] fuerit carior.

2. Pater mature decessit. Ipse adulescentulus
propter adfinitatem P. Sulpicii, qui tribunus plebi
interfectus est, non expers fuit illius periculi; namque
Anicia, Pomponii consobrina, nupserat Servio,[2]
2 fratri Sulpicii. Itaque interfecto Sulpicio, posteaquam vidit Cinnano tumultu civitatem esse pertur-
batam neque sibi dari facultatem pro dignitate
vivendi quin alterutram partem offenderet, dissociatis
animis civium cum alii Sullanis, alii Cinnanis faverent
partibus, idoneum tempus ratus studiis obsequendi
suis, Athenas se contulit. Neque eo setius adules-
centem Marium hostem iudicatum iuvit opibus suis,
3 cuius fugam pecunia sublevavit. Ac ne illa pere-
grinatio detrimentum aliquod adferret rei familiari,
eodem magnam partem fortunarum traiecit suarum.

Hic ita vixit, ut universis Atheniensibus merito
4 esset carissimus; nam praeter gratiam, quae iam

---

[1] perpetua, *A, Voss. I*; perpetua vita, *Fleck.*
[2] Servio, *Lambin*; M. Servilio, *Leid.*; M. Servio, *the other MSS.*

---

[1] In 88 B.C. he caused the command in the war against
Mithridates to be transferred from Sulla to Marius.

agreeable enunciation and quality of voice, so that he not only quickly learned passages that were set, but also declaimed them admirably.   Hence in childhood he was conspicuous among those of his own age, and showed greater superiority than his high-born schoolfellows could accept with indifference.   Consequently, he inspired them all with a spirit of rivalry; and among them were Lucius Torquatus, the younger Gaius Marius, and Marcus Cicero, with all of whom he became so intimate that as long as he lived no one was dearer to them.

2. His father died early.   He himself, when a mere youth, because he was related by marriage to Publius Sulpicius, who was killed while tribune of the commons,[1] was involved in the same danger; for Anicia, cousin german of Atticus, had married Servius, the brother of Sulpicius.   Therefore, after Sulpicius had been killed, seeing that the state was in disorder because of the rebellion of Cinna, and that no opportunity was given him of living as his rank demanded without offending one or the other faction —for the feelings of the citizens were at variance, some favouring the party of Sulla, the others that of Cinna—he thought it was a favourable opportunity for gratifying his tastes, and went to Athens.   But 86 B.C. nevertheless when the younger Marius had been pronounced a public enemy, he aided him with his resources and facilitated his flight by furnishing money.   And in order that his sojourn abroad might not inflict any loss upon his property, he transported a great part of his fortunes to Athens.

There he lived in such a manner that he was deservedly very dear to all the Athenians.   For not to mention his influence, which was great even in

in adulescentulo magna erat, saepe suis opibus
inopiam eorum publicam levavit. Cum enim versuram facere publice necesse esset neque eius condicionem aequam haberent, semper se interposuit,
atque ita, ut neque usuram umquam iniquam [1] ab
iis acceperit neque longius quam dictum esset debere
5 passus sit. Quod utrumque erat iis salutare; nam
neque indulgendo inveterascere eorum aes alienum
patiebatur neque multiplicandis usuris crescere.
6 Auxit hoc officium alia quoque liberalitate; nam
universos frumento donavit, ita ut singulis VI [2]
modii tritici darentur, qui modus mensurae medimnus
Athenis appellatur.

3. Hic autem sic se gerebat, ut communis infimis,
par principibus videretur. Quo factum est ut huic
omnes honores, quos possent, publice haberent
civemque facere studerent; quo beneficio ille uti
noluit, quod consulti [3] ita interpretantur amitti civi-
2 tatem Romanam alia ascita. Quamdiu affuit, ne
qua sibi statua poneretur restitit, absens prohibere
non potuit. Itaque aliquot ipsi et Piliae [4] locis
sanctissimis posuerunt; hunc enim in omni pro-
curatione rei publicae actorem auctoremque habe-
3 bant. Igitur primum illud munus fortunae, quod in
ea urbe potissimum natus est in qua domicilium
orbis terrarum esset imperii, ut eandem et patriam
haberet et domum; hoc specimen prudentiae, quod,
cum in eam se civitatem contulisset quae antiquitate,

---

[1] umquam iniquam *Gottschalch*; numquam *A B R H* (*H
before* usuram); umquam, *the other MSS.*

[2] sex, *Faērnus*; septem *or* VII, *MSS.*; seni, *Fleck.*

[3] consulti, *Wagner*; nonnulli, *MSS.*

[4] Piliae, *Lambin*; Phidiae (Fid-), *MSS.*; ipsi effigies,
Wagner.

---

[1] There is a word-play on *opibus* and *inopia.*

his youth, he often relieved their public necessities by his wealth.[1] For example, when the state needed to negotiate a loan and could not do so on fair terms, he always came to the rescue, and in such a way that he never exacted from them excessive interest, nor would he allow them to remain in debt beyond the stipulated time. And both those conditions were to their advantage, since he did not by indulgence allow their debt to grow old, nor yet to increase by the piling up of interest. He added to this service still another act of generosity; for he made a distribution of grain to the entire people, giving each man six bushels of wheat, the equivalent of the measure which at Athens is called a *medimnus*.

3. Furthermore, his conduct in Athens was such that he showed himself gracious to the humble and on an equality with the great. The result was that the state conferred upon him all possible honours and wished to make him a citizen of Athens. But that favour he declined to accept, because the jurists hold that if one becomes a citizen elsewhere, Roman citizenship is lost. So long as he was in Athens, he opposed the erection of any statue in his honour; but he could not prevent it after he left. And so they set up several to himself and Pilia [2] in their most sacred places; for they found him an adviser and a help in all the administration of their state. Thus in the first place it was a gift of fortune that he was born in no other city than that which was the abode of universal empire, and that it was at once his native land and his home. And it was a mark of his wisdom that when he had gone to the city which

---

[2] The wife of Atticus; the MSS. give the name of an otherwise unknown Phidias.

humanitate doctrinaque praestaret omnes unus ei
fuit [1] carissimus.

4. Huc ex Asia Sulla decedens cum venisset,
quam diu ibi fuit, secum habuit Pomponium, captus
adulescentis et humanitate et doctrina. Sic enim
Graece loquebatur, ut Athenis natus videretur;
tanta autem suavitas erat sermonis Latini, ut appareret in eo nativum quemdam leporem esse, non
ascitum. Idem poemata pronuntiabat et Graece
2 et Latine sic ut supra nihil posset addi. Quibus
rebus factum est ut Sulla nusquam eum [2] ab se
dimitteret cuperetque secum deducere. Qui cum
persuadere temptaret, " Noli, oro te," inquit Pomponius, " adversum eos me velle ducere cum quibus
ne contra te arma ferrem, Italiam reliqui." At
Sulla, adulescentis officio collaudato, omnia munera
ei quae Athenis acceperat proficiscens iussit deferri.
3 Hic complures annos moratus, cum et rei familiari
tantum operae daret quantum non indiligens deberet
pater familias, et omnia reliqua tempora aut litteris
aut Atheniensium rei publicae tribueret, nihilo
4 minus amicis urbana officia praestitit; nam et ad
comitia eorum ventitavit, et si qua res maior acta
est, non defuit. Sicut Ciceroni in omnibus eius
periculis singularem fidem praebuit; cui ex patria
fugienti HS [3] ducenta et quinquaginta milia donavit.

[1] fuit, *Heusinger*; fuerit, *MSS.*
[2] eum, *added by Lambin.*
[3] HS, *Lambin*; sextertia(-cia), *MSS.*

surpassed all others in antiquity, culture and learning, he was dearer to it than all other men.

4. When Sulla had come to Athens on his way home from Asia, so long as he remained there he kept Atticus with him, attracted by the young man's refinement and culture. For he spoke Greek so well that one would have thought that he had been born in Athens, while on the other hand he used the Latin language with such grace that it was clear that the elegance of his diction was native and not the result of study. He recited poems, too, both in Greek and in Latin, in a manner which left nothing to be desired. The effect of this was, that Sulla would not be parted from him and wished to take him in his company to Rome. But when he tried to persuade him, Atticus answered: " Do not, I pray you, try to lead me against those with whom I refused to bear arms against you but preferred to leave Italy." Whereupon Sulla praised the young man for his sense of duty and gave orders, when he left, that all the gifts that he had received in Athens should be taken to Atticus.

During his residence of many years in Athens, Atticus gave to his property as much attention as was the duty of a careful head of a family and devoted all the rest of his time either to literature or to the public business of the Athenians. At the same time he rendered service to his friends in Rome; for he always appeared on the occasion of their candidacy for office, and was at hand whenever any important action was taken. Thus to Cicero in all his times of peril he showed unparalleled loyalty, and when the orator was on his way to exile, he made him a present of two hundred and fifty thousand

5 Tranquillatis autem rebus Romanis, remigravit
Romam, ut opinor L. Cotta et L. Torquato consulibus; quem discedentem[1] sic universa civitas
Atheniensium prosecuta est, ut lacrimis desiderii
futuri dolorem indicaret.

5. Habebat avunculum Q. Caecilium, equitem
Romanum, familiarem L. Luculli, divitem, difficillima
natura; cuius sic asperitatem veritus est, ut quem
nemo ferre posset, huius sine offensione ad summam
senectutem retinuerit benevolentiam. Quo facto
2 tulit pietatis fructum. Caecilius enim moriens testa-
mento adoptavit eum heredemque fecit ex dodrante;
ex qua hereditate accepit circiter centiens sestertium.
3 Erat nupta soror Attici Q. Tullio Ciceroni, easque
nuptias M. Cicero conciliarat, cum quo a condis-
cipulatu vivebat coniunctissime, multo etiam familiarius quam cum Quinto; ut iudicari possit plus in
amicitia valere similitudinem morum quam adfini-
4 tatem. Utebatur autem intime Q. Hortensio, qui
iis temporibus principatum eloquentiae tenebat, ut
intellegi non posset uter eum plus diligeret, Cicero
an Hortensius; et, id quod erat difficillimum, efficie-
bat ut inter quos tantae laudis esset aemulatio nulla
intercederet obtrectatio essetque talium virorum
copula.

6. In re publica ita est versatus, ut semper optima-

---

[1] discedentem, *Aldus*; diem, *MSS*.

---

[1] It is strange that Nepos did not verify this date by ques-
tioning Atticus. The sentence may have been added in his
second edition.

sesterces. After calm had been established at Rome
he returned to the city, in the consulship, I believe,[1]
of Lucius Cotta and Lucius Torquatus. When he left 65 B.C.
Athens, all the citizens attended[2] him, showing
by tears the grief that they would feel at losing
him.

5. His maternal uncle was Quintus Caecilius, a
Roman knight and a friend of Lucius Lucullus, rich
but very hard to please. Atticus treated the sour-
tempered old man with such deference, that although
no one else could endure him, his nephew retained
his good-will without giving him any offence until he
reached extreme old age. By such conduct he reaped
the fruits of his devotion; for Caecilius on his death- 58 B.C.
bed adopted him by will and made him heir to three-
fourths of his estate; and his share came to about
ten million sesterces. Atticus' sister was married to
Quintus Tullius Cicero; the marriage was arranged
by Marcus Cicero, with whom Atticus had lived in the
closest intimacy from the time when they were
schoolfellows, much more intimately than with
Quintus; which shows that likeness of character is of
more weight in friendship than family alliances.
He was also a close friend of Quintus Hortensius,
who in those days held the first rank in eloquence—
so dear a friend that it was uncertain which loved
him the better, Cicero or Hortensius. He even
accomplished the difficult task of preventing any ill-
feeling between those rivals for a position of such
glory,[3] and was the bond of union between those great
men.

6. In public life he so conducted himself as always

[2] On his way to the ship.
[3] That is, the first rank in eloquence.

rum partium et esset et existimaretur, neque tamen
se civilibus fluctibus committeret, quod non magis
eos in sua potestate existimabat esse qui se his
2 dedissent, quam qui maritimis iactarentur. Honores
non petiit, cum ei paterent propter vel gratiam vel
dignitatem, quod neque peti more maiorum neque
capi possent, conservatis legibus, in tam effusi
ambitus largitionibus neque geri[1] e re publica sine
3 periculo corruptis civitatis moribus. Ad hastam
publicam numquam accessit. Nullius rei neque
praes neque manceps factus est. Neminem neque
suo nomine neque subscribens accusavit, in ius de
4 sua re numquam iit, iudicium nullum habuit. Multorum consulum praetorumque praefecturas delatas
sic accepit, ut neminem in provinciam sit secutus,
honore fuerit contentus, rei familiaris despexerit
fructum; qui ne cum Q. quidem Cicerone voluerit
ire in Asiam, cum apud eum legati locum obtinere
posset. Non enim decere se arbitrabatur, cum
praeturam gerere noluisset, adseclam esse praetoris.
5 Qua in re non solum dignitati serviebat, sed etiam
tranquillitati, cum suspiciones quoque vitaret crimi-
num. Quo fiebat ut eius observantia omnibus esset

---

[1] geri, *added by Lambin.*

---

[1] *Optimarum partium* is equivalent to *optimatium partium,*
the self-applied designation of the senatorial party.

[2] The *hasta publica* was a spear set up to announce the sale
of booty taken in war. Then it came to denote a public
auction of any kind.

[3] That is, he took no part in the farming of the revenues,
either as a principal (*manceps*) or as a surety or bondsman
(*praes*); the latter shared in the profits.

[4] These were positions of the third rank under governors
of provinces, the second rank being that of the *legatus.* They

to be, and to be regarded as being, on the side of the best men,[1] yet he did not trust himself to the waves of civic strife, since he thought that those who had delivered themselves up to them had no more control of themselves than those who were tossed on the billows of the sea. He did not seek offices, although they were open to him either through influence or merit, because they could not be canvassed for in the traditional way, nor gained amid such unlimited bribery and corruption without violence to the laws, nor administered to the advantage of the state without risk in so debauched a condition of public morals. He was never present at an auction sale of confiscated property.[2] He never acted as a public contractor or a surety.[3] He accused no one either in his own name or in partnership with another. He never went to law about his own property, he never acted as judge. He accepted the prefectures [4] offered him by numerous consuls and praetors on the condition that he should accompany no one to his province, being content with the honour and disdaining to increase his means. He would not even consent to go with Quintus Cicero [5] to Asia, although he might have had the post of his lieutenant-governor. For he did not think it becoming, after having declined a praetorship, to become the attendant of a praetor. In so acting he had an eye, not only to his dignity, but to his peace of mind as well, since he thus avoided even the suspicion of wrong-doing.[6] The result was that his attentions were more highly valued by all, since 61 B.C.

were commonly held by Roman knights and offered numerous opportunities for personal profit.

[5] He was propraetor in 61 B.C.

[6] That is, of maladministration in the provinces.

carior, cum eam officio, non timori neque spei tribui
viderent.

7. Incidit Caesarianum civile bellum. Cum haberet annos circiter sexaginta, usus est aetatis vacatione
neque se quoquam movit ex urbe. Quae amicis suis
opus fuerant ad Pompeium proficiscentibus, omnia
ex sua re familiari dedit, ipsum Pompeium coniunc-
2 tum non offendit. Nullum ab eo habebat orna-
mentum, ut ceteri, qui per eum aut honores aut
divitias ceperant; quorum partim invitissimi castra
sunt secuti, partim summâ cum eius offensione domi
3 remanserunt. Attici autem quies tanto opere Caesari
fuit grata, ut victor, cum privatis pecunias per
epistulas imperaret, huic non solum molestus non
fuerit, sed etiam sororis filium et Q. Ciceronem ex
Pompei castris concesserit. Sic vetere instituto
vitae effugit nova pericula.

8. Secutum est illud tempus,[1] occiso Caesare, quo[2]
res publica penes Brutos videretur esse et Cassium
2 ac tota civitas se ad eos convertisse videretur. Sic
M. Bruto usus est, ut nullo ille adulescens aequali
familiarius quam hoc sene, neque solum eum princi-
3 pem consilii haberet, sed etiam in convictu. Excogi-
tatum est a quibusdam, ut privatum aerarium
Caesaris interfectoribus ab equitibus Romanis con-
stitueretur. Id facile effici posse arbitrati sunt, si[3]
principes eius ordinis pecunias contulissent. Itaque

---

[1] illud tempus, *Cod. Mon.* 433; tempus *omitted by*
A B H R θ λ.
[2] quando, *R*; quom, *Fleck.*
[3] si, *Nipp.*; si et, *MSS.*

---

[1] That is, he remained neutral.
[2] Namely, Marcus and Decimus Brutus.

they saw that they were inspired by a desire to be of service and not by fear or hope.

7. Caesar's civil war broke out when Atticus was 49 B.C. about sixty years old. He took advantage of the exemption due his years and did not stir from the city. Whatever his friends needed when they went out to join Pompey he supplied from his own means, and he escaped giving offence to Pompey himself.[1] He had no emolument at his friend's hands, as the rest had who through him had gained either offices or riches, some of whom joined his army most reluctantly, while others bitterly offended him by remaining at home. Moreover, Atticus' neutrality so gratified Caesar, that after his victory, when he made written demand of contributions from private citizens, he not only caused Atticus no trouble, but even granted to his entreaties the pardon of his nephew and of Quintus Cicero, who were in Pompey's camp. Thus by the long-standing policy of his life he avoided the new dangers.

8. There followed that period after the death of 44 B.C. Caesar, when the government was apparently in the hands of the Brutuses[2] and Cassius, and all the state seemed to have espoused their cause. Atticus' relations with Marcus Brutus were such, that there were none of his own age with whom the younger man was more intimate than with the old knight,[3] whom he made, not only his chief adviser, but also his boon companion. Certain men had formed the plan of making up a private fund for the assassins of Caesar through the Roman knights. They thought that their purpose could easily be effected, if the leading men of that order would contribute. Accordingly,

---

[3] Brutus was thirty-four, and Atticus was thirty-one years his senior.

appellatus est a C. Flavio, Bruti familiari, Atticus,
4 ut eius rei princeps esse vellet. At ille, qui officia
amicis praestanda sine factione existimaret semperque a talibus se consiliis removisset, respondit: si
quid Brutus de suis facultatibus uti voluisset, usurum
quantum eae paterentur, sed neque cum quoquam
de ea re collocuturum neque coiturum. Sic ille
consensionis globus huius unius dissensione disiectus
est.
5 Neque multo post superior esse coepit Antonius,
ita ut Brutus et Cassius destituta tutela[1] provinciarum, quae iis dicis[2] causa datae erant a consule,
desperatis rebus, in exsilium proficiscerentur; neque
eo magis potenti adulatus est Antonio neque
6 desperatos reliquit.[3] Atticus, qui pecuniam simul
cum ceteris conferre noluerat florenti illi parti, ab-
iecto Bruto Italiaque cedenti HS[4] centum milia
muneri misit. Eidem in Epiro absens trecenta
iussit dari.
9. Secutum est bellum gestum apud Mutinam.
In quo si tantum eum prudentem dicam, minus
quam debeam praedicem, cum ille potius divinus

---

[1] destituta tutela, *H*; *the other MSS. omit*; omissa cura,
Halm.
[2] dicis, *Cuiacius*; necis, *MSS.*
[3] neque . . . reliquit, *transposed by Guill.*; *after* dari,
MSS.
[4] HS, *Lambin*; sextertia (-cia), *MSS.*

---

[1] *Provinciarum* here has the meaning of "spheres of duty";
Brutus was to send grain to Rome from Asia, Cassius from
Sicily.
[2] They had left Rome through fear of Caesar's veterans,
although as praetors it was unlawful for them to be absent

Gaius Flavius, a friend of Brutus, appealed to Atticus to consent to take the initiative in the enterprise. He, however, thinking that he ought to render service to his friends, but not join parties, and having consistently held aloof from such measures, replied that if Brutus wished to make any use of his means, he might do so to the limit of his resources, but that he would neither confer with anyone on the subject nor meet with anyone. Thus the unanimity of that clique was broken by the disagreement of this one man.

Not long after that, Antony began to gain the upper hand, to such a degree that Brutus and Cassius ceased to perform the duties[1] which had been assigned them as a pretext[2] by the consul, and in utter despair went into exile.[3] But Atticus did not the more on that account flatter the power of Antony or abandon the lost cause. In fact, the man who had declined to join with the rest in contributing money when the party was prosperous, after Brutus had fallen from power and was leaving Italy sent him a gift of a hundred thousand sesterces; and again, when Brutus was in Epirus,[4] he sent orders from Rome that three hundred thousand more be given to the regicide.

9. After that came the war at Mutina. In the 43 B.C. course of which if I were merely to say that he showed foresight, I should give him less credit than I ought, since it was more properly divination, if the term

from the city for more than ten days. To conceal the real reason for their departure, Antony had given them the charge mentioned in note 1.

[3] That was their version of their action; in reality, they took possession of Syria and Macedonia, which had been assigned them as provinces by Caesar, and prepared for war.

[4] Atticus had a large estate in Epirus; see 14. 3.

fuerit, si divinatio appellanda est perpetua naturalis bonitas, quae nullis casibus agitur neque minuitur.

2 Hostis Antonius iudicatus Italia cesserat; spes restituendi nulla erat. Non solum inimici, qui tum erant potentissimi et plurimi, sed etiam qui adversariis eius se dabant et in eo laedendo aliquam consecuturos sperabant commoditatem, Antonii familiares insequebantur, uxorem Fulviam omnibus rebus spoliare cupiebant, liberos etiam exstinguere parabant.

3 Atticus cum Ciceronis intima familiaritate uteretur, amicissimus esset Bruto, non modo nihil iis indulsit ad Antonium violandum, sed e contrario familiares eius ex urbe profugientes, quantum potuit, texit,

4 quibus rebus indiguerunt, adiuvit. P. vero Volumnio ea tribuit, ut plura a parente proficisci non potuerint. Ipsi autem Fulviae, cum litibus distineretur magnisque terroribus vexaretur, tanta diligentia officium suum praestitit, ut nullum illa steterit vadimonium sine Attico, Atticus [1] sponsor omnium rerum fuerit.

5 Quin etiam, cum illa fundum secunda fortuna emisset in diem neque post calamitatem versuram facere potuisset, ille se interposuit pecuniamque sine faenore sineque ulla stipulatione credidit, maximum existimans quaestum memorem gratumque cognosci simulque aperiens [2] se non fortunae, sed hominibus solere esse amicum.

6 Quae cum faciebat, nemo eum temporis causa facere poterat existimare; nemini enim in opinionem

7 veniebat Antonium rerum potiturum. Sed sensim

---

[1] Atticus, *added by Lambin*; hic, *Bosius.*
[2] aperiens, *Hofman-Peerlkamp*; aperire, *MSS.*

---

[1] He went to join Lepidus in Cisalpine Gaul.

divination ought to be applied to an invariable natural goodness which is shaken or diminished by nothing that happens. When Antony was judged a public enemy and had left Italy,[1] no one expected to see his power restored. Not only his personal enemies, who were then very numerous and powerful, but also those who joined his opponents and hoped to gain some advantage by injuring him persecuted his friends, tried to rob his wife Fulvia of all her possessions, and were even preparing to destroy his children.

Although Atticus was very intimate with Cicero and a close friend of Brutus, so far was he from being induced to help them injure Antony, that on the contrary he protected the latter's friends as much as he could in their flight from the city, and gave them what help they required. To Publius Volumnius, indeed, he rendered as great service as could come from a parent. Further, to Fulvia herself, when she was distracted by lawsuits and tormented by great anxiety, he was so unremitting in his attentions, that she never appeared in court without Atticus, Atticus was her surety in all cases. Nay, more, when she had bought an estate in the time of her prosperity with a fixed date for payment, and after her reverses was unable to negotiate a loan, he came to the rescue and lent her the money without interest and without any contract, considering it the greatest profit to be known as mindful and grateful, and at the same time desiring to show that it was his way to be a friend to mankind and not to their fortunes.

In so doing he could not be suspected by anyone of being a time-server; for no one had any idea that Antony would regain his power. But gradually

is a nonnullis optimatibus reprehendebatur, quod parum odisse malos cives videretur. Ille autem, vir [1] sui iudicii, potius quid se facere par esset intuebatur quam quid alii laudaturi forent.

10. Conversa subito fortuna est. Ut Antonius rediit in Italiam, nemo non magno in periculo Atticum putarat propter intimam familiaritatem 2 Ciceronis et Bruti. Itaque ad adventum imperatorum de foro decesserat, timens proscriptionem, latebatque apud P. Volumnium, cui, ut ostendimus, paulo ante opem tulerat—tanta varietas iis temporibus fuit fortunae, ut modo hi, modo illi in summo essent aut fastigio aut periculo—habebatque secum Q. Gellium Canum, aequalem simillimumque sui. 3 Hoc quoque sit Attici bonitatis exemplum, quod cum eo, quem puerum in ludo cognorat, adeo coniuncte vixit, ut ad extremam aetatem amicitia eorum creverit.

4 Antonius autem, etsi tanto odio ferebatur in Ciceronem, ut non solum ei, sed etiam omnibus eius amicis esset inimicus eosque vellet proscribere, multis hortantibus, tamen Attici memor fuit officii, et ei, cum requisisset ubinam esset, sua manu scripsit, ne timeret statimque ad se veniret: se eum et illius causa [2] Canum de proscriptorum 5 numero exemisse. Ac ne quod periculum incideret,

---

[1] vir, *addidi, but cf. Suet. Tib. 18. 1.*
[2] illius causa, *Mon. 433;* illius *omitted by R;* causa, *by most MSS.*

---

[1] The opposite of *boni* (*cives*) (cf. note 1, p. 296) from the point of view of the *optimates.*
[2] See 9. 3–5.

criticism of him arose from some of the aristocrats, because in their opinion he was not sufficiently hostile to bad citizens.[1] But Atticus, being a man of independent judgment, had an eye rather to what it was right for him to do than to what others were likely to commend.

10. There came a sudden change of fortune. Antony returned to Italy, and there was no one but thought that Atticus was in extreme danger because of his intimacy with Cicero and Brutus. Therefore, on the eve of the arrival of the triumvirs he had retired from public life, fearing proscription, and was in hiding at the house of Publius Volumnius, to whom, as I have stated, he had shortly before rendered aid— such were the changes of fortune in those times that now these, now those, were at the summit of power or the extremity of danger—and he had with him Quintus Gellius Canus, a man of his own age and of very similar opinions. This too is an indication of Atticus' good-heartedness, that he lived in such harmony with this man, whom he had known as a boy in school, that their friendship increased constantly up to extreme old age.

Antony felt such hatred of Cicero that he was the personal enemy, not only of the orator himself, but of all his friends, and desired to proscribe them— a course to which many urged him. But never-theless he was mindful of the services rendered him by Atticus.[2] Therefore, when he learned where Atticus was, he wrote to him with his own hand, telling him not to be afraid but to come to him at once; that he had erased his name, and for his sake that of Canus, from the list of the proscribed. And that no danger might befall him—for this happened

quod noctu fiebat, praesidium ei misit. Sic Atticus
in summo timore non solum sibi, sed etiam ei quem
carissimum habebat praesidio fuit. Neque enim
suae solum a quoquam auxilium petit salutis,[1] ut
appareret nullam seiunctam sibi ab eo velle fortunam.
6 Quod si gubernator praecipua laude effertur,[2] qui
navem ex hieme marique scopuloso servat, cur non
singularis eius existimetur prudentia qui ex tot
tamque gravibus procellis civilibus ad incolumitatem
pervenit?

11. Quibus ex malis ut se emersit, nihil aliud egit
quam ut quam[3] plurimis, quibus rebus posset, esset
auxilio. Cum proscriptos praemiis imperatorum
vulgus conquireret, nemo in Epirum venit cui res
ulla defuerit, nemini non ibi perpetuo manendi
2 potestas facta est; quin etiam post proelium Philippense interitumque C. Cassii et M. Bruti L. Iulium
Mocillam praetorium et filium eius Aulumque
Torquatum ceterosque pari fortuna perculsos instituit[4] tueri atque ex Epiro iis omnia Samothraciam
supportari iussit.[5] Difficile est omnia persequi et
3 non necessarium. Illud unum intellegi volumus,
illius liberalitatem neque temporariam neque calli-
4 dam fuisse. Id ex ipsis rebus ac temporibus iudicari
potest, quod non florentibus se venditavit, sed
afflictis semper succurrit; qui quidem Serviliam,

---

[1] *After* salutis *the MSS. have* sed coniuncti, *which was
deleted by Vielhaber;* neque ... coniuncti, *deleted by Eber-
hard.*

[2] effertur, *Eussner;* fertur, *MSS.*

[3] quam, *added by Grasberger.*

[4] instituit, *Lambin;* instituerit, *MSS.*

[5] iussit, *Lambin;* iusserit, *MSS.*

---

[1] See note on 8. 6 (p. 301).

at night—he sent him an escort. Thus it was that Atticus in a time of extreme anxiety saved not only himself but also his dearest friend. For he did not seek aid from anyone for his own safety alone, thus making it clear that he desired no good fortune that was not shared by his friend. But if that pilot is extolled with the highest praise who saves his ship from the storm in a rock-strewn sea, why should not that man's skill be regarded as without parallel, who from such numerous and terrible civil tempests comes safe into port?

11. Once escaped from those evils, Atticus' sole effort was to help as many as possible in whatever manner he could. At a time when the rewards offered by the triumvirs caused a general hounding of the proscribed, no one came to Epirus [1] who did not get everything that he needed, no one who was not given the opportunity of living there permanently. Nay, more, after the battle of Philippi and the death 42 B.C of Gaius Cassius and Marcus Brutus he undertook to protect the ex-praetor Lucius Julius Mocilla and his son, as well as Aulus Torquatus and the other victims of the same ill-fortune, ordering that all that they needed should be sent for them from Epirus to Samothrace. It is difficult to enumerate everything, and needless besides. This one thing I wish to make clear, that his generosity was neither time-serving nor calculated.[2] This may be inferred from the circumstances themselves and from the times, because he never bought the favour of those in power, but always succoured the afflicted; for example, he showed no less regard to Servilia, the

[2] Here, as elsewhere, Nepos gives Atticus too much credit. The keynote of his character appears in 6. 5, *tranquillitati serviebat.*

Bruti matrem, non minus post mortem eius quam florentem coluerit.

5 Sic liberalitate utens nullas inimicitias gessit, quod neque laedebat quemquam, neque, si quam iniuriam acceperat, non malebat oblivisci quam ulcisci. Idem immortali memoria percepta retinebat beneficia; quae autem ipse tribuerat, tam diu meminerat quoad ille gratus erat qui acceperat.
6 Itaque hic fecit ut vere dictum videatur:

Sui cuíque mores fíngunt fortunam hóminibus.

Neque tamen ille prius fortunam quam se ipse finxit, qui cavit ne qua in re iure plecteretur.

12. His igitur rebus effecit ut M. Vipsanius Agrippa, intima familiaritate coniunctus adulescenti Caesari, cum propter suam gratiam et Caesaris potentiam nullius condicionis non haberet potestatem, potissimum eius deligeret adfinitatem praeoptaretque equitis Romani filiam generosarum
2 nuptiis. Atque harum nuptiarum conciliator fuit —non est enim celandum—M. Antonius, triumvir rei publicae constituendae.[1] Cuius gratia cum augere possessiones posset suas, tantum afuit a cupiditate pecuniae, ut nulla in re usus sit ea, nisi in deprecandis amicorum aut periculis aut incommodis.
3 Quod quidem sub ipsa proscriptione perillustre fuit. Nam cum L. Saufei equitis Romani, aequalis

----

[1] constituendae, *added by Lambin.*

----

[1] The author of this iambic senarius is unknown; it is attributed by Cicero (*Parad.* v. 34) to *sapiens poeta.*
[2] Octavian, the future emperor Augustus.

mother of Brutus, after her son's death than at the
height of her prosperity.

Practising generosity in that way, he made no
enemies; for he never wronged anyone, and if he
had suffered any injury, he preferred to forget it
rather than take vengeance. He had besides an
unfailing memory for kindnesses received; but as
for those which he himself bestowed, he remembered
them only so long as the recipient was grateful.
Thus he showed the truth of the adage :

'Tis each man's character his fortune makes.[1]

And yet, before fashioning his fortune, Atticus so
fashioned his character as to make it impossible for
him ever to be injured justly.

12. It was by such conduct, then, that he led Marcus
Vipsanius Agrippa, the intimate friend of the young
Caesar,[2] although through his own influential position
and the power of Caesar he might have made any
match he desired, to choose an alliance by marriage
with the family of Atticus, and prefer the daughter of
a Roman knight to women of noble birth. And the
one who arranged the marriage (we must admit it)[3]
was Marcus Antonius, one of the triumvirs for re-
organizing the government; but although Antony's
influence might have increased his possessions,
Atticus was so far from desiring money, that he never
resorted to that influence except to save his friends
from danger or annoyance.

This, in fact, was clearly evident at the very time 43 B.C.
of the proscriptions. For example, Lucius Saufeius,

---

[3] This apologetic remark is due to the fact that when
Nepos wrote, Octavian and Antony were at odds; the
marriage was probably arranged in 37 B.C.

sui, qui complures annos, studio ductus philosophiae, Athenis habitabat habebatque in Italia pretiosas possessiones, triumviri bona vendidissent consuetudine ea qua tum res gerebantur, Attici labore atque industria factum est ut eodem nuntio Saufeius fieret certior se patrimonium amisisse et recuperasse.

4 Idem L. Iulium Calidum, quem post Lucretii Catullique mortem multo elegantissimum poetam nostram tulisse aetatem vere videor posse contendere, neque minus virum bonum optimisque artibus eruditum; quem post proscriptionem equitum propter magnas eius Africanas possessiones in proscriptorum numerum a P. Volumnio, praefecto fabrum Antonii, absentem

5 relatum expedivit. Quod in praesenti utrum ei laboriosius an gloriosius fuerit, difficile est [2] iudicare, quod in eorum periculis non secus absentes quam praesentes amicos Attico esse curae cognitum est.

13. Neque vero ille vir minus bonus pater familias habitus est quam civis; nam cum esset pecuniosus, nemo illo minus fuit emax, minus aedificator. Neque tamen non in primis bene habitavit omnibusque

2 optimis rebus usus est; nam domum habuit in colle Quirinali Tamphilianam, ab avunculo hereditate relictam, cuius amoenitas non aedificio, sed silva constabat—ipsum enim tectum antiquitus constitutum plus salis quam sumptus habebat—in quo

---

[1] est, *Fleck.*; fuit, *MSS.*

---

[1] The tenses in 13–18 indicate that those chapters were revised in Nepos' second edition.

a Roman knight of the same age as Atticus, who because of his devotion to philosophy had lived for several years in Athens, had valuable possessions in Italy. When the triumvirs sold his property, after the manner in which things were done at that time, it was due to the efforts and energy of Atticus that the same messenger brought Saufeius news of the loss of his property and of its recovery. He was equally helpful to Lucius Julius Calidus, who since the death of Lucretius and Catullus is, I think I may truly say, by far the most graceful poet that our age has produced, in addition to being a good man and endowed with the highest culture. This Calidus, after the proscription of the knights was completed, because of his extensive possessions in Africa was added to the list by Publius Volumnius, Antony's chief of engineers, although he was out of the country; but he was saved by Atticus. Whether this conduct caused Atticus more trouble at the moment or gave him greater glory, it is not easy to decide, since at the time of the perils of these men it became known that his friends, whether present or absent, were the object of his care.

13. And indeed this great man was considered[1] to be as good as head of a family as he was as a citizen. For although he had an abundance of money, no one was less inclined to excess in buying or in building. At the same time, he had as fine a dwelling as anyone, and he enjoyed the best of everything. He had his home on the Quirinal in the villa built by Tamphilus, which was left him in his uncle's will, the charm of which consisted less in its construction than in its park; for the building itself was put up in early times and was rather tasteful than costly.

nihil commutavit, nisi si quid vetustate coactus est.
3 Usus est familia, si utilitate iudicandum est, optima;
si forma, vix mediocri. Namque in ea erant pueri
litteratissimi, anagnostae optimi et plurimi librarii,
ut ne pedisequus quidem quisquam esset qui non
utrumque horum pulchre facere posset; pari modo
artifices ceteri, quos cultus domesticus desiderat,
4 apprime boni. Neque tamen horum quemquam nisi
domi natum domique factum habuit; quod est
signum non solum continentiae, sed etiam diligentiae.
Nam et non intemperanter concupiscere quod a
plurimis videas continentis debet duci, et potius
industria[1] quam pretio parare non mediocris est
5 diligentiae. Elegans, non magnificus, splendidus,
non sumptuosus; omnisque diligentia munditiam,
non adfluentiam adfectabat. Supellex modica, non
multa, ut in neutram partem conspici posset.
6 Nec praeteribo, quamquam nonnullis leve visum
iri putem, cum in primis lautus esset eques Romanus
et non parum liberaliter domum suam omnium
ordinum homines invitaret, scimus non amplius quam
terna milia[2] peraeque in singulos menses ex ephe-
7 meride eum expensum sumptui ferre solitum. Atque
hoc non auditum, sed cognitum praedicamus; saepe
enim propter familiaritatem domesticis rebus inter-
fuimus.

14. Nemo in convivio eius aliud acroama audivit
quam anagnosten, quod nos quidem iucundissimum

---

[1] industria . . . diligentiae, *Nipp.*; diligentia . . . in-
dustriae, *MSS.*

[2] milia aeris, *MSS.*; aeris *omitted by Manutius.*

But he made no changes in it, except such as lapse of time compelled. He had slaves that were excellent in point of efficiency, although in personal appearance hardly mediocre; for there were among them servants who were highly educated, some excellent readers and a great number of copyists; in fact, there was not even a footman who was not expert in both those accomplishments. In the same way, the other artisans required by the management of a house were of first-rate quality. In spite of this, however, he possessed no slave who was not born in his house and trained at home, which is a sign, not only of his self-control, but also of his spirit of economy. For not to desire immoderately what you see coveted by many ought to be considered a mark of self-control, and to acquire property by labour rather than by money is a token of no slight regard for economy. He was tasteful rather than magnificent, distinguished rather than extravagant; and all his efforts were in the direction of elegance, not of excess. His furniture was modest, not abundant, so that it attracted attention in neither direction.

I shall not pass over the fact, although I suppose that some will regard it as trivial, that although he was one of the richest of the Roman knights, and with no little generosity invited to his house men of all ranks, we know from the entries in his day-book that he consistently limited his expenses to not more than three thousand sesterces each month. And this I state not from hearsay, but from actual knowledge; for because of our intimacy I was often familiar with the details of his domestic life.

14. No one at a dinner-party of his heard anything but a reader, which is the most agreeable form

arbitramur; neque umquam sine aliqua lectione apud eum cenatum est, ut non minus animo quam 2 ventre convivae delectarentur. Namque eos vocabat, quorum mores a suis non abhorrerent. Cum tanta pecuniae facta esset accessio, nihil de cottidiano cultu mutavit, nihil de vitae consuetudine, tantaque usus est moderatione ut neque in sestertio viciens, quod a patre acceperat, parum se splendide gesserit neque in sestertio centiens adfluentius vixerit, quam instituerat, parique fastigio steterit in utraque 3 fortuna. Nullos habuit hortos, nullam suburbanam aut maritimam sumptuosam villam, neque in Italia, praeter Arretinum et Nomentanum, rusticum praedium, omnisque eius pecuniae reditus constabat in Epiroticis et urbanis possessionibus. Ex quo cognosci potest usum eum pecuniae non magnitudine, sed ratione metiri solitum.

15. Mendacium neque dicebat neque pati poterat. Itaque eius comitas non sine severitate erat neque gravitas sine facilitate, ut difficile esset intellectu utrum eum amici magis vererentur an amarent. Quidquid rogabatur, religiose promittebat, quod non liberalis, sed levis arbitrabatur polliceri quod 2 praestare non possent. Idem in nitendo quod semel adnuisset tanta erat cura, ut non mandatam, sed suam rem videretur agere. Numquam suscepti negotii eum pertaesum est; suam enim existimationem in ea re agi putabat, qua nihil habebat

---

[1] By the inheritance from his uncle; see 5. 2.
[2] He did, however, have a villa, as we see from Cicero, *ad Att.* xii. 36. 2 and elsewhere.

of entertainment, at least in my opinion; and dinner was never served at his house without reading of some kind, so that his guests enjoyed the gratification of the mind as well as of the appetite. For he invited those whose tastes did not differ from his own. When that great addition was made to his fortune,[1] he made no change in his daily habits, none in his manner of life; in fact, he showed such moderation that he did not live without distinction on the two million sesterces which he received from his father, nor on ten millions more extravagantly than before; but he maintained the same elevation with both fortunes. He had no gardens, no expensive villa[2] in the suburbs or on the sea, no country estates in Italy except his properties at Arretium and Nomentum; all his income came from his possessions in Epirus and in the city of Rome. From this it can be seen that it was his habit to regulate his expenses, not by the amount of his wealth, but by reason.

15. He never lied, nor could he tolerate falsehood. Hence his affability was tempered with austerity and his dignity by good-nature, so that it was difficult to know whether his friends felt for him greater love or respect. Whenever anything was requested of him, he was circumspect in promising, because he thought that to make a promise that one could not keep was a mark of weakness rather than of generosity. He was also so careful in endeavouring to carry through what he had once consented to undertake, that he seemed to be attending, not to another's commission, but to an affair of his own. He never wearied of an enterprise which he had once undertaken; for he thought that his own reputation was involved, and there was nothing that he held dearer.

3 carius. Quo fiebat ut omnia Ciceronum, Catonis
Marci, Q. Hortensii, Auli Torquati, multorum praeterea equitum Romanorum negotia procuraret. Ex
quo iudicari poterat non inertia, sed iudicio fugisse
rei publicae procurationem.

16. Humanitatis vero nullum adferre maius testimonium possum, quam quod adulescens idem seni
Sullae fuit[1] iucundissimus, senex adulescenti M.
Bruto, cum aequalibus autem suis Q. Hortensio et
M. Cicerone sic vixit,[2] ut iudicare difficile sit cui
2 aetati fuerit aptissimus. Quamquam eum praecipue
dilexit Cicero, ut ne frater quidem ei Quintus carior
3 fuerit aut familiarior. Ei rei sunt indicio praeter
eos libros in quibus de eo facit mentionem, qui in
vulgus sunt editi, XVI[3] volumina epistularum, ab
consulatu eius usque ad extremum tempus ad
Atticum missarum; quae qui legat non multum
desideret historiam contextam eorum temporum.
4 Sic enim omnia de studiis principum, vitiis ducum,
mutationibus rei publicae perscripta sunt, ut nihil
in iis non appareat et facile existimari possit prudentiam quodam modo esse divinationem. Non
enim Cicero ea solum quae vivo se acciderunt futura
praedixit, sed etiam quae nunc usu veniunt cecinit
ut vates.

17. De pietate autem Attici quid plura com-
memorem? Cum hoc ipsum vere gloriantem audie-

---

[1] fuit, *Fleck.*; fuerit, *MSS.*
[2] vixit, *Fleck.*; vixerit *MSS.*
[3] XVI, *Aldus*; XI, *MSS.*

---

[1] Cato Uticensis, great-grandson of Cato the Censor. The
inversion of the names is unusual, but not unexampled. Nepos
seems to have tried to vary the forms of the names in this list—
if the text is sound.

Hence it was that he managed all the business affairs of the Ciceros, of Marcus Cato,[1] of Quintus Hortensius, of Aulus Torquatus, and of many Roman knights besides; and from this it may be judged that it was not from indolence, but from conviction that he held aloof from affairs of state.

16. To his amiability I can bring no stronger testimony than to say that when he was a young man he was greatly beloved by the aged Sulla, and when he was old, by the young Marcus Brutus; and with the men of his own age, Quintus Hortensius and Marcus Cicero, his relations were such that it is difficult to determine with what time of life he was most congenial. And yet it was Cicero who loved him more than all others, so much so that not even his brother Quintus was dearer to the orator or more intimate. This is shown, not only by those published works in which Cicero mentions him, but also by the sixteen volumes of letters sent to Atticus from the time of his consulship to the end of his life.[2] One who reads these does not feel great need of a connected history of those times; for such complete details are given of the rivalry of the chief men, the faults of the leaders, the changes of government, that there is nothing that they do not make clear, and it may readily appear that Cicero's foresight was almost divination. For he not only predicted the events that actually happened during his lifetime, but, like a seer, foretold those which are now being experienced.[3]

17. Why should I say more about Atticus' devotion to his family than this? He himself, in my hearing,

---

[2] Really, from 68 B.C., five years after the consulship, to 44 B.C., the year before Cicero's death.

[3] This, like many of Nepos' statements, is exaggerated.

rim in funere matris suae, quam extulit annorum
XC, cum esset [1] VII et LX, se numquam cum matre
in gratiam redisse, numquam cum sorore fuisse in
2 simultate, quam prope aequalem habebat. Quod
est signum aut nullam umquam inter eos queri-
moniam intercessisse, aut hunc ea fuisse in suos
indulgentia, ut, quos amare deberet, irasci iis nefas
3 duceret. Neque id fecit natura solum, quamquam
omnes ei paremus, sed etiam doctrina; nam principum philosophorum ita percepta habuit praecepta,
ut iis ad vitam agendam, non ad ostentationem
uteretur.

18. Moris etiam maiorum summus imitator fuit
antiquitatisque amator, quam adeo diligenter habuit
cognitam, ut eam totam in eo volumine exposuerit
2 quo magistratus ordinavit.[2] Nulla enim lex neque
pax neque bellum neque res illustris est populi
Romani, quae non in eo suo tempore sit notata, et,
quod difficillimum fuit, sic familiarum originem
subtexuit, ut ex eo clarorum virorum propagines
3 possimus cognoscere. Fecit hoc idem separatim
in aliis libris, ut M. Bruti rogatu Iuniam familiam
a stirpe ad hanc aetatem ordine enumeraverit,
notans qui [3] a quoque ortus, quos honores quibusque
4 temporibus cepisset; pari modo Marcelli Claudii de
Marcellorum, Scipionis Cornelii et Fabii Maximi

---

[1] cum ipse esset, *Dietsch.*
[2] ordinavit, *J. G. Voss*; ornavit, *MSS.*
[3] quis, *Wölfflin*; but cf. xvii. 1. 3 (*Nipp.-W.*).

---

[1] This is the work referred to in xxiii. 13. 1, *in suo Annali.*
It was published in 47 B.C. It gave a history of Rome, probably to 49 B.C., with the names of the curule magistrates of
each year.

justly prided himself at the funeral of his mother, whom he buried at the age of ninety, being himself sixty-seven, that he had never had occasion to seek a reconciliation with his mother, and had never quarrelled with his sister, who was about his own age. That is an indication either that no cause of complaint ever arose among them, or else that he was so indulgent towards them as to think it impious to get angry with those whom it was his duty to love. And this conduct was due, not only to Nature, although we all obey her, but also to training; for he had so thoroughly mastered the precepts of the great philosophers, that he made use of them in the conduct of his life and not merely for display.

18. He was a great imitator of the customs of the men of old and a lover of the early times, of which he had such a thorough knowledge that he gave a full account of them in the work in which he set down the chronological order of the magistrates.[1] For there is no law, no treaty of peace, no war, no illustrious deed of the Roman people, which is not mentioned in that work at its proper date, and—a most difficult task—he has so worked out the genealogies of the families, that from it we can learn the descendants of our famous men. He has treated this same subject by itself in other books; for example, at the request of Marcus Brutus he gave an account of the Junii in order, from their origin down to our own time, noting the parentage of each member of the family and the offices which he had held, with their dates. He did the same at the request of Claudius Marcellus for the Marcelli, at that of Cornelius Scipio [2] and

[2] Scipio Africanus the younger, who was an Aemilius adopted by a Scipio.

Fabiorum et Aemiliorum. Quibus libris nihil potest
esse dulcius iis qui aliquam cupiditatem habent
notitiae clarorum virorum.

5 Attigit quoque poeticen, credimus, ne eius expers
esset suavitatis. Namque versibus [1] qui honore
rerumque gestarum amplitudine ceteros populi
6 Romani praestiterunt exposuit ita, ut sub singulorum
imaginibus facta magistratusque eorum non amplius
quaternis quinisque [2] versibus descripserit; quod
vix credendum sit tantas res tam breviter potuisse
declarari. Est etiam unus liber Graece confectus,
de consulatu Ciceronis.

19. Hactenus Attico vivo edita a nobis sunt.
Nunc, quoniam fortuna nos superstites ei esse voluit,
reliqua persequemur et, quantum potuerimus, rerum
exemplis lectores docebimus, sicut supra signifi-
cavimus, suos cuique mores plerumque conciliare
2 fortunam. Namque hic, contentus ordine equestri
quo erat ortus, in adfinitatem pervenit imperatoris,
Divi filii, cum iam ante familiaritatem eius esset
consecutus nulla alia re quam elegantia vitae, qua
ceteros ceperat principes civitatis dignitate pari,
3 fortuna humiliores. Tanta enim prosperitas Caesarem est consecuta, ut nihil ei non tribuerit fortuna
quod cuiquam ante detulerit, et conciliarit quod
4 nemo adhuc civis Romanus quivit consequi. Nata

---

[1] namque de viris, *Halm*; namque versibus de iis, *Nipp.*
[2] quinisve, *Bosius.*

---

[1] The *Imagines* of Varro was a similar work, and the so-called
epitaphs in Gellius i. 24 are believed by some to have come
from Varro's book. At any rate, these and the epitaphs of the
Scipios give an idea of what could be said of a man in four or
five lines.

Fabius Maximus for the Fabii and the Aemilii.
There can be no more agreeable reading than these
books for those who have any desire to know the
history of distinguished men.

He also dipped into poetry; in order, I suppose,
to have a taste of its charm. For he celebrated in
verse those men who in distinction and in the greatness of their exploits surpassed the rest of the Roman
people, recording under the portrait of each of them
his deeds and his honours in not more than four or
five verses; this he did so well that it could hardly
be believed that such important events could be
described so briefly.[1] There is also a single book
of his written in Greek, on Cicero's consulship.

19. Here ends what I wrote during the lifetime of
Atticus.[2] Now, since it was Fortune's decree that I
should survive him, I will finish the account, and so
far as I can, will show my readers by examples that
as a rule—as I indicated above [3]—it is the character
of every man that determines his fortune. Thus,
although Atticus was content with the equestrian
rank to which he was born, he attained relationship by marriage with the emperor, son of the
deified Julius, after having previously won his friendship through no other cause than the refinement of
his life, by which he had charmed other great men,
of equal worth but of less lofty estate. For such
prosperity attended Caesar, that Fortune refused
him nothing which she had conferred on anyone else
and granted him what up to our time no other Roman
citizen has been able to gain. Furthermore, Atticus

[2] Chapters 19 and 20 were added in the second edition;
see Introd. p. xi.
[3] See 11. 6.

est autem Attico neptis ex Agrippa, cui virginem
filiam conlocarat. Hanc Caesar vix anniculam Ti.
Claudio Neroni, Drusilla nato, privigno suo, despon-
dit; quae coniunctio necessitudinem eorum sanxit,
familiaritatem reddidit frequentiorem.

20. Quamvis ante haec sponsalia non solum cum
ab urbe abesset, numquam ad suorum quemquam
litteras misit quin Attico scriberet quid ageret, in
primis quid legeret quibusque in locis et quam diu
2 esset moraturus, sed etiam cum esset in urbe et
propter infinitas suas occupationes minus saepe quam
vellet Attico frueretur, nullus dies temere intercessit [1] quo non ad eum scriberet, cum modo aliquid
de antiquitate ab eo requireret, cum modo [2] aliquam
quaestionem poeticam ei proponeret, interdum
3 iocans eius verbosiores eliceret epistulas. Ex quo
accidit, cum aedis Iovis Feretrii in Capitolio, ab
Romulo constituta, vetustate atque incuria detecta
prolaberetur, ut Attici admonitu Caesar eam reficien-
4 dam curaret. Neque vero a M. Antonio minus
absens litteris colebatur, adeo ut accurate ille ex
ultumis terris [3] quid ageret curae sibi haberet
5 certiorem facere Atticum. Hoc quale sit, facilius
existimabit is qui iudicare poterit quantae sit sapien-
tiae eorum retinere usum benevolentiamque, inter
quos maximarum rerum non solum aemulatio, sed
obtrectatio tanta intercedebat, quantam fuit intercedere [4] necesse inter Caesarem atque Antonium,

---

[1] intercessit, *Lambin and Cod. Schotti*; intercesserit, *the
other MSS.*

[2] cum modo, *Leid.*; quo mo, *A*; quo non, *the other
MSS.*

[3] ex ultumis (ultimis, *Roth*) terris, *Aldus*; exul tum (cum,
B H) his terris, *A B H*; exul cum litteris, *F R.*

had a grand-daughter by Agrippa, to whom he had
united his daughter in her first marriage. This
grand-daughter, when she was barely a year old,
Caesar betrothed to his stepson Tiberius Claudius
Nero, son of Drusilla, a union which sealed the friendship of the ruler with Atticus and made their intercourse more frequent.

20. Even before this betrothal, when Octavian was
absent from the city, he never sent a letter to any
one of his friends without letting Atticus know what
he was doing, in particular what he was reading, where
he was going, and how long he intended to stay; and
even when he was in Rome, but because of his count-
less engagements could not enjoy Atticus' society as
often as he wished, hardly even a single day passed
that he did not write to him, now asking some question
about ancient history, now putting before him some
difficult passage in the poets, sometimes in jesting
fashion trying to induce him to write longer letters.
It was owing to that intimacy that when the temple
of Jupiter Feretrius, which had been built on the
Capitol by Romulus, through lapse of time and neglect
was without a roof, and was falling into ruin, Caesar
was led by Atticus' advice to have it restored. Mark
Antony too, although far away, carried on a corre-
spondence with Atticus, and even took pains to send
him word from the ends of the earth of what he was
doing. What this means will more easily be understood by one who can judge how great tact it requires
to retain the intimacy and good-will of men who were
not only rivals in affairs of the greatest importance,
but also such enemies as Caesar and Antony inevit-

---

⁴ intercedere, *Aldus*; incidere, *MSS.*, *omitted by Bosius.*

cum se uterque principem non solum urbis Romae,
sed orbis terrarum esse cuperet.

21. Tali modo cum VII et LXX annos complesset
atque ad extremam senectutem non minus dignitate
quam gratia fortunaque crevisset—multas enim
hereditates nulla alia re quam bonitate consecutus
est [1]—tantaque prosperitate usus esset [2] valetudinis,
2 ut annis triginta medicina non indiguisset, nactus
est morbum, quem initio et ipse et medici con-
tempserunt; nam putarunt esse tenesmon, cui
3 remedia celeria faciliaque proponebantur. In hoc
cum tres menses sine ullis doloribus, praeterquam
quos ex curatione capiebat consumpsisset, subito
tanta vis morbi in imum [3] intestinum prorupit, ut
extremo tempore per lumbos fistulae puris eruperint.
4   Atque hoc priusquam ei accideret, postquam in
dies dolores accrescere febresque accessisse sensit,
Agrippam generum ad se accersi iussit et cum eo
L. Cornelium Balbum Sextumque Peducaeum.
5 Hos ut venisse vidit, in cubitum innixus, " Quantam,"
inquit, " curam diligentiamque in valetudine mea
tuenda hoc tempore adhibuerim, cum vos testes
habeam, nihil necesse est pluribus verbis com-
memorare. Quibus quoniam, ut spero, satisfeci,
me nihil reliqui fecisse quod ad sanandum me
pertineret, reliquum est ut egomet mihi consulam.
Id vos ignorare nolui; nam mihi stat alere morbum
6 desinere. Namque his diebus quidquid cibi sumpsi,

---

1 est, *added by Fleckeisen*, *before* consecutus, *Lambin.*
2 esset, *Lambin*; est, *MSS.*
3 imum, *Ascensius*; unum, *MSS.*

ably became, when each desired to be the ruler, not only of the city of Rome, but of the whole world.

21. In this fashion Atticus completed seventy-seven years, and up to that advanced age increased in dignity, as well as in importance and fortune—for he acquired many inheritances through no other cause than his good qualities. He also enjoyed such excellent health that for thirty years he required no medical treatment. But just at that time he fell ill of a complaint of which at first both he himself and his physicians made light; for they thought it was a dysentery, for which speedy and easy remedies were usually available. When he had suffered from this trouble for three months without any pain except what was caused by his treatment, suddenly such a violent form of the disease attacked his rectum, that finally fistulas discharging pus broke out through the lower part of his back.

Even before this occurred, feeling a daily increase of pain attended with fever, he gave orders that his son-in-law Agrippa should be summoned, and with him Lucius Cornelius Balbus and Sextus Peducaeus. As soon as he saw that they had arrived, raising himself upon his elbow, he said: "How much care and attention I have devoted to trying to restore my health at this time, it is not necessary for me to tell you at more length, since you have been witnesses to my efforts. Having by these, as I hope, satisfied you that I have left nothing undone which would tend to restore me, it remains for me to consider my own welfare. I did not wish you to be ignorant of my purpose; for I am resolved to cease to nourish my malady. As a matter of fact, whatever food I have taken during these last days, by prolonging my

ita produxi vitam ut auxerim dolores sine spe salutis.
Qua re a vobis peto, primum ut consilium probetis
meum, deinde ne frustra dehortando impedire
conemini.''

22. Hac oratione habita, tanta constantia vocis
atque vultus, ut non ex vita, sed ex domo in domum
2 videretur migrare, cum quidem Agrippa eum flens
atque osculans oraret atque obsecraret ne id [1] quod
natura cogeret ipse quoque sibi acceleraret,[2] et,
quoniam tum quoque posset temporibus superesse,
se sibi suisque reservaret, preces eius taciturna sua
3 obstinatione depressit. Sic cum biduum cibo se
abstinuisset, subito febris decessit leviorque morbus
esse coepit. Tamen propositum nihilo setius peregit
itaque die quinto postquam id consilium inierat,
pridie Kal. Apriles Cn. Domitio C. Sosio consulibus
4 decessit. Elatus est in lecticula, ut ipse praescrip-
serat, sine ulla pompa funeris, comitantibus omnibus
bonis, maxima vulgi frequentia. Sepultus est iuxta
viam Appiam ad quintum lapidem in monumento
Q. Caecilii, avunculi sui.

FRAGMENTA

1. Verba ex epistula Corneliae Gracchorum matris
ex libro Corneli Nepotis de Latinis Historicis ex-
cerpta.[3]

1. Dices pulchrum esse inimicos ulcisci. Id neque
maius neque pulchrius cuiquam atque mihi esse

---

[1] ne id, *Lambin;* ne ad id, *MSS.*
[2] *A and B have a blank space of about half a line after*
acceleraret.
[3] *Cod. Gif., according to Savaro and Patavius.*

---

[1] For the meaning of *bonis,* see note 1, p. 304.

life has increased my suffering without hope of a cure. Therefore I beg you, first, that you approve my resolution; then, that you do not try by useless exhortations to shake it."

22. When he had finished this speech with such firmness of voice and expression that he seemed, not to be quitting life, but moving from one dwelling to another, Agrippa for his part with tears and kisses begged and implored him not to hasten by his own act the decree of nature, but since even then it was possible that he might survive the crisis, to preserve his life for his own sake and that of his loved ones; but Atticus discouraged his prayers by his obstinate silence. Accordingly, when he had abstained from food for two days, on a sudden the fever abated and the disease began to be less violent. Nevertheless, he persisted in his resolution, and so died, on the fifth day after he had made his decision, which was the thirty-first of March, in the consulship of Gnaeus 32 B.C. Domitius and Gaius Sosius. He was carried to the grave in a modest litter, as he himself had directed, without any funeral procession, but attended by all the good citizens [1] and a great throng of the commons. He was buried near the fifth milestone of the Appian Way in the tomb of Quintus Caecilius, his maternal uncle.

FRAGMENTS

1. Extract from a letter of Cornelia, mother of the Gracchi, from the book of Cornelius Nepos on the Latin Historians.

1. You will say that it is glorious to take vengeance on one's enemies. That seems to no one greater and more glorious than it does to me, but only if it can be

videtur, sed si liceat re publica salva ea persequi.
Sed quatenus id fieri non potest, multo tempore
multisque partibus inimici nostri non peribunt, atque
uti nunc sunt erunt potius quam res publica pro-
fligetur atque pereat.

Eadem alio loco.

2. Verbis conceptis deierare ausim, praeterquam
qui Tiberium Gracchum necarunt, neminem inimicum [1] tantum molestiae tantumque laboris, quantum
te ob has res, mihi tradidisse; quem oportebat
omnium eorum [2] quos antehac habui liberos partis [3]
tolerare atque curare ut quam minimum sollicitudinis
in senecta haberem, utique quaecumque ageres, ea
velles maxime mihi placere atque uti nefas haberes
rerum maiorum adversum meam sententiam quicquam facere, praesertim mihi cui parva pars vitae
superest. Ne id quidem tam breve spatium potest
opitulari, quin et mihi adversere et rem publicam
profliges? Denique quae pausa erit? ecquando
desinet familia nostra insanire? ecquando modus
ei rei haberi poterit? ecquando desinemus et habentes et praebentes molestiis insistere? [4] ecquando
perpudescet miscenda atque perturbanda re publica?
Sed si omnino id fieri non potest, ubi ego mortua ero,
petito tribunatum; per me facito quod lubebit,
cum ego non sentiam. Ubi mortua ero, parentabis
mihi et invocabis deum parentem. In eo tempore
non pudet te eorum deum preces expetere, quos
vivos atque praesentes relictos atque desertos

---

[1] inimicum, *omitted by Gif.* (?).   [2] meorum, *Roth.*
[3] partis eorum, *MSS.*; *omitted in ed. of Savaro.*
[4] insistere, *Nipp.*; desistere, *MSS.*

---

[1] For *multis partibus = multo,* see Cic. *Epist.* i. 2. 2, *multis
partibus plures*; and viii. 9. 3.
[2] With *habentes* and *praebentes* supply *molestias* from
molestiis.

done without injury to one's country. But inasmuch as that cannot be, long and surely [1] shall our enemies not perish but remain as they now are, rather than that our country should be ruined and perish.

Another passage from the same letter:

2. I would not hesitate to take oath in set terms that except for the murderers of Tiberius Gracchus no enemy has caused me so much annoyance and trouble as you have because of these events—you who ought, as the only survivor of all the children that I have had in the past, to have taken their place and to have seen to it that I had the least possible anxiety in my old age; you, who ought to have wished that all your actions should above all be agreeable to me, and should consider it impious to do anything of great importance contrary to my advice, especially when I have so brief a portion of my life left. Cannot even that brief span aid me in preventing you from opposing me and ruining your country? Finally, where will you make an end? Will our family ever cease from madness? Will it ever be possible to observe moderation? [2] Shall we ever cease to insist on causing and suffering trouble? Shall we ever be ashamed of embroiling and harassing our country? [3] But if any change is impossible, sue for the tribunate after I am dead; do whatever you like, so far as I am concerned, when I shall no longer be aware of it. When I am no more, you will offer funerary sacrifices in my honour, and invoke the god of our family. Are you not ashamed at that time to ask for the prayers of those as gods, whom you abandoned and deserted when they were alive and present with you? [4] May great

---

[3] *Miscenda atque perturbanda re publica* is ablative of cause; for the construction cf. Plautus, *Bacch.* 379.

[4] The *di parentes* were the shades of deceased ancestors.

habueris? Ne ille sirit Iuppiter te ea perseverare
nec tibi tantam dementiam venire in animum. Et
si perseveras, vereor ne in omnem vitam tantum
laboris culpa tua recipias uti in nullo tempore tute
tibi placere possis.

2. Cornelius Nepos in libro De Historicis Latinis
de laude Ciceronis.[1]

1. Non ignorare debes unum hoc genus Latinarum
litterarum adhuc non modo non respondere Graeciae,
sed omnino rude atque inchoatum morte Ciceronis
relictum. Ille enim fuit unus qui potuerit et etiam
debuerit historiam digna voce pronuntiare, quippe
qui oratoriam eloquentiam rudem a maioribus acceptam perpoliverit, philosophiam ante eum incomptam
Latinam sua confirmarit[2] oratione. Ex quo dubito,
interitu eius utrum res publica an historia magis
doleat.

Idem.

2. Locuples ac divina natura, quo maiorem sui
pareret admirationem ponderatioraque sua essent
beneficia, neque uni omnia dare nec rursus cuiquam
omnia voluit negare.

3. Nepos Cornelius ad . . . Ciceronem ita scribit.[3]
Tantum abest ut ego magistram esse putem vitae
philosophiam beataeque vitae perfectricem, ut nullis
magis existimem opus esse magistros vivendi quam
plerisque qui in ea disputanda versantur. Video
enim magnam partem eorum qui in schola de pudore
et continentia praecipiant argutissime, eosdem in
omnium ibidinum cupiditatibus vivere.[4]

---

[1] *On the first page of Cod. Guelferbytanus Gudianus,* 278,
*saec. xiii, of Cicero's "Philippics." Apparently formed part
of the preface of the book " De Historicis Latinis."*

[2] confirmarit, *Lieberkühn;* confirmavit, *MSS.*

[3] *Lactantius, Inst. Div. iii. 15. 10.*

[4] *See for other brief quotations Suetonius and Gellius, Index,
s.v. Cornelius Nepos.*

Jupiter forbid you to persist in that course or to allow
such madness to enter your mind. But if you do
persist, I fear that through your own fault you may
bring such trouble upon your whole life that you can
never make peace with yourself.

2. Eulogy of Cicero from the book of Cornelius
Nepos on the Latin Historians.

1. You ought not to be unaware that this [1] is the
only branch of Latin literature that even in my own
time cannot be compared with what the Greeks
accomplished, and that it was left wholly rude and unfinished by the death of Cicero. For he was the only
man who could, or even sought to, give history a
worthy utterance, since he highly polished the rude
eloquence handed down from our forefathers, and
gave Latin philosophy, which before his time was
uncouth, the finish of his style. Which leads me to
doubt whether his loss brought greater grief to our
country or to history.

2. Another extract from the same :

Bountiful and divine mother Nature, in order to
win greater admiration and make a better distribution of her gifts, has chosen neither to give everything to one man, nor, on the contrary, to refuse
everything to anyone.

3. Cornelius Nepos wrote as follows to Cicero :

So far am I from thinking that philosophy can teach
how to live and is the perfecter of a happy life, that
I believe that none have more need of learning how
to live than the greater number of those who are
engaged in teaching philosophy. In fact, I observe
that a great part of those same men who in the schools
argue most subtly about moderation and self-restraint
pass their lives a prey to all the passions.

[1] Namely, history.

INDEX [1]

OF PROPER NAMES

[1] The references are to the number of the Life, followed by the chapter and section; e.g. X. 5. 1 = Life of Dion, chapter 5, section 1.

INDEX

Andocides, VII. 3. 2 (*bis*). A celebrated Athenian orator, also general in the time of the Peloponnesian war

Anicia, XXV. 2. 1

Annales, XXIII. 13. 1. A work of T. Pomponius Atticus; *see* note 1, p. 684.

Antigenes, XVIII. 5. 1; 7. 1

Antigonus, XVIII. 5. 2, 7 (*bis*); 7. 1; 8. 1, 4; 9. 1, 3, 5; 10. 2–4; 11. 3; 12. 1, 4; 13. 1, 3, 4; XXI. 3. 1, 2. One of Alexander's greatest generals. He became king of Syria and was slain in the battle of Ipsus, 301 B.C.

Antiochus, XXIII. 2. 1; 7. 6; 8. 1–3; 9. 1. Antiochus III, or the Great, king of Syria

Antipater, XVIII. 2. 2; 3. 3; 4. 3; 5. 1; XIX. 2. 2. A friend and general of Philip and later of Alexander the Great. After the latter's death he made himself king of Macedonia. He died in 319 B.C.

Antonius, M., XXV. 8. 5, 6; 9. 2 (*bis*), 3, 6; 10. 1, 4; 12. 2; 20. 4, 5. Mark Antony, the triumvir

Apollo, II. 2. 7; IV. 1. 3

Apollocrates, X. 5. 6. Eldest son of Dionysius the younger, tyrant of Syracuse

Appenninus, XXIII. 4. 2

Appia, via, XXV. 22. 4. The Appian Way, running in a south-easterly direction from Rome to Capua

Aprilis, Kalendae, XXV. 22. 3. The first day of April

Apulia, XXIII. 4. 4. A district in the south-eastern part of Italy

Arcades, XV. 6. 1, 2. The people of Arcadia

Arcadia, VII. 10. 5. A district of Greece, situated in the centre of the Peloponnesus

Archias, XVI. 3. 2. Boeotarch at Thebes in 379 B.C.

Archinus, XVI. 3. 2

Arete, X. 1. 1 (*bis*); 4. 3; 8. 4. Daughter of Dionysius the elder, tyrant of Syracuse, and wife of Dion

Argi, *see* Argos

Argilius, IV. 4. 1, 4, 5; 5. 1. A native of Argilus, a city of Thrace near the Strymonian Gulf

Argivi, XV. 6. 1 (*bis*). The inhabitants of Argolis

Argos, only nom. and acc. neut., also Argi, -orum, m. pl., II. 8. 1, 3; XXI. 2. 2. The chief city of Argolis in the north-eastern part of the Peloponnesus

Ariobarzanes, XIII. 1. 3; XIV. 2. 5; 5. 6; 10. 1. Satrap of Lydia, Ionia and Phrygia under Artaxerxes II

Aristides (III), III. 1–4; 2. 3; 3. 1

Aristomache, X. 1. 1; 8. 4. Sister of Dion and wife of Dionysius the elder

Armenii, XIV. 8. 2. Inhabitants of Armenia, a country south of the Caucasus Mountains

Arretinum praedium, XXV. 14. 3. An estate at Arretium, a town in the eastern part of Etruria; modern Arezzo

Arsidaeus, XIV. 6. 1. Son of Datames

Artabanus, XXI. 1. 5. Brother of Darius I.

Artabazus, IV. 2. 5; 4. 1. A Persian satrap

Artaphernes, I. 4. 1. Nephew of Darius Hystaspis; one of the two commanders of the Persians at Marathon

Artaxerxes I, Macrochir, II. 9. 1; 10. 2; XXI. 1. 3, 4. Son of Xerxes; king of Persia from 465 to 424 B.C.

Artaxerxes II, Mnemon, IX. 2. 2; 3. 1; XI. 2. 4; XII. 2. 3; XIV. 1. 1; 5. 1; 7. 1; 8. 6; XV. 4. 1; XVII. 2. 1; XXI. 1. 3, 4. Son of Darius Nothus; king of Persia from 405 to 362 B.C.

Artemisium, II. 3. 2, 4. A promontory at the north-eastern end of the island of Euboea

Asia, I. 3. 1, 2, 4; 4. 1, 2; II. 5. 1–3; 9. 1, 3; 10. 2; VI. 2. 2; VII. 5. 6; 7. 1; 9. 3; 10. 1; IX. 2. 2, 3; XVII. 2. 1, 2; 3. 6; 4. 3; XVIII. 3. 2; 6. 1; 8. 2; XXIII. 8. 4; 12. 1; 13. 2; XXV. 4. 1; 6. 4. Asia, referring to Asia as distinguished from Europe, to Asia Minor, or to the Roman province

Aspendii, XIV. 8. 2. The people of Aspendos, a town of Pamphylia

Aspis, XIV. 4. 1, 2, 4, 5; 5. 1. A satrap of Cataonia in southern Cappadocia

Athamanes, XIII. 2. 1. A people of Epirus dwelling near the boundary of Acarnania and Aetolia

INDEX

INDEX

Capitolium, XXV. 20. 3. The Capitol, a temple on the south-western part of the Capitoline hill at Rome, dedicated to Jupiter, Juno and Minerva; also the hill on which the temple stood

Cappadoces, XIV. 8. 2. The people of Cappadocia

Cappadocia, XIV. 1. 1; 4. 1; 5. 6; 7. 1; XVIII. 2. 2; 13. 4. A country in the eastern part of Asia Minor

Captiani, XIV. 8. 2. An unknown people of Asia

Capua, XXIII. 5. 1. The principal city of Campania, 136 miles south-east of Rome

Car, XIV. 1. 1; Cares, I. 2. 5. The people of Caria

Cardaces, XIV. 8. 2. A force of mercenaries recruited from the barbarians of the Persian empire. The word was said to mean "The Valiant"

Cardianus, XVIII. 1. 1. A native of Cardia, a town of the Thracian Chersonese

Caria, XVII. 3. 1, 5. A province in the south-western part of Asia Minor, south of Lydia

Carthaginienses, see Karthaginienses

Carthago, see Karthago

Cassandrus, XVIII. 13. 3; XIX. 2. 4; 3. 1, 2. Son of Antipater. He became ruler of Greece and Macedonia after the death of his father and died in 279 B.C.

Cassius (Longinus), O., XXV. 8. 1, 5; 11. 2. The author of the conspiracy against Caesar

Cataonia, XIV. 4. 1. A division of southern Cappadocia, afterwards a part of Cappadocia

Cato, see Porcius

Catullus, see Valerius

Catulus, see Lutatius

Centenius, O., XXIII. 4. 3. A Roman praetor, defeated by Hannibal in 216 B.C.

Ceraunus, see Ptolemaeus

Cethegus, see Cornelius

Chabrias (XII), XII. 1. 1, 3; 2. 1, 3; 3. 1 (bis), 3; 4. 1 (bis); XIII. 4. 4; XV. 4. 3

Chalcioicos, IV. 5. 2. A surname of Minerva; see note 3, p. 420.

Chalcis, XIII. 3. 5. The chief city of the island of Euboea

Chaones, XIII. 2. 1. The people of Chaonia, a country in north-western Epirus

Chares, XII. 3. 4 (bis); XIII. 3. 1, 3; XIX. 2. 3. An Athenian general of the time of Philip II of Macedon. He apparently fell in the battle of Chaeronea, 338 B.C.

Charon, XVI. 2. 5. A Theban

Chersonesus, I. 1. 1, 4, 6; 2. 4 (bis); 8. 3; see note 2, p. 372.

Chius, XII. 4. 1. An island in the Aegean Sea, near the coast of Ionia

Cicero and Cicerones, see Tullius

Cilices, XIV. 8. 2. The people of Cilicia

Cilicia, VIII. 4.4; XIV. 1. 1; 4. 1, 4. A province in the south-eastern part of Asia Minor. Ciliciae portae, XIV. 7. 2. A mountain-pass in the eastern part of Cilicia, leading through the Taurus Mountains to Cappadocia

Cimon, I. 1. 1. Father of Miltiades

Cimon (V), Praef. 4; V. 1. 1 (bis), 3; 2. 1. Son of Miltiades

Cinnanus, -a, -um, adj. from (L. Cornelius) Cinna, the colleague of Marius in his contest with Sulla; partes, XXV. 2. 2; tumultus, XXV. 2. 2; see note

Citium, V. 3. 4. A seaport in the south-eastern part of the island of Cyprus

Clastidium, XXIII. 4. 1. A town in Cisalpine Gaul

Claudius Marcellus, O., XXV. 18. 4. Consul in 50 B.C.

Claudius Marcellus, M., XXIII. 5. 3; XXIV. 1. 2. Five times consul, first in 222 B.C., when he won the spolia opima; he captured Syracuse in 212 B.C., and fell in battle with Hannibal in 208

Claudius Marcellus, M., XXIII. 7. 6; 13. 1. Consul in 196 and 183 B.C.

Claudius Nero, O., XXIV. 1. 2. Consul in 207 B.C., when he defeated Hasdrubal at the Metaurus river

Claudius Nero, Ti., XXV. 19. 4. Emperor of Rome from 14 to 37 A.D.

Cleon, VI. 3. 5. A rhetorician of Halicarnassus in Caria

336

INDEX

337

INDEX

Delphi, I. 1. 2; II. 2. 6; IV. 1. 3. A town in Phocis in central Greece, seat of the oracle of Apollo

Delphicus, -a, -um, adj. from Delphi: *deus*, IV. 5. 5; *oraculum*, VI. 3. 2

Delus, III. 3. 1. Delos, the centre of the Cyclades in the Aegean Sea

Demades, XIX. 2. 2. An Athenian orator contemporary with Demosthenes

Demaenetus, XX. 5. 3. A Syracusan

Demetrius Phalereus, I. 6. 4; XIX. 3. 1, 2. Demetrius of Phalerum, famous as orator, statesman, philosopher and poet. He lived from 345 to about 283 B.C., and governed Athens for Cassander from 317 to 307

Demetrius (Poliorcetes), XXI. 3. 1, 3. Demetrius, the Taker of Cities. He made himself ruler of Macedonia in 294 B.C., but was deposed and imprisoned by Seleucus; he died in 284 B.C.

Demosthenes, XIX. 2. 2, 3. The celebrated Athenian orator (381–322 B.C.)

Dercylus, XIX. 2. 4. An Athenian envoy

Diana, XXIII. 9. 2

Dinon, IX. 5. 4. The author of a history of Persia; he lived about 350 B.C.

Diomedon, XV. 4. 1, 2, 4. A man of Cyzicus

Dion (X), X. 1. 1 (*ter*), 2, 4; 2. 2, 3 (*ter*), 4, 5; 3. 1 (*bis*); 4. 1–3; 5. 1, 3, 5, 6; 6. 3, 4; 8. 1, 3–5; 9. 1, 3, 6; 10. 1; XX. 2. 1

Dionysii, X. 1. 1; XX. 2. 2

Dionysius (Maior), X. 1, 3 (*bis*), 5; 2. 1, 4; XX. 2. 2; XXI. 2. 2. Tyrant of Syracuse from 405 to 367 B.C.

Dionysius (Minor), X. 1. 1; 2. 5; 3. 1 (*bis*), 3; 4. 2; 5. 1, 4, 5, 6 (*bis*); XX. 2. 1 (*bis*), 3 (*ter*); 3. 3. Tyrant of Syracuse from 367 to 344 B.C.

Dionysius, XV. 2. 1. A musician of Thebes

Dodona, VI. 3. 2. A city of Epirus with a celebrated oracle of Zeus (Jupiter)

Dolopes, V. 2. 5. A Thessalian people, settled also in the island of Scyrus

Domitius, Cn., XXV. 22. 3. Consul in 32 B.C.

Drusilla, XXV. 19. 4. Surname of Livia Drusilla, wife of the emperor Augustus and mother of Tiberius

E

Elis, VII. 4. 4. A division of Greece, in the north-western part of the Peloponnesus

Elpinice, V. 1. 2, 4. Daughter of Miltiades; sister and wife of Conon

Ennius, Q., XXIV. 1. 4. The celebrated Roman epic and dramatic poet (239–169 B.C.)

Epaminondas (XV), Praef. 1; XI. 2. 5; XV. 1. 1, 3; 4. 1; 5. 3; 6. 3; 7. 1, 3, 5; 8. 1, 3; 9. 1, 3; 10. 3, 4; XVI. 4. 1 (*bis*), 2, 3; 5. 2; XVII. 6. 1

Ephesus, II. 8. 7; XVII. 3, 2. A city on the western coast of Asia Minor, famous for its temple of Artemis (Diana)

Epirotes, sing. (sc. *rex*), XXI. 2. 2. Of Epirus, Epirote; plur., XIII. 2.1. The people of Epirus

Epiroticae possessiones, XXV. 14. 3

Epirus, XVIII. 6. 1; XXV. 8. 6; 11. 1, 2. A country north-west of central Greece and west of Thessaly

Eretria, I. 4. 2. A city of Euboea

Eretriensis, IV. 2. 2. A native of Eretria

Eryx, XXII. 1. 2, 5. A mountain of north-western Sicily, famous for its temple of Venus

Etruria, XXIII. 4. 2. A country of Italy, north-west of Rome, modern Tuscany

Euagoras, XII. 2. 2. King of Salamis in Cyprus

Euboea, I. 4. 2; II. 3. 2, 3. A large island off the eastern coast of Boeotia and Locris

Eumenes (XVIII), XVIII. 1. 1; 2. 2, 4; 3. 3, 4; 4. 1–4; 5. 1; 6. 3, 5; 7. 3; 9. 1, 2; 10 1, 4; 11. 2, 3, 5; 12. 2; 13. 1, 2

Eumenes, XXIII. 10. 2, 3, 5; 11. 1–4. Eumenes II, king of Pergamum from 197 to 158 B.C.

Eumolpidae, VII. 4. 5; 6. 5. A family of priests at Athens, descendants of

INDEX

Eumolpus, the reputed founder of the Eleusinian mysteries

Euphiletus, XIX. 4. 3. An Athenian

Europa, I. 3. 1, 4; 4. 1; II. 2. 4; 5. 3; XII. 2. 1; XVII. 2. 1

Europaei adversarii, XVIII. 3. 2

Eurybiades, II. 4. 2. A Spartan admiral

Eurydice, XI. 3. 2. Mother of Philip II, king of Macedon

Eurysthenes, XVII. 1. 2; 7. 4. A king of Sparta

F

Fabiani milites, XI. 2. 4. Soldiers of Fabius, referring to Q. Fabius Maximus Cunctator; see note.

Fabii, XXV. 18. 4

Fabius Labeo, XXIII. 13. 1. Consul in 183 B.C.

Fabius Maximus (Cunctator), Q., XXIII. 5. 1, 2; XXIV. 1. 2. Appointed dictator in 217 B.C. after the battle at Lake Trasumenus; famous for his policy of delay in dealing with Hannibal

Fabius Maximus, Q., XXV. 18. 4. Consul in 45 B.C.

Falernus ager, XXIII. 5. 1. A district in north-western Campania and south-eastern Latium, famous for its wine

Feretrius, XXV. 20. 3. A surname of Jupiter, as God of Trophies

Flaccus, see Valerius

Flamininus, see Quintius

Flaminius, C., XXIII. 4. 3. Consul in 217 B.C.; defeated by Hannibal at Lake Trasumenus

Flavius, C., XXV. 8. 3. A friend of Brutus

Fregellae, XXIII. 7. 2. A city in south-eastern Latium on the river Liris

Fulvia, XXV. 9. 2, 4. Wife of Mark Antony

Furius, L., XXIII. 7. 6. Consul in 196 B.C.

G

Galba, see Sulpicius

Gallia, XXIII. 3. 4

Gellius Canus, Q., XXV. 10. 2, 4. A friend of Atticus

Geminus, see Servilius

Gongylus, IV. 2. 2. An Eretrian

Gortynii, XXIII. 9. 1, 4. The people of Gortyn, a city of Crete

Gracchus, see Sempronius

Graece, XXV. 4. 1 (bis); 18. 6. Adv. to Graecus

Graeci, I. 3. 4; IV. 4.4; VII. 2. 2; XI. 2. 4; XV. 1. 2. The Greeks

Graecia, Praef. 5, 7; I. 3. 3; 4. 1; 6. 3; II. 2. 4, 6; 3. 2; 4. 5; 5. 3; 7. 4, 6; 8. 2; 9. 4; 10. 2, 4; III. 1. 5; 2. 2, 3; IV. 1. 2; 2. 4; VI. 1. 3; VII. 9. 3; IX. 4. 4; 5. 2; XI. 2. 1, 3; XII. 1. 3; XIV. 8. 2; XV. 2. 3; 5. 4, 6 (bis); 8. 4; 10. 4; XVI. 2. 4; XVII. 2. 1; 4. 7; 5. 2 (bis), 3; XXI. 1. 3; Frag. 2. 1

Graecus, -a, -um, adj. to Graecia: civitas, VII. 7. 4; IX. 5. 2; gens, XXI. 1. 1; historici, X. 3. 2; lingua, I. 3. 2; VII. 2. 1; X. 1. 5; litterae, Praef. 2; XVI. 1. 1; XXIII. 13. 3; res, XXIV. 3. 2; sermo, XXIII. 13. 2; urbes, VII. 5. 6

Graii, Praef. 3; II. 9. 2; VII. 7. 4; XVIII. 1. 5. An old form equivalent to Graeci

Graius, -a, um, adj. to Graii: Hercules, XXIII. 3. 4.; saltus, XXIII. 3. 4

Grynium, VII. 9. 3. A town of Phrygia, famous for its temple of Apollo

H

Hadrumetum, XXIII. 6. 3, 4. A city of northern Africa, not far from Carthage

Haliartus, VI. 3. 4. A city of Boeotia, on Lake Copais

Halicarnasius, VI. 3. 5. A native of Halicarnassus, a city of Caria.

Hamilcar (XXII), XIII. 4. 5; XXI. 3. 5; XXII. 1. 1, 3; 2. 3; 3. 2, 3; 4. 1; XXIII. 1. 1; 2. 3. Father of Hannibal

Hammon, VI. 3. 2. A surname of Jupiter; really an Egyptian deity, Amon or Amun, identified with Jupiter by the Romans

Hannibal, XXII. 1. 1. Father of Hamilcar

Hannibal (XXIII), XIII. 4. 5; XXI. 3. 5; XXII. 3. 1, 3; 4. 3; XXIII. 1. 1 (bis); 2. 2 (bis); 3. 2; 7. 4, 6; 8. 1,

INDEX

340

INDEX

341

INDEX

(Manlius) Torquatus, L., XXV. 1. 4;
4. 5. Consul in 65 B.C.

(Manlius) Torquatus, A., XXV. 11. 2;
15. 3

Manlius Volso, Cn., XXIII. 13. 2.
Consul in 189 B.C.

Mantinea, XV. 9. 1. A city of Arcadia

Marathon, I. 4. 2. A plain on the
eastern coast of Attica

Marathonius, -a, -um, adj. from
Marathon: *pugna*, I. 6. 3; II. 2. 6;
tropaeum, II. 5. 3; *victoria*, II. 6. 3

Marcelli, XXV. 18. 4

Marcellus, *see* Claudius

Mardonius, III. 2. 1, 2; IV. 1, 2. Commander of the Persians at Plataea
in 479 B.C.

Marius, C., XXV. 1. 4; 2. 2. Son of
the famous Marius

Maximus, *see* Fabius

Massagetae, XXI. 1. 2. A nomadic
people of Scythia living in the plains
north-east of the Caspian Sea

Media, XVIII. 8. 1. A country of
Asia, on the southern coast of the
Caspian Sea

Medica vestis, IV. 3. 2

Medus, IV. 1. 2; *Medi*, XVIII. 8. 4;
Medi satellites, IV. 3. 2

Meneclides, XV. 5. 2, 5 (*ter*). A Theban
orator

Menelai portus, XVII. 8. 6. A harbour
on the northern coast of Africa,
between Egypt and Cyrenae, where
Menelaus, was said to have landed
on his way home from Troy

Menestheus, XI. 3. 4; XIII. 3. 2. Son
of Iphricrates

Mercurius, VII. 3. 2

Messena, XVI. 4. 3, or Messene, XV. 8. 5.
Capital of Messenia in the south-
western part of the Peloponnesus,
restored by Epaminondas in 369 B.C.

Micythus, XV. 4. 1 (*bis*), 3. A Theban
youth

Milesius, I. 3. 5. A native of Miletus,
a city on the western coast of Asia
Minor

Miltiades (I), I. 1. 1, 3, 4, 6; 3. 2, 6;
4. 4, 5; 5. 2; 6. 1, 3; 7. 1, 4; 8. 2,
4; II. 8. 1; V. 1. 1, 4

Minerva, IV. 5. 2; XVII. 4. 6

Minucius Rufus, M., XXIII. 5. 3.
Master of horse with Q. Fabius
Maximus

Minucius (Thermus), Q., XXIII. 8. 1.
Consul in 193 B.C.

Mithridates, XIV. 4. 5; 10. 1; 11. 2, 3.
An officer of Datames

Mithrobarzanes, XIV. 6. 3–5. Father-
in-law of Datames

Mnemon, *see* Artaxerxes II

Mocilla, *see* Iulius

Molossi, II. 8. 3. A people of Epirus

Munychia, VIII. 2. 5. A peninsula on
the coast of Attica near Athens,
forming a harbour also called Munychia

Mutina, XXV. 9. 1. A city of Cisalpine
Gaul, modern Modena

Mycale, V. 2. 2. A promontory on the
coast of Ionia opposite Samos

Mytilenaei, VIII. 4. 2. The people of
Mytilene, the principal city of the
island of Lesbos

Myus, II. 10. 3. A city of Caria, on
the river Meander

N

Naxus, II. 8. 6. Naxos, the largest of
the Cyclades

Nectanabis or Nectenebis, XII. 2. 1;
XVII. 8. 6. A king of Egypt in the
first half of the fourth century B.C.

Neocles, II. 1. 1, 2. Father of Themistocles

Neontichos, VII. 7. 4. A town of
Thrace on the Propontis

Neoptolemus, XVIII. 4. 1. One of
Alexander's generals

Neptunus, IV. 4. 4

Nero, *see* Claudius

Nicanor, XIX. 2. 4, 5; 3. 4. A Macedonian officer

Nicias, VII. 3. 1. An Athenian statesman and general at the time of the
Peloponnesian war

Nilus, XVIII. 5. 1. The Nile

Nisaeus, X. 1. 1. Son of Dionysius the
elder, of Syracuse

Nomentanum praedium, XXV. 14. 3.
An estate at Nomentum, a town in
the Sabine district north-east of
Rome

Nora, XVIII. 5. 3. A fortress on the
boundary between Lycaonia and
Cappadocia

Numidae, XXIII. 6. 4. Inhabitants of
Numidia in northern Africa

INDEX

343

INDEX

Persia, a country of Asia north of the Persian Gulf

Peucestes, XVIII. 7. 1. One of Alexander's body-guard

Phalereus, *see* Demetrius I

Phalericus portus, II. 6. 1. One of the seaports of Athens

Pharnabazus, VI. 4. 1 (*bis*), 3; VII. 9. 3; 10. 1, 2, 6; IX. 2. 1, 2; 3. 2; 4. 1, 2, 5; XIV. 3. 4, 5. A Persian satrap who governed the northwestern provinces of Asia Minor from 412 to 377 B.C.

Pherae, IX. 1. 1. A town of Messenia

Pheraeus, XVI. 5. 1. Of Pherae, a town in the eastern part of Thessaly

Phidippus, I. 4. 3. A famous Athenian courier

Philippense proelium, XXV. 11. 2. The battle at Philippi, a town of Macedonia, 42 B.C.

Philippus, XI. 3. 2; XIII. 3. 1; XVIII. 1, 4, 6; 6. 3: 13. 1; XIX. 1. 3; XXI. 2. 1 (*bis*). Philip II, king of Macedonia from 360 to 336 B.C.; father of Alexander the Great

Philippus, XXIII. 2. 1. Philip V, king of Macedonia from 220 to 197 B.C.

Philippus (Arrhidaeus), XIX. 3. 3. Illegitimate son of Philip II. He was made king of Macedonia in 323 B.C. as Philip III, and was put to death by Olympias in 317

Philistus, X. 3. 2, 3. An historian of Syracuse

Philocles, VII. 8. 1, 4. An Athenian general

Philostratus, X. 9. 2. A Syracusan

Phocion (XIX), XIX. 1. 1; 2. 4; 3. 1, 2 (*bis*); 4. 3

Phoebidas, XVI. 1. 2. A Spartan general

Phoenices, V. 2. 2; IX. 4. 2. Natives of Phoenicia on the eastern coast of the Mediterranean Sea

Phryges, XIV. 8. 2. Natives of Phrygia

Phrygia, VII. 9. 3; 10. 3; XIV. 2. 5; 8. 6; XVII. 3. 2; XVIII. 5. 3. An inland province in the western part of Asia Minor

Phyle, VIII. 2. 1. A fortress in Attica on the Boeotian frontier

Pilia, XXV. 3. 2. Wife of Atticus

Piraeus, II. 6. 1; VII. 6. 1, 3; VIII. 2. 5;

IX. 4. 5; XIX. 2. 4, 5; 3. 4; 4. 1. The principal seaport of Athens

Pisander, VII. 5, 3. An Athenian general

Pisander, IX. 4. 4. A Spartan general

Pisidae, XIV. 4. 4; 6. 1, 6, 7; 8. 2. Inhabitants of Pisidia, a mountainous country in the southern part of Asia Minor

Pisistratus, I. 8. 1. Tyrant at Athens for three periods between 560 and 527 B.C.

Pittacus, VIII. 4. 2. A sage of Mitylene, one of the Seven Wise Men of Greece

Plataeae, III. 2. 1; IV. 1. 2, 3. Plataea, a town in the southern part of Boeotia

Platacenses, I. 5. 1. The people of Plataea

Plato, VII. 2. 2; X. 2. 2, 3: 3. 1, 3. The celebrated Greek philosopher, who lived from 429 to about 348 B.C.

Poicile, I. 6. 3; *see* note

Poeni, XXII. 1. 2; 2. 3; XXIII. 7. 7; 8. 2; *Poenus*, XXIII. 10. 1. The Carthaginians, so called because of their Phoenician origin

Poenicum bellum, XXII. 1. 1; 4. 3; XXIV. 3. 3

Polybius, XXIII. 13. 1. A celebrated historian of Megalopolis in Arcadia, sent as a hostage to Rome in 169 B.C.

Polymnis, XV. 1. 1. Father of Epaminondas

Polyperchon, XIX. 3. 1–3. One of Alexander's generals

Pompeius (Magnus), Cn., XXV. 7. 1 (*bis*), 3. Pompey the Great

Pomponius Atticus, T., (XXV), Praef. 1; XXIII. 13. 1; XXIV. 3. 5; XXV. 1. 1; 2. 1; 4. 1, 2; 5. 3; 7. 3; 8. 3, 6; 9. 3, 4 (*bis*); 10. 1, 3–5; 12. 3, 5; 16. 3; 17. 1; 19. 1, 4; 20. 1–4

Pontus, XXIII. 10. 1. A country of north-eastern Asia Minor, south of the Pontus Euxinus, or Black Sea

Porcius Cato (Censorius), M. (XXIV), XXIV. 1. 1; 2. 3; 3. 5.

(Porcius) Cato (Uticensis), M., XXV. 15. 3. Great-grandson of Cato the Censor; he committed suicide at Utica in 46 B.C.

INDEX

Procles, XVII. 1. 2. Founders of one of the lines of Spartan kings

Propontis, VII. 9. 1. A sea between the Euxine and the Thracian Bosphorus, now called the Sea of Marmora

Proserpina, X. 8. 5

Prusias or Prusia, XXIII. 10. 1; 12. 1 (bis), 3. A king of Bithynia

Ptolemaeus, XVIII. 3. 2; 10. 3; 13. 3; XXI. 3. 1, 4. Ptolemy I, son of Lagus, one of Alexander's generals, afterwards king of Egypt

Ptolemaeus Ceraunus, XXI. 3. 4. Son of Ptolemy I; he became king of Macedonia in 280 B.C., but died in battle the next year

Pydna, II. 8. 5. A town of Macedonia, in Pieria on the Thermaic Gulf

Pylaemenes, XIV. 2. 2. A king of Paphlagonia at the time of the Trojan war

Pyrenaeus saltus, XXIII. 3. 3. The Pyrenees mountains

Pyrrhus, XXI. 2. 2. King of Epirus, killed at Argos in 272 B.C.

Pythagoreus, XV. 2. 2. A Pythagorean or follower of Pythagoras, the celebrated philosopher, born at Samos in 550 B.C.

Pythia, I. 1. 3; II. 2. 7. The priestess of the Delphic oracle

Q

Quinctius Flamininus, T., XXIII. 12. 1, 2. Conqueror of Philip V of Macedon in 197 B.C.

Quirinalis collis, XXV. 13. 2. The Quirinal hill at Rome

R

Rhodanus, XXIII. 4. 1; 6. 1. The Rhone

Rhodii, XXIII. 8. 4; 13. 2. The people of Rhodes, an island south of the western part of Asia Minor

Roma, XXIII. 5. 1; 7. 2, 4, 6; 12. 1; XXIV. 1. 1; XXV. 4. 5; 20. 5

Romani, Praef. 6; XVIII. 1. 5; 3. 4; XXII. 1. 3, 4; 2. 2, 3; 3. 1; 4. 3 (bis); XXIII. 1. 2, 3 (bis); 2. 3, 4, 6; 5. 2; 7. 1, 5; 10. 1-3; 12. 4; 13. 4

Romanus, -a, -um, adj. from Roma ;

civis, XXV. 19. 3 ; civitas, XXV. 3. 1; dictator, XXIII. 5. 1; eques, XXV. 5.1; 12. 1, 3; 13. 6; 15. 3; equites, XXV. 8. 3; legati, XXIII. 7. 3; nomen, XXIII. 7. 3; populus, I. 6. 2: XXI. 2. 2; XXIII. 1. 1 (bis); 7. 2; XXIV. 3. 3; XXV. 18. 2, 5; res, XXV. 4. 5; stirps, XXV. 1. 1

Romulus, XXV. 20. 3

Rubrum mare, XXIII. 2. 1. The Red Sea, a name applied to the Red Sea and to the Persian Gulf by the Romans

Rufus, see Minucius

S

Sabini, XXIV. 1. 1. The Sabines; a people of Central Italy, north-east of Latium

Saguntum, XXIII. 3. 2. A town in the eastern part of Spain near the coast

Salaminia victoria, II. 6. 3

Salamis, II. 2. 8; 3. 4; 5. 3; 9. 3; III. 2. 1. An island in the Saronic Gulf, near Athens

Samothracia, XXV. 11. 2. An island in the northern part of the Aegean Sea, opposite the mouth of the river Hebrus

Samus, VII. 5. 3, 4; XIII. 1. 2; 3. 1, 3, 4. Samos, an island on the western coast of Asia Minor, opposite Ephesus

Sardes or Sardis, I. 4. 1; IX. 5. 3; XVII. 3. 5. The capital of Lydia

Sardinia, XXIV. 1. 4. An island west of Italy

Sardiniensis triumphus, XXIV. 1. 4

Saufeius, L., XXV. 12. 3. A friend of Atticus

Scipio, see Cornelius

Scyrus, V. 2. 5. An island in the Aegean Sea, north-east of Euboea

Scythae, I. 3. 1, 3. The people of Scythia, a country north-east of the Caspian Sea

Scythissa, XIV. 1. 1. A Scythian woman

Seleucus, XVIII. 5. 1; 10. 3; 13. 3; XXI. 3. 1, 2 (bis), 3, 4. One of Alexander's generals, afterwards king of Syria and founder of the dynasty of the Seleucids

INDEX

(Sempronius) Longus, Ti., XXIII. 4. 2.
Consul in 218 B.C.

Sempronius Gracchus, Ti., XXIII. 5. 3.
Consul in 213 B.C.

(Sempronius) Gracchus, Ti., Frag. 1. 2.
Tribune of the commons in 133 B.C.

Sena, XXIV. 1. 2. A town of Umbria in
north-eastern Italy

Servilia, XXV. 11. 4. Mother of M.
Iunius Brutus

Servilius Geminus, Cn., XXIII. 4. 4.
Consul in 217 B.C.

Sestus, XIII. 1. 3. A town on the
eastern coast of the Thracian Chersonese, opposite Abydos

Seuthes, VII. 8. 3; XI. 2. 1. A Thracian
king

Sicilia, VII. 4. 3 (bis); 5. 3; 6. 2; X. 2.
2; 5. 3, 5, 6; 8. 1; 10. 3; XX. 1. 1;
2. 1, 4 (bis); 4. 3; 5. 1, 4; XXII. 1.
1, 2, 5; XXIV. 1. 2

Siculi, XX. 3. 1, 4; Siculus, XXI. 2. 2.
Sicilian

Sigeum, XII. 3. 4. A promontory and
city of the Troad, in north-western
Asia Minor

Silenus, XXIII. 13. 3. A Greek historian

Socrates, VII. 2. 1, 2 (bis). The celebrated Athenian philosopher (469–
399 B.C.)

Socraticus, XVII. 1. 1. A disciple of
Socrates

Sophrosyne, X. 1. 1. Daughter of
Dionysius the elder of Syracuse, and
wife of Dionysius the younger

Sosius, C., XXV. 22. 3. Consul in 32
B.C.

Sosylus, XXIII. 13. 3 (bis). A Greek
historian

Sparta, IV. 2. 3, 4; 3. 3; XI. 2. 5; XV.
6. 4; 8. 4; XVI. 4. 3; XVII. 1. 2;
4. 2; 6. 1 (bis); 8. 7. The capital
of Laconia

Spartani, XVI. 2. 4; XXI. 1. 2. The
citizens of Sparta

Spinther, see Cornelius

Stesagoras, I. 7. 5. Brother of Miltiades

Strymon, V. 2. 2. One of the principal
rivers of Thrace

Sulla, see Cornelius

Sullanae partes, XXV. 2. 2

Sulpicius, P., XXIII. 7. 1. Consul in
200 B.C.

Sulpicius Blitho, XXIII. 13. 1. A Roman
historian

(Sulpicius) Galba, Ser., XXIV. 3. 4.
Governor of Lusitania in 151 B.C.

Sulpicius (Rufus), P., XXV. 2. 1 (bis),
2. Tribune of the commons in 88
B.C.

(Sulpicius Rufus), Ser., XXV. 2. 1.
Brother of P. Sulpicius Rufus

Susamithres, VII. 10. 3. A Persian

Symposium, a work of Plato

Syracusae, X. 2. 2; 3. 2; 5. 3, 5, 6;
6. 5; XX. 2. 1 (bis); 3. 1, 3–5. The
famous city on the eastern coast of
Sicily

Syracusani, VII. 3. 1; X. 3. 3; XX. 1.
1; 5. 3, 4; Syracusanus, X 1. 1;
9. 6

Syria, XXIII. 7. 6; 8. 4. A country
in Asia between the Euphrates and
the Mediterranean

Sysinas, XIV. 7. 1. Son of Datames

T

Tachus, XVII. 8. 2. King of Egypt in
362 B.C.

Taenarum, IV. 4. 4. A promontory of
Laconia, on the south-eastern shore
of the Peloponnesus

Tamphiliana domus, XXV. 13. 2. A
house built by Baebius Tamphilius
and later owned by Atticus

Tamphilus, see Baebius

Tarentinus, XV. 2. 2. A native of
Tarentum

Tarentum, X. 2. 2. A city of Calabria
in southern Italy, on the Gulf of Tarentum

Taurus, IX. 2. 3; XIV. 4. 4; XVIII. 3. 2.
A range of mountains in the south-
eastern part of Asia Minor

Terentius (Varro), C., XXIII. 4. 4.
Consul in 216 B.C.

Thasii, V. 2. 5; VI. 2. 3. The people
of Thasos

Thasus, VI. 2. 2. An island in the
northern part of the Aegean Sea,
near the coast of Thrace

Thebae, VII. 4. 4; 11. 3; XII. 1. 1;
XV. 4. 1; 5. 2; 6. 2; 7. 5; 8. 4;
10. 3, 4; XVI. 1, 2; 2. 2, 5; 3. 2;
4. 1, 3. Thebes, the chief city of
Boeotia

346

INDEX

INDEX

X

Xenophon, XVII. 1. 1. An Athenian, celebrated as a writer and for his conduct of the retreat of the ten thousand in 400 B.C.

Xerxes, II. 2. 4; 4. 1; 9. 1; III. 1. 5; IV. 2. 2; XVII. 4. 4; XXI. 1. 3 (*bis*). King of Persia from 485 to 465 B.C.

Z

Zacynthii, X. 9. 3. Of Zacynthus, an island off the coast of Elis, modern Zante

Zama, XXIII. 6. 3 (*bis*). A town of Numidia on the frontier of the territory of Carthage, the scene of the defeat of Hannibal by Scipio in 202 B.C.